LIBRARIAN'S HANDBOOK FOR SEEKING, WRITING, AND MANAGING GRANTS

LIBRARIAN'S HANDBOOK FOR SEEKING, WRITING, AND MANAGING GRANTS

*Sylvia D. Hall-Ellis,
Stacey L. Bowers,
Christopher Hudson,
Claire Williamson, and
Joanne Patrick*

LIBRARIES UNLIMITED

AN IMPRINT OF ABC-CLIO, LLC
Santa Barbara, California • Denver, Colorado • Oxford, England

Copyright 2011 by Sylvia D. Hall-Ellis, Stacey L. Bowers, Christopher Hudson, Claire Williamson, and Joanne Patrick

All rights reserved. No part of this publication may be reproduced, stored in a retrieval system, or transmitted, in any form or by any means, electronic, mechanical, photocopying, recording, or otherwise, except for the inclusion of brief quotations in a review or reproducibles, which may be copied for classroom and educational programs only, without prior permission in writing from the publisher.

Library of Congress Cataloging-in-Publication Data

Librarian's handbook for seeking, writing, and managing grants / Sylvia D. Hall-Ellis ... [et al.].
 p. cm.
Includes bibliographical references and index.
 ISBN 978–1–59158–870–2 (hard copy : alk. paper) – ISBN 978–1–59158–872–6 (ebook)
 1. Project management—Finance. 2. Project management—Evaluation. 3. Education—Research—Finance. 4. Proposal writing for grants. I. Hall-Ellis, Sylvia D.
HD69.P75L533 2011
025.1′1–dc22   2011005085

ISBN: 978–1–59158–870–2
EISBN: 978–1–59158–872–6

15 14 13 12 11   1 2 3 4 5

This book is also available on the World Wide Web as an eBook.
Visit www.abc-clio.com for details.

Libraries Unlimited
An Imprint of ABC-CLIO, LLC

ABC-CLIO, LLC
130 Cremona Drive, P.O. Box 1911
Santa Barbara, California 93116-1911

This book is printed on acid-free paper ∞

Manufactured in the United States of America

Excerpts from *Grants for School Libraries* by Sylvia D. Hall-Ellis and Ann Jerabek. Copyright © 2003 by Sylvia D. Hall-Ellis and Ann Jerabek. Reproduced with permission of ABC-CLIO, LLC.

CONTENTS

Preface	xi
Introduction	xv
Part 1: Grant Development	1
1 Planning: The Core of Proposal Development	3
Planning Defined	5
The Rationale for Planning	6
Readiness for Planning	7
Historical Commitment to Planning	10
The Reward System for Staff Contributions	10
Culture and Complexity of the Organization	11
Rate of Growth	12
Financial Resources	14
Ready Reference Handbooks and Tools	14
Access and Availability of Information	15
Willingness to Take Risks	16
General Guidelines for the Predevelopment Planning Process	16
Calculating the Funding Potential	18
Managing Proposal Development	19
Selecting Partner Organizations	19
Calendar Development	28
Planning Meetings	33
Initial Planning Meeting	34
Conceptual Design Meeting	35
Working Meetings	35

Decisions Relating to Proposal Preparation	35
Writing and Editing Issues	37
Document Formatting Issues	39
2 Project Design	**41**
Needs Statement	42
Context of the Problem	43
Justification for the Project	44
Aspect to be Addressed	44
The Importance of a Lucid Mission Statement	44
Project Goal Development	45
The Relationship of the Goal and Objectives	47
Conceptual Design of the Project	50
Preliminary Checklists	50
Methodologies	50
The Dynamic Process Underlying Project Design	53
Laying the Groundwork for a Collaborative Effort	53
Steps to Prepare the Project Design	54
Project Management	58
Establishing an Advisory Group	59
Orientation for the Advisory Group	60
Parental Involvement with the Project	60
3 Project Narrative	**65**
Proposal Functions	66
Components of the Proposal	67
Cover Sheet (Face Sheet)	70
Abstract	70
Table of Contents	71
Introduction	71
Needs Assessment	71
Goals, Objectives, and Activities	72
Service Programs	74
Evaluation Design and Research Implications	75
Dissemination of Findings, Results, and Products	77
Plan for Continued Support (Sustainability)	78
Budget	78
Appendices	80
Letter of Transmittal	80
Proposal Writing, Design, and Organizational Guidelines	81
4 Project Personnel	**85**
Project Staffing Requirements	85
Requirements from the Funding Agency	87
Requirements from the Applicant	90

Contents   vii

Capabilities Statements for Key Project Personnel	90
Principal Investigator (or Project Director)	93
Support Staff	94
Local Personnel Available to the Project	94
Library Administrators	94
Librarians in Public Library and Academic Library Settings	97
School Librarians	98
Instructional Personnel	98
Parents	99

5 Project Evaluation 101
  Overview of the Evaluation Process 102
  Evaluation Methods 102
    Formative Evaluation 103
    Summative Evaluation 104
  The Basics of Evaluation 106
    Selecting an Evaluator 127
    Internal Evaluation Teams 127
    External Evaluation Teams 132
  Planning the Evaluation 132
  Analyzing Evaluation Data 136
  Writing the Evaluation Report 137
    Executive Summary 137
    Formative Evaluation 137
    Summative Evaluation 138

6 Budget Development 141
  The Role of the Budget 142
  Budget Preparation 143
    Ground Rules for Budget Preparation 144
    Identify the Costs 145
    Drafting the Budget 147
    Reviewing the Budget 163
  Additional Budgeting Considerations 163
    The Influence of Funding Agencies on Budget Formatting 163
    Budget Adjustments and Amendments 164
    Subcontracts 164

7 Appendices 167
  The Roles of Appendices 167
  Grant Compliances and Assurances 168
  Demographic Data and Community Descriptions 170
  Profiles of Participating Institutions 170
  Curriculum Vitae and Job Descriptions 170
  Standards, Benchmarks, and Academic Achievement 173

Literature Review, "Best Practices," and Models	173
Letters of Commitment and Letters of Support	179
Bibliography of Resources Consulted	180

Part 2: Implementation and Management — 183

8 After the Proposal — 185
- Activities Between the Submission and Decision — 186
- Strategies for Successful Grant Recipients — 187
- Strategies for Organizations Failing to Obtain Grant Funding — 189
- Poor Grantmanship Practices — 190
  - The Narrative — 190
  - The Budget — 191
  - The Details — 192
- Resubmitting the Proposal — 193

9 Implementing the Project — 195
- Getting Started: Celebrate, Praise, and Communicate — 195
  - Notifying Partners — 197
  - Accepting the Award — 199
  - Review Project Award Information and Documents Provided by the Grantor — 200
- The Project Handoff — 200
  - Acceptance Paperwork — 201
  - Internal Accounts and Fiscal Paperwork — 201
- Staffing and Training — 201
  - Hiring Project Personnel — 204
  - Employees, Consultants, and Volunteers — 207
  - Developing Position Descriptions — 209
  - Advertising the Position — 211
  - The Interview Process — 213
  - Developing Interview Questions — 214
  - After the Hiring Decision Is Made — 217
- Setting Up the Project Office — 218
- Announcing the Grant Award — 219
  - Internal Promotion of the Grant Award — 219
  - Traditional Ways of Promoting the Grant Project — 219
  - Web Sites and Other Electronic Publications — 220
  - Online Surveys — 220
  - Promoting the Grant Project Using Social Media — 221
  - Building an Online Community to Support the Grant Project — 222
  - Overlooked Opportunities to Promote the Grant Project — 222

10 Managing the Project Day-to-Day — 225
- Organizational Structure: The Big Picture — 225
- Roles and Responsibilities: The Details — 227

	Operations	230
	Managing People	231
	Management Styles	231
	Leadership and Team Building	234
	Deadlines, Calendars, and Timelines	235
	Planning for the Unexpected	249
11	Project Accountability	253
	Fiscal Management	254
	Accounting and Financial Management	255
	Budget Modifications	260
	Cost Share	262
	Legal Overview and Issues	267
	Components of a Contract	269
	Contract Terms and Their Importance	270
	General Contract Tips	272
	Grants versus Contracts	272
	Specific Types of Agreements in the Grant Context	273
	Project Evaluation	282
	Conducting Evaluations	283
	Writing Project Reports	284
	Deliverables	286
12	Project Closeout	289
Glossary of Grant Terms		291
Bibliography		299
Index		305

PREFACE

Success in writing and winning grants comes through practice-based effort, sustained enthusiasm, tenacity, and a commitment to turn temporary setbacks (i.e., proposal rejections) into renewed efforts and grant awards. Few educators or librarians begin their professional careers prepared to participate in the grant seeking process. As their careers evolve, they recognize and understand economic realities. Without supplemental funding, schools and their media centers are often forced to choose between essential and desirable programs. Consequently, the importance of identifying and securing supplemental financial resources increases as tax revenues, formula-driven state support, and mandated monies decrease. Challenged to pay for a portion of programs and services with non-institutional funds, including their own paychecks, educators and media specialists seek supplemental funding. Their dedication to students' academic and personal successes frequently drives them to investigate the grant-making process. This interest may begin during professional development sessions, conferences, or site-based committee work. Or interest can begin in response to an administrator's decision to seek additional funds.

Larger public, academic, and specialized libraries have historically participated in the writing and winning of grants. However, as school media centers increase institutional participation in the grant arena, staff predictably lack resources and expertise required to compete with their larger colleagues. Novice grant writers seek opportunities to gain knowledge about funding and grantors, "best practices" research, and writing skills. They need encouragement to manage proposal development, project design, evaluation techniques, and articulate collaborative arrangements among partner organizations.

Inexperienced grant writers are likely to find the process confusing, time-consuming, and intimidating. We have made significant efforts to cover the full spectrum of the process in a lucid, succinct format. In short, this book is designed to provide the information necessary for educators and media specialists to become effective members of grant development teams.

This book is a desktop, ready-reference handbook. The text may be used for casual inquiry or as a guide during grant writing. Its scope embraces all aspects of the proposal development process and the requirements for grant management regardless of the size of library or level of K-12 education. Teachers, elementary and secondary education administrators, librarians, library coordinators, and others involved in the "community of learners" will find this handbook valuable. The authors bring together information designed to prepare readers with the following skills:

- to identify potential funding sources in federal and state arenas;
- to organize and manage the proposal development process;
- to establish and encourage representative participation on local development teams;
- to compile relevant research, standards, and Internet resources to support grant requests; and
- to recommend professional reading materials to individuals and groups interested in grant writing.

Recognizing that grants are developed through a sequential process, *Librarian's Handbook for Seeking, Writing, and Managing Grants* focuses on its fundamental components. Presuming little or no background knowledge, the book is organized to guide the reader through the primary stages comprising the grant development process. Each chapter in part one discusses the elements of these sections:

- planning;
- project design;
- project narrative;
- project personnel;
- budget development;
- project evaluation; and
- supplementary materials.

Each chapter in part two discusses the elements of these sections:

- project implementation;
- managing the grant day-to-day;

- grant accountability; and
- closing out the grant.

The insights included in the chapters are taken from the authors' experiences as professional grant writers, readers, and researchers. Their backgrounds include work with school districts, state educational agencies, regional education services centers, public libraries and multi-county systems, institutions of higher education, private consulting, fee-based information services, and graduate teaching. The text also synthesizes selected information that is readily available in a number of expensive, out-of-print, and proprietary publications.

INTRODUCTION

Few educators or librarians begin their professional careers prepared to participate in the grant-seeking process. From start to finish, grant development and management require a diverse skill set not generally possessed by those new to such endeavors. Good writing and editing habits, efficient project management, and careful long-term budgeting and planning skills are needed to successfully compete for grant awards. Knowledge of reporting and formal evaluation standards, experience hiring and supervising personnel, and familiarity with relevant governmental and institutional policies, regulations, and laws are required for the management and administration of funded projects.

It is the rare individual who is the master of all facets of the grant process. For this reason, *Librarian's Handbook for Seeking, Writing, and Managing Grants* emphasizes the importance of teamwork and collaboration in all stages of development and management. Including individuals with varying backgrounds and expertise on the grant team provides a framework of skill and experience necessary for the creation and management of funded projects. As economic realities encourage more institutions to seek outside funding, competition for limited resources becomes increasingly keen. Utilizing the collective knowledge and expertise of co-workers and colleagues will allow smaller institutions and those with limited experience or institutional support to have success.

In addition to capitalizing on collective skill, cooperation and teamwork foster creativity and encourage accountability among team members. With many projects to choose from, funding agencies are especially responsive to those that address documented needs in novel and creative ways. Funding agencies also look for proposals that are well reasoned, well written, and free of errors. Including individuals of varying experience ensures consideration of diverse points of view. Further, working with close colleagues and peers from other professional backgrounds encourages increased attention to detail and presents learning opportunities for all involved.

Although an unsought obligation at many institutions, grant seeking and management should not be overwhelming or overly burdensome. Successful grant seeking is a sequential process that can be learned by anyone willing to devote the time needed for research and development of skills. This text is designed as a step-by-step guide for those new to the field. From identifying funding sources to disseminating results, *Librarian's Handbook* covers all of the fundamentals in an easy-to-understand format. For those already familiar with the process, the text will provide new perspective and serve as a handy ready reference.

PART 1
Grant Development

CHAPTER 1

Planning: The Core of Proposal Development

Creativity and entrepreneurial approaches to promoting services and programs that contribute to the library mission are essential. Ideas and creative approaches to problem solving can originate with anyone. When an individual identifies an idea that evolves into an appropriate service or program for the organization, but implementation cannot be undertaken without additional resources, a grant can provide them. The key components for grant-seeking success include strong, dynamic leadership, shared vision for the proposed project, and the dedicated investment of time, resources, and effort from team members. The individual whose idea is the foundation for the grant typically serves as a team leader (Principal Investigator or Project Director).

Writing a successful grant proposal that results in funding requires a well-executed plan. The planning process represents the combined efforts of individuals, representatives of key constituencies, and community partners working on the grant development team. Group members share a strong commitment to funding their project. They provide the energy and commitment required to write and submit a grant proposal. Working collaboratively, team members develop project goals, objectives, and activities; divide research and writing responsibilities; and secure partnerships within the applicant organization and among partner community organizations, higher education institutions, and not-for-profit groups.

The composition of a grant team depends on the type of funding opportunity and the organization that leads the project implementation, evaluation activities, and grant management responsibilities. A wide variety of funding opportunities from government agencies, private foundations, and philanthropic individuals offer possibilities for libraries of all types to partner with school campuses, districts, non-profit organizations, state and local government agencies, departments within colleges and universities, and citizen groups. Regardless of the identified library need, the potential to seek and secure grant funding exists.

Self-directed, local teams are the key to effective grant preparation. Working together or independently, team members can perform the various tasks that underpin the final document. These tasks include (but are not limited to) the identification of potential funding sources (particularly within federal and state governments and the private sector), the evaluation of Requests for Proposals (RFPs) and Requests for Applications (RFAs), execution of local needs assessments, a survey of the education and library literature to identify research-based models and "best practices," the establishment of partnerships in support of projects, and preparation for the proposal document.

In a public library system or district, the ideal grant development team includes administrators (the director, supervising librarians, department or branch managers), librarians (the local experts with regard to working with patrons, the library's collection of resources, and current services and programs), school teacher-librarians (partners in teaching and learning), program directors, support staff, faculty members from institutions of higher education, business and industry leaders, library computer systems, networking, and technology specialists, evaluators, the library coordinator for grants development and management, and neighborhood representatives.

Within a school campus, charter school, or district, a grant development team ideally includes administrators (principals, assistant principals, department or grade-level chairpersons), teachers (the local experts with regard to the use of instructional strategies and the integration of technologies into the learning environment), school librarians (partners in teaching), curriculum specialists, program directors, district library coordinators, support staff, faculty members from institutions of higher education, business and industry leaders, technology specialists, evaluators, the district coordinator for grants development and management, students, and parents.

Academic librarians find themselves in a unique situation with regards to grant funding opportunities. While a selected number of funding opportunities focused exclusively on the library exist, the number is significantly greater when the college or university library joins one or more academic units and partners in a funding proposal. On the college or university campus, the ideal grant development team includes the Principal Investigator (a faculty member seeking grant funding to further an established research agenda and support for students); faculty colleagues who share research components and bring complementary aspects to the initiative; librarians (the local experts with regard to working with the academic community, the library's collection of resources, and current services and programs); department chairs; support staff; faculty members from other institutions of higher education; business and industry leaders; library computer systems, networking, and technology specialists; and, evaluators.

All academic units on campus, including the library, work through an office of sponsored programs or funded research. The Office of Research and Sponsored Programs (ORSP) coordinates grant seeking, management, and compliance across the campus. Coordinating grant applications across the campus benefits each member of the team and streamlines the administrative tasks after funding is secured. When research funding includes participation of human subjects, the Principal Investigator (or Project Director) is required to work through the local Institutional Review Board (IRB). Defined in the National Research Act of 1974, institutional IRBs are governed by Title 45 CFR (Code of Federal Regulations).[1] All research that receives funding, directly or indirectly, from the Department of Health and Human Services (HHS) must work through an IRB according to the regulations of the Office for Human Research Protections (OHRP) within HHS.[2]

PLANNING DEFINED

Team members may begin their tasks after they reach a mutual commitment to planning. In general, planning is a defined strategy for doing an activity, arranging items or materials, or producing a product. In a library or educational environment, planning customarily results in providing a service or imparting knowledge and skills to a specific target group or audience. In the context of grant proposal development, planning is ongoing and continuous. Specific planning activities include grant seeking, proposal preparation, funding, evaluation, and reporting.

Planning activities include these distinct components:

1. conceptualizing the program and its budget;
2. securing organizational approval to submit a proposal;
3. identifying potential funding sources;
4. requesting guidelines and application forms;
5. writing the grant proposal;
6. submitting the proposal by the deadline;
7. waiting for proposal review and evaluation;
8. receiving notification of a grant award;
9. negotiating the award;
10. celebrating the award;
11. implementing the project;
12. conducting formative and summative evaluations;

13. submitting programmatic and financial reports; and
14. completing final documents for the funding entity and project partners.

Figure 1.1 provides a visual representation of the planning process.

THE RATIONALE FOR PLANNING

Grant seeking is a continuous process. The time required to develop innovative projects is not related to predefined dates of the calendar or academic year. Grant seekers are cautioned to avoid the practice of formulating a project in response to a funding announcement. Proposals written during the final days before the submission deadline generally do not reflect the collaborative planning that is characteristic of successful applications. Funding bodies issue announcements and invitations to submit proposals according to their organizational timelines. Government agencies publish dates for the submission of grant applications on a timeline driven by legislative appropriations and departmental workloads. Consequently, routine monitoring of funding announcements is an appropriate albeit time-consuming task. Experienced grant seekers gain the knowledge to anticipate upcoming opportunities so that work can begin well in advance of the formal announcement.

Anecdotal evidence throughout the library practitioner community indicates that administrators traditionally have considered grant seeking peripheral to assigned job responsibilities. Consequently, seeking and applying for additional funds has occurred without adequate planning and attention to detail. Grant proposals prepared in these situations are not frequently funded. However, after the economic downturns and significant cuts to library funding, staff members with experience in fundraising and grant writing have been encouraged to pursue these activities more formally. Position descriptions for librarians more frequently include grant writing as a preferred skill or as a potential assignment upon hiring.

Without supplemental monies from government agencies, foundations, corporations, and other supporters, libraries in the twenty-first century have been forced to reduce services and programs. The decline in state and federal funding since the mid-1990s and the economic downturns of the first decade in the twenty-first century forced librarians in libraries of all types and sizes across the United States to focus their efforts on the procurement of outside funding. These positions carry various titles, including Grant Writer, Proposal Development Specialist, Development Officer, Grants and Grant Development and Management Specialist, and Grants Administrator.

Regardless of the job title, the individual oversees a number of tasks in support of grant seeking, application writing, and management. Responsibilities include the establishment of an office, routine monitoring and identification of potential funding sources, overseeing the preparation and coordination of proposal writing, and managing grant awards.

Principal Investigator and Team creates idea, writes abstract, drafts approval form

Administrator reviews funding opportunity & approves proposal preparation

Principal Investigator and Team write the proposal

Grants Office reads, edits, critiques proposal, serves as liaison with funder

Principal Investigator and Team complete the proposal

Grants Office submits the proposal to Chief Administrator for signatures

Chief Administrator authorizes submission

Grants Office submits proposal

Principal Investigator and Grants Office negotiate award with funding entity, request reviewers' comments on declined proposal, recommend improvements, seek alternative funding

Principal Investigator and Project Staff implement project, revise project and/or proposal for resubmission or submission to new funder

Figure 1.1   Grant Development Process Flowchart

READINESS FOR PLANNING

The commitment to a successful grants program results in changes within the organizational culture as priorities shift. Time and resources must be allocated differently, and new systems and procedures will need to be implemented. Building an efficient organizational infrastructure to support grant seeking and management is a challenge, especially as library administrators strive to train and provide professional development opportunities for the affected staff. Library administrators, managers, and grant team leaders should anticipate and prepare for organizational resistance. However, a well-developed, successful process that results in additional funding usually convinces administrators.

Each library faces its own set of unique and uncertain events. Popular strategic remedies to cope with them include total quality management, continuous improvement, benchmarking, re-engineering, downsizing, learning organizations, groupware, customer focus, core competencies, self-directed teams, just-in-time inventories, scenario planning, activity-based costing, outsourcing, and strategic alliances.[3] Because local circumstances are unique, a successful librarian will develop a tailored approach to strategic planning. Seeking grant funds should be incorporated into the library's long-range strategic plan. As part of the fact finding about the needs of the library's target service community, assessments of current library operations, and accountability to funding bodies, administrators can identify the areas that current financial resources cannot be stretched to support. Incorporating the potential opportunities for seeking and procuring grant funds emphasizes the importance of the effort and enables librarians to identify how current services and programs will be enhanced through new, externally funded initiatives.

Successful strategies share three characteristics. First, team members will formulate long-term goals, followed by the identification and allocation of resources.[4] Second, group members will participate in conversations to create a "vision of success" and articulate clearly how to realize its achievement.[5] Third, group members will create a clear and realistic strategic plan. A successful strategic planning process includes the following elements:

- formulating a clear future direction;
- establishing a set of priorities;
- making coherent decisions;
- including all levels and functions in decisions;
- addressing significant problems;
- improving performance;
- building teamwork and expertise;
- thinking and behaving strategically; and
- preparing appropriate responses to changes in the environment.

At its best, strategic planning pulls the library and its partners together as a single unit working toward a common vision of the future. The library's administrators, its governing body, and community partners will consider issues horizontally and vertically. Incentives can promote cooperation and the ability to respond effectively and rapidly to the unexpected.

In the end, ideas matter. Strategic planning inspires and promotes ideas. The successful library administrator inspires participation and contributions from each member of the staff. The formulation of strategies focuses on local leadership and the inclusive involvement of the entire library community. Effective strategic planning empowers the library and its community partners to meet identified needs and expectations. Ideas evolving from strategic planning inspire everyone and give participants a unified sense of purpose.

Because successful grant seeking is a collaborative process, individuals throughout the organization must be motivated to participate. The following steps can help lay the groundwork for a favorable climate:

- Encourage the chief executive officer (i.e., library director, superintendent, dean) to issue (or endorse) a policy statement indicating that grant seeking is an organizational priority.
- Provide the time, resources, personnel, and training to support grant development teams.
- Recognize and reward grant team preparation activities within the organization.
- Employ in-house newsletters or letters from the chief executive officer to recognize the grant development team for its efforts.
- Share grant awards with others in the organization and the community. Enthusiasm is contagious!
- Start small and build. Select a core staff to act as local experts. As they achieve success, others will want to get involved.

The potential for success is significantly increased when the grant development team collaborates to design a service, program, or project that reflects an understanding of the institutional mission (see Chapter 2), responds to the needs of the library's clientele, and motivates employees (achievement, recognition, responsibility). A number of organizational characteristics should be considered as part of the effort to achieve a match between project objectives and organizational missions.

Librarians have the option to work through a proposal-specific group or with an established grant team. Some librarians choose to hire a professional grant-writing firm. If the librarian brings together individuals based on their content expertise or work experience to prepare a specific grant application, then they face a steep learning curve about the actual application process. An established grant team has the potential to learn through consistent efforts by applying for and procuring funding. A seasoned grant team has the advantage of developing standard language about the library, its mission, services and programs, and the community it serves. In addition, the team gains an understanding of the budgetary and financial requirements that must be followed. Consequently, this will significantly reduce the learning curve for the content experts who develop the programs and services, as they can rely on the support of the grant team. A for-hire grant writer brings experience to the process but does not possess an in-depth understanding of the library and its operations. Turning over the responsibility to an outside consultant may be expedient, but it can be costly and does not guarantee success.

Once an organizational team is formed, the project planning for the grant begins. An effective planning process is not a given. In fact, the need to plan effectively may be ignored, discounted, or underestimated by inexperienced grant seekers. Team efficiency and success will be curtailed if the level of support and commitment within the organization is limited. Changes in the library environment during the planning process have the potential to cause failure for a grant development team. The team must recognize and respond to a notable principle of behavior: organization prevents reorganization.

Historical Commitment to Planning

A library with a history of effective planning provides significant documentation for the grant development team to use in its work. On the other hand, the lack of materials about the library, partner organizations, and community indicates a diminished importance for planning. The library's unwillingness to adopt a plan of continuous planning for improvement to programs, services, and community-based collaborations reflects a lack of commitment. A file cabinet filled with plans that have never been implemented represents another danger sign. Reliance upon outside "experts" to write plans can contribute to failure. Without an insider's knowledge of the organization, a consultant may produce a document (i.e., a plan) but the probability of adoption and implementation by the library, its governing body, and the community is limited. The successful implementation of funded projects reflects the involvement and endorsement of the entire library community.

The Reward System for Staff Contributions

Successful organizations routinely reward employees for their efforts. Inspirational administrators engage in five practices of exemplary leadership:

- Model the way;
- Inspire a shared vision;
- Challenge the process;
- Enable others to act; and
- Encourage the heart.[6]

Hard work and the sharing of creative ideas to solve problems are essential for organizational success. On the other hand, the lack of recognition to deserving librarians, faculty members, teachers, teacher-librarians, staff, community partners, residents, and parents compromises future efforts.

While some employees are strongly self-motivated, the majority of librarians, managers, teachers, and teacher-librarians require encouragement. Motivation may be extended through a variety of mechanisms, including (but not limited to): recognition by the governing body and chief executive officer; increased influence within the library system, school district and school, or campus; nomination or appointment to key task forces and committees at the district, system, or campus level; increased responsibilities; paid release time for outside assignments, including grant preparation tasks; access and support for special training opportunities and professional development activities to increase an employee's skills; merit salary increases; perks such as financial travel support for attendance at conferences; "chits" for resources or additional funds for library or classroom supplies or enrichment materials; a liberalized dress code; the availability of recreational facilities; and gift certificates to suppliers or bookstores.

Culture and Complexity of the Organization

Organizational culture reflects shared beliefs. Libraries are "communities of practice," reflecting common interests and expertise.[7] Library staff members articulate their shared vision and philosophy through a mission statement. Their collective energies must be focused on the delivery of services and programs designed to transform this mission into realistic goals and objectives.

Regardless of an organization's size or complexity, the mission statement functions as a cornerstone for the proposal development process. Significant grant development support should go to initiatives designed to secure additional funding for services and programs directly supported by the library's mission. Library service area, number of library card holders, and project implementation strategies need to be considered when determining organizational priorities. Larger organizations have the resources required to offer an extensive array of services and programs. These libraries can employ a correspondingly large number of administrators to oversee specific instructional, financial, and management functions. Smaller organizations may need to limit development to essential services and programs.

In a public library system or district, the traditional hierarchy is characterized as "top down." Lead by the library director, the administrative team includes an associate director, supervising librarians (e.g., division heads for several departments), department heads, and branch managers. Librarians are the local experts with regard to working with patrons, the library's collection of resources, and current services and programs. Department and branch staffs include paraprofessionals (library assistants, clerks, and shelvers), physical plant workers, and custodians.

Within a school district or charter school, the educational leader is the superintendent, working with a central administrative team, including assistant (or area) superintendents, and directors of large initiatives (curriculum, assessment, Title I, etc.). A principal leads the campus cadre of experts that includes assistant principals, department or grade-level chairpersons, teachers, and school librarians. The campus staff includes paraprofessionals (classroom assistants, office staff, and clerks), and custodians.

Academic libraries find themselves in a unique situation with regard to organizational structure. The enrollment for the college or university generally dictates the size of the library and its staff. However, regardless of size, the traditional hierarchy is characterized as "top down." Lead by the library dean or director, the administrative team includes an associate dean or director, departmental library managers, and department heads within the main library. Librarians are the local experts with regard to working with students and faculty, the collection of print, online, and electronic resources, and services and programs. Staff members include paraprofessionals (library assistants, clerks, and shelvers), physical plant workers, and custodians.

The Principal Investigator should seek approval from the administrative team early in the planning stage (see Form 1.1). Knowing the library's culture and organizational structure will ensure the inclusion of necessary and/or influential individuals in these discussions. The grant development team needs to consider the project focus and its relationship to the library mission within the context of the organizational vision, values, and goals statements. Without approval, the allocation of the library's resources into the effort is inappropriate. After the library administrator approves the preparation of a grant application, supervisors and staff from participating units should be invited and encouraged to participate. Smaller libraries employ fewer staff members and administrators. However, the importance of their participation in the grant development process is critical and cannot be overlooked.

Rate of Growth

A library experiencing rapid growth within its diverse user community tends to focus its attention on the management of expansion. When the growth occurs outside of the library's span of control (e.g., population explosion caused by the influx of new residents or increased use of the library due to economic downturns), administrators will feel pressured to redistribute resources which otherwise would have been available to the grant development team. If the number of new patrons is pronounced, administrators will be forced respond. While the library service area is expanding, the chief executive officer and other administrators will need to expand its internal capacity to accommodate increased planning, including grant development activities. Regardless of the growth rate, the grant development team needs to have an in-depth understanding of the library's climate in order to design a project that reflects both support needs and services for users.

A. Description of Funding Opportunity
   1. Title:_____
   2. Funder:_____
   3. Due date:_____ Dollar value: _____ Indirect rate: _____
   4. Starting date:_____ Ending date:_____ Duration:_____

B. Bid Evaluation
   1. What is the project goal? _____
   _____
   2. What are the project objectives? _____
   _____
   _____
   3. Who are the institutional or community partners?_____
   _____
   4. Do we meet every requirement in the evaluation criteria? Yes___ No___ Don't know___
   5. Will subcontractors/consultants be required? Yes___ No___

C. Proposal Team

Team Member	Organizational Affiliation	Role
		Principal Investigator

D. Describe how this project supports the library mission.
   _____
   _____
   _____
   _____
   _____
   _____

   Library staff conversation date: _____ Supervisor: _____
   Principal Investigator: _____
   Administrator: _____ Date: _____

Form 1.1   Bid Decision Form

Financial Resources

The library must underwrite grant development costs. When the project includes partner organizations, these preparatory expenses can be shared. Grant preparation costs typically include staff salaries and benefits, office space, equipment use, photocopying, communications (e.g., telephone, FAX, Internet access), travel to "best practices" sites, and attendance at meetings.

Funding agencies do not underwrite proposal preparation costs. While this fact does not pose a serious problem for less ambitious activities, comprehensive projects encompassing collaborative efforts across a geographically dispersed area can require the investment of considerable resources.

The Principal Investigator is responsible for negotiating sufficient support for the proposal writing process. During initial planning stages, team members should identify all anticipated proposal development costs. The Principal Investigator should compile the projected expenses and forward them to the appropriate administrator. When the lead agency (i.e., grant applicant) is unable to underwrite anticipated costs, the project costs may be paid by partner organizations or a related group. However, it is important to bear in mind that encouraging the grant development personnel to work without adequate financial support represents unsound management practice. Many experts feel that if the school district or campus cannot support grant development the process should be terminated.

Ready Reference Handbooks and Tools

Grant writing is a specialized form of technical writing. Successful grant writers need to understand the funding announcement and response process, political activities that impact legislation and appropriations, and the local community. In addition to understanding the educational environment, proposal developers are proficient writers and editors. To support their work a majority of grant writers maintain a collection of ready reference handbooks and tools. These materials typically include (but are not limited to) the following items:

- a style manual (*Publication Manual of the American Psychological Association* or *The Chicago Manual of Style*);
- *The New York Public Library Writer's Guide to Style and Usage*;
- *The New York Public Library Desk Reference*;
- a dictionary (*American Heritage*, *Webster's*, or the like);
- *Roget's Thesaurus*;
- *Statistical Abstract of the United States*;
- *U.S. Government Organization Manual*;
- *Yearbook of Mental Measurement*;

Planning: The Core of Proposal Development

- books about writing (*Write Tight* by William Brohaugh, *A Writer's Reference* by Diana Hacker, or similar title);
- *The Foundation Center Directory*;
- subscriptions to *Education Week, The Chronicle of Philanthropy, Grants Alert, Educational Leadership*, and similar professional continuing resources;
- *Catalog of Federal Domestic Assistance*;
- *The Federal Register*;
- *EDGAR*;
- local telephone book;
- professional organization directories;
- current and retrospective data from the U.S. Bureau of the Census;
- content standards for curricular areas published by the local school district, the state department of education, and national organizations;
- standardized test results for the school district, campuses, the state, and the nation;
- school district and campus demographic data;
- school district policies and procedures; and
- community, regional, and state economic development data, including forecasts and historical perspectives.

Access and Availability of Information

The proposal development process requires access to a minimum of two types of information. First, the team needs comprehensive background information describing the library and its parent organization, including its service area, demographics, recent standardized test scores for students, levels and types of available technologies in libraries (at the public library, within classrooms and the school library, and the college or university), funding history, key personnel, staffing patterns, grant management experience, and overall services and programs. When this information is compiled, it should be organized to optimize reference and access. Relevant new and revised documents should be added to the reference (or "record") set upon publication by the library. When these reference documents are properly maintained, these data can be used in the development of every proposal.

The second type of required information includes research findings, "best practices," and other relevant material focused on the area addressed in the proposal. In the competitive environment characterizing twenty-first century grant seeking, development team members require access to significant amounts of up-to-date information.

The grant development leader needs to encourage team members to become proficient computer and Internet users. An understanding of what is available as well as a mastery of search and retrieval techniques requires significant time and effort. Reference librarians understand educational technologies, offer access to the Internet, and possess skills in information seeking and retrieval. Their specialized skills make them particularly valuable members of the grant team.

Electronic resources available through the Internet (see bibliography) are essential to keep current with grant-seeking institutions, newly released funding announcements, research findings, training and professional development opportunities, technical assistance sessions, and "best practices" sites.

Willingness to Take Risks

Funding agencies do not financially support routine, ongoing activities. Librarians who lack a commitment to change or are unwilling to take risks are not likely to be successful in the grants arena. Historically, a number of libraries, school districts, and educational consortia have built significant reputations through their long-standing grant-funded instructional programs, technology initiatives, and supplementary student services.

The decision to maintain a conservative stance is appropriate to selected libraries. However, a dynamic external environment has motivated many library administrators to use self-assessment tools to assure continued organizational vitality. Self-assessments frequently provide a mandate for change. In such instances, the grant development team is responsible for the incorporation of the commitment to change into funding proposals. In conclusion, the analysis of a library's preparedness to change may best be handled through the use of the instrument included in Form 1.2.

GENERAL GUIDELINES FOR THE PREDEVELOPMENT PLANNING PROCESS

Library administrators should be encouraged to participate in the ongoing review of funding opportunities. Administrative involvement can motivate library staff members and heighten general interest in grant development, diminishing the possibility of overlooking viable funding sources. Particular attention should be given to those administrators who oversee programs focusing on key target service and program areas and groups. If a funding source appears promising, the information needs to be shared with library administrators, campus leaders, and members of the grant development team.

Information describing potential funding entities and their interests is available primarily in two formats: electronic and printed. Both formats include continuing resources (serials, periodicals, newsletters, documents, and subscription services) that distribute regular announcements of upcoming grant opportunities (see bibliography).

After identifying potential funding sources, the team needs to request formal grant announcements. These announcements customarily contain the

Part I. To determine your library's strengths and weaknesses, check the space between each pair of descriptors to reflect your assessment.

Library Leadership Position

Leader : : : : : : Follower

Response to Change Capability

Rapid : : : : : : Slow

Response to Change Capacity

Broad : : : : : : Narrow

Library Name Recognition in State

High : : : : : : Low

Library Name Recognition in Region

High : : : : : : Low

Library Name Recognition in Nation

High : : : : : : Low

Capacity Utilization

High : : : : : : Low

Library Infrastructure

Strong : : : : : : Weak

Library Operations

Deficit : : : : : : No deficit

Access to Capital

High : : : : : : Low access

Library Facilities

Expandable : : : : : : Static

Library Technology and Telecommunications Infrastructure

Strong : : : : : : Weak

Library Collection Area Expertise

High : : : : : : Low

Library Technology Expertise

High : : : : : : Low

Library Reputation

Ethical : : : : : : Unethical

Project Staff Recruitment Potential

Good : : : : : : Poor

(*Continued*)

> Summarize strengths and weaknesses.
> _____
> _____
> _____
>
> Part II. Based upon the above analysis of organizational strengths and weaknesses, consider the following opportunities for expansion. Please indicate the extent to which your library could expand.
>
> ---
>
> Provide new services and programs
> Great   :   :   :   :   :   :   Minimal
> Increase number of patrons served regularly
> Great   :   :   :   :   :   :   Minimal
> Improve existing technologies
> Great   :   :   :   :   :   :   Minimal
> Enhance current services and programs
> Great   :   :   :   :   :   :   Minimal
> Enter into new collaborations or partnerships
> Great   :   :   :   :   :   :   Minimal
> Use personnel more effectively
> Great   :   :   :   :   :   :   Minimal
>
> ---
>
> Based on the above analyses, our library strengths can best be summarized as follows:
> _____
> _____
> _____

Form 1.2 Library Self-Assessment Tool

guidelines, eligibility and program requirements, and the required forms to submit with the proposal. Upon arrival, copies of the announcements need to be distributed to team members and administrators for review and evaluation.

Calculating the Funding Potential

Only those funding opportunities deemed attainable by the library and its collaborating partners should be pursued. Administrators are encouraged to consider the following issues while making a decision regarding the appropriateness of a funding source:

- The library or a collaborating partner must be an eligible applicant as defined by the funding agency.
- The project requirements must be acceptable within the context of the library's mission.
- When matching funds are required, the library and its collaborating partners must be able to raise them.

The pre-proposal checklist in Form 1.3 shows additional support that the Principal Investigator and grant team may request from administrators during proposal development.

Managing Proposal Development

If a potential funding source looks promising after a formal review and analysis, the team needs to explore levels of interest among the library and its partners. Oral and written comments, suggestions, and concerns should be solicited and encouraged from administrators, librarians, teachers, the school librarian, support staff, parents, and potential partner organizations at this fact-finding stage of the process. Securing a definite commitment necessitates bridging the gap between a general interest in grant seeking and a focused conversation concerning the proposed project.

Because conceptualization requires significant time and effort, it is imperative that the proposal development process be seen an opportunity to serve the community and meet needs in an innovative way. Proposal writing involves the construction of many seemingly unrelated parts; therefore, the crafting of a coherent document cannot be accomplished without making an effort to envision the grant development process as a whole. The Principal Investigator can use the pre-proposal checklist to ensure that all of the steps necessary for successfully planning and writing a fundable proposal are taken (see Form 1.4).

Selecting Partner Organizations

The importance of working with partnerships cannot be ignored in twenty-first century grant proposal development. Historically, an applicant could identify a funding opportunity, prepare a proposal, submit the document, and receive funding independently. However, contemporary proposal development practices assume that the applicant will collaborate with partner organizations formally and informally.

The selection process for a grant proposal does not differ from other collaborative endeavors. Library administrators and the Principal Investigator should select potential partners to represent the constituencies directly

A. Description of Funding Opportunity
   1. Title:_____
   2. Funder:_____
   3. Due date:_____ Dollar value:_____ Indirect rate: _____
   4. Starting date:_____ Ending date:_____ Duration:_____
B. Assistance for the Principal Investigator (check all that apply)

Activity	Notes and Comments
☐ Literature review	
☐ Conducting online	
☐ Updating my literature review	
☐ Statistical data	
☐ Compiling statistical data (national, state, local)	
☐ Preparing statistical data (graphic representation)	
☐ Analyzing data	
☐ Concept development	
☐ Implementation strategy	
☐ Project staffing	
☐ Personnel costs (coordinator, support staff)	
☐ Position descriptions (drafts)	
☐ Expenses	
☐ Timeline development (start-up / implementation / end)	
☐ Evaluation design	

Activity	Notes and Comments
☐ Formative	
☐ Summative	
☐ Data collection	
☐ Focus groups	
☐ Others	
☐ Partners (support / contribute / sub-agreement)	
☐ Identifying potential partners	
☐ Community partners	
☐ Institutional partners	
☐ Partnership agreement (draft)	
☐ Budget development	
☐ Tuition (current & future academic years)	
☐ Travel (per diem rates)	
☐ Expenses (pro-forma budget)	
☐ Library indirect rate calculations	
☐ Cost share calculations	
☐ Proposal editing and/or proofing	
☐ Library submission process	
Submitted by: _____ Date: _____	

Form 1.3   Pre-Proposal Assistance Request Form

Item	Notes	Dates	Who
☐ RFP arrives			
☐ Attend bidders' conference			
☐ Acknowledge RFP			
☐ Submit "Letter of Intent"?			
☐ Qualify funding opportunity			
☐ 1st analysis of RFP			
☐ Copy RFP and distribute			
☐ Bid/No bid decision			
☐ 2nd analysis of RFP			
☐ Administration			
☐ Library Services and Programs			
☐ Business Office			
☐ Send "no bid" letter?			
☐ Administration approval			
☐ Assemble proposal team			
☐ Identify outside evaluator			
☐ Prepare proposal status form			
☐ Outline RFP			
☐ Identify proposal resources			
☐ Writing team members			
☐ Review team members			
☐ Budget team members			

Item	Notes	Dates	Who
☐ Computer software			
☐ Printer			
☐ "War room"			
☐ Develop proposal schedule			
☐ Writing			
☐ Reviewing			
☐ Approving			
☐ Printing			
☐ Sending			
☐ Hold "kick-off" meeting			
☐			
☐			
☐			
☐			

Form 1.4 Pre-Proposal Checklist form

impacted by the proposed project. Potential partners include school district administrators (superintendent, principals, teachers, and school librarians), college and university representatives (dean, department heads, and faculty in specific departments associated with the grant focus), research organizations (regional educational laboratories, "think tanks," and commercial firms), boards of cooperative education services (BOCES, educational service centers, and the like), parents, and community leaders.

Members of the proposal development team are selected to represent identified constituencies in the community. Parents may be self-identified, nominated by the parent-teacher organization, volunteer, or secure recommendations from teachers and administrators. Community representatives may include members of service clubs, not-for-profit agencies, chambers of commerce, churches and faith-based groups, school-to-career (workforce development) partnerships, civic organizations, and professional associations.

Ideally, proposal development team members participate during the entire process. Together they review partners' mission statements, meet and discuss potential contributions, determine levels of commitment, negotiate each partner's role, and solicit ideas and suggestions. During the document drafting process, team members consider the funding limit over a period of years, project costs, and identify realistic goals, objectives, and outcomes to justify the investment. An outline of the steps that the group can follow during this process appears in Figure 1.2.

Step 1. Understand the Problem

Identify the problem in terms of library and patron constituency ensuing from the absence of knowledge, skills, or a particular social difficulty. In order to take the proper action, project designers must identify all aspects of the problem through a review of the available data and an assessment of contributing factors and root causes.

Step 2. Brainstorm Potential Solutions

The preconditions for success at this stage involve the development of the following intangible skills:

- listening;
- observing;
- sensing community enthusiasm and support; and
- trusting one's own intuition related to the viability of program ideas.

The key here is to allow project designers the freedom to think and innovate without self-imposition of any inhibiting factors. Avoid confining project designers to past ways of addressing the problem.

Focus on the underlying or unifying features of team members' ideas. Combine these ideas with the recurring themes expressed by others who attempt to solve the problem.

Integrate the ideal perspective derived from these ideas with the practical considerations emerging from the library, patrons, community, and collaborating partners. The proposal will undergo modification as it is viewed from the context of each of these areas.

Employing the library's perspective requires the following background information:

- History and mission statement;
- Service area (in geographic terms);
- Population served;

- Current library services, resources, and programs;
- Current staffing (workload, interests, relationships, qualifications, etc.);
- Future plans;
- Funding sources (percent of total budget of each); and
- Other community and not-for-profit organizations providing similar services.

Another important consideration is the degree to which the library possesses the resources (facilities, personnel, and time), competencies, connections, and staff capabilities to execute the proposed project.

As part of the process to determine the library's capacity to manage supplemental grant-funded projects, begin by analyzing the past performance record:

- What types of programs has it run successfully?
- What kinds of programs were difficult for the library to run?
- Where are the majority of the library's contacts in the community?

Cooperative programming may be necessary in response to three areas of pressure:

- diminishing financial resources;
- increasing magnitude of social problems; and
- responding to increasing service delivery and reducing social problems.

Relationships between the library, collaborating partners, and community-based organizations tend to be fragile in nature, requiring a heightened political awareness. The implementation of a grant-funded project currently offered by another organization may be unwise and redundant. The established program may manipulate public opinion so as to neutralize such a move. On the other hand, such competition can be healthy where one of the following factors applies:

- a program is copied or duplicated because it serves a different target group;
- the library possesses technologies needed to improve the service or program; or
- the library will deliver the service or program more effectively.

Competition among organizations within a comparatively small geographic area for limited funding is counterproductive. If a need is not likely to be met with a new approach, collaborative services and programs may represent a viable alternative. Central to understanding a problem is the ability to ascertain the readiness of the community at

(*Continued*)

(*Continued*)

large. To achieve the project goal, the library must reach a critical mass of community support. When community support is sufficient, the library can identify potential grantors. The availability of grant monies often stimulates an emphasis on particular features of the planned project. Although it is wise to position the library to take advantage of funding opportunities, grant seekers should be wary of modifying the project focus to the extent that the library takes the wrong path. A satisfactory compromise between the grant seeker's vision and the grantor's perspective is most likely to be reached when the latter's viewpoint is clearly understood by the proposal development team.

Funding entities are inclined to favor proposals that fit within their mission or the developed guidelines and come from applicants with strong community support and a solid, long-standing reputation for successful project implementation and responsible fiscal stewardship.

Step 3. Identify Solutions

From the pool of brainstormed solutions, select the one(s) deemed most promising. Include a rationale for this choice. The following queries can function as a guide in the evaluation of proposal solutions:

___Y ___N Does the program idea fit within the library's mission?
___Y ___N Does the project address aspects of community need?
___Y ___N Can this need be documented?
___Y ___N Does the program idea have a well-defined target group (population who will receive and benefit from this service or program)?
___Y ___N Does the idea fit within the acceptable range of the library? (Consider staffing, space, and experience requirements.)
___Y ___N Do you know what neighboring libraries are doing to address this need?
___Y ___N Does your program idea excite the library administrator and governing body?
___Y ___N Will the library's patrons use, like, and support this service or program?
___Y ___N Does your program idea meet the needs of the grantor? (Is it a good investment of public or private dollars?)
___Y ___N Does your program enhance and support future library developments?

Step 4. Describe Expected Results and Benefits

Describe the changes likely to take place and who will be affected as a result of the project or service programs. Attempt to view the benefit from the patron, student, parent, and/or community member perspective in terms of changes in knowledge, attitudes, and beliefs; the acquisition of skills; current program and service enhancements; physical, economic, or social conditions; the learning environment; and whether or not the targeted group will receive a single or multiple effects and/or benefits.

Step 5. Determine Tasks to Accomplish Solutions

Also identified as "implementation," "project activities," "service programs," or the methodology section, this step looks at each task concerned with the preparation of program and service activities and the service delivery strategy. These tasks include (but are not limited to) the following:

- recruitment of project staff;
- material development;
- public relations and outreach activities;
- professional development sessions, workshops, trainings, etc.; and
- public relations tools (Web site, blog, wiki, listserv, newsletter, etc.).

Step 6. Estimate Resources Needed

The identification of the resources required for operating a service or program is essential to construct a rough estimate of project expenses. These resources include personnel and non-staffing categories. They include (but are not limited to) the following: professional and support staff; volunteers; office supplies; equipment; support of technologies; and facilities.

Step 7. Reassess Viability of Solutions

The data derived from prior steps may require a modification of the proposed service or program or a reconsideration of another solution or strategy. Discussing the problems with other staff may result in the realignment of perspectives.

Step 8. Reassess Expected Benefits

Determine whether the proposed service or program adequately accommodates the identified need(s) and facilities desired outcome. The key concern is to ensure that the library and its collaborating partners do not lose direction with regard to the provision of the appropriate service to patrons, students, parents, faculty, and community members.

Step 9. Identify Measurement Outcomes

It is imperative to note the evaluation strategies, data collection instruments, collection methods, and analysis that will be used to measure the project success and effectiveness.

Figure 1.2   Steps in Conceptualization of Proposal Development

During the deliberations and drafting processes, team members typically read the school district and campus improvement plans, survey colleagues to identify programmatic modifications and enhancements, identify resources within the school district and partner agencies, solicit ideas and suggestions from members of their respective governing bodies, and discuss planning activities with focus groups, public forums, and open meetings.

CALENDAR DEVELOPMENT

A proposal development calendar is essential. Without such a calendar, team members may have difficulties coordinating activities and completing the document in time for submission. The calendar should be developed early in the grant development process and record key stages and milestones. The proposal development calendar enables team members to make schedule adjustments, coordinate activities, and conduct related research while maximizing their efforts.

Starting with the deadline for submission is an effective approach to constructing the proposal development calendar. If the grant team works backwards chronologically from this date, key time frames can be identified and included. This strategy enables the team to allow adequate time for each activity. A sample proposal development calendar appears in Figure 1.3.

The number of required copies and method of delivery to the funding agency must be considered in the proposal development calendar. Scheduling involves consideration of the time to prepare electronic files (usually in Adobe, Word, or Excel) or the pickup and delivery times for each common carrier (e.g., U.S. mail, overnight delivery and priority mail; Federal Express; United Parcel Service, and other commercial firms). Delivery times vary around holidays and these schedule modifications need to be considered. A recommended practice is to designate an individual who will be responsible for submission of the proposal, whether it is sent electronically or picked up by a common carrier.

Regardless of the team's resolve to follow the calendar, experienced grant writers typically take the prudent step of inserting an additional week at the end of the process to accommodate unpredictable events. Without this cushion, the final days can become frantic. The Principal Investigator can monitor the proposal development process through the use of a proposal status worksheet (see Form 1.5).

Above all, the team must realize that planning and proposal writing typically require significant time. Time management is a central concern for team members. They are encouraged to make optimum use of the time available by adopting a number of recommended and proven strategies:

- **Recommendation 1.** Enjoy what you are doing. Individuals who dislike proposal development or delegated tasks are unlikely to devote more than the minimum amount of time necessary to carry out their

Key Dates	Actions
February 5–9	Name team members
February 12–16	Share with colleagues
February 19–23	Share & gather data
February 26–March 1	Compile & write
March 4–8	Final review & edit
March 11–15	Spring break
March 14	Last day to send

Potential Calendar Problems

Deadline at the end of spring break
Signing and review by administration requires time
Coordination with partners

Possible Solutions

Decide whether or not to proceed. Is there adequate time?
Assign tasks to be accomplished to a small group of team members in order to expedite completion.
Contact potential team members and partners with modified calendar.
Schedule additional work sessions in the evenings and weekends.
Solicit support for additional work sessions.

Figure 1.3 Sample Proposal Development Calendar

respective responsibilities. Their resulting performance in such situations is unlikely to approach true capabilities.
- **Recommendation 2.** Recognize that there is always time for important things. Professional individuals are subjected to a wide array of distractions. Successful librarians, educators, and higher education faculty tend to be those who have ordered their priorities and focused efforts accordingly.
- **Recommendation 3.** Allot time to concentrate on high priority items. It is vital to identify just what constitutes a "high priority" item. Because all grant proposal activities constitute a key component of the completed document, the priority status accorded each activity needs to represent its importance as negotiations change.

Section	Title	Leader	Draft #1 Due Date	Review Deadline	Draft #2 Due Date	Final Version	Proof read Date
Proposal Narrative							
1	Executive Summary						
2	Needs Assessment						
3	Goal(s) and Objectives						
4	Service Programs						
5	Roles of Collaborating Partners						
6	Key Staff						
7	Evaluation						
8	Budget						
Appendices							
	Appendix A						

(*Continued*)

	Appendix B					
	Appendix C					
	Timeline					
	Resumes or Curriculum Vitae					
	Community Support					
	Alignment Chart					
	Budget Narrative					

Form 1.5 Proposal Status Worksheet

- **Recommendation 4.** Jot down ideas as they occur. Many good ideas have been lost due to the failure to record and organize them for future use. Documented material can save time in the planning process.
- **Recommendation 5.** Recall long-term goals while doing small tasks. All activities should contribute to the accomplishment of the team's major goals. Tasks that do not fit this pattern should be promptly discarded.
- **Recommendation 6.** Set priorities daily. The execution of key tasks does not always take place exactly as planned. Therefore, flexibility in each team member's approach should be maintained.
- **Recommendation 7.** Be prepared to make adjustments in the project agenda as needed.
- **Recommendation 8.** Do first things first. Each activity builds upon its predecessor and moves the effort closer to a final product. The failure to carry out each stage before beginning the subsequent task will impact a later phase of the process.
- **Recommendation 9.** Quickly eliminate unproductive activities. These activities fail to move the project closer to completion and may not be identified as extraneous during initial planning. When such activities are retained because of their value in past projects, team members may not have the comfort level necessary to discard them. Once their minimal value is identified, any additional time expended on them could be directed more effectively elsewhere.
- **Recommendation 10.** Focus on one thing at a time. Attempts to execute two or more activities simultaneously are likely to dilute effectiveness. One means of assuring adherence to this principle is to delegate whenever that option appears viable.
- **Recommendation 11.** Delegate whenever possible. When a team has assembled to maximize individual skills and capabilities, members should focus primarily on those activities for which they are most qualified or for which they have been specifically selected. Other activities should be delegated to the team members designated to carry them out. If the team lacks understanding and skills, additional members or outside "experts" should be recruited or contracted to fill this void.
- **Recommendation 12.** Think online. Effective communication among team members is essential to ensure high quality in the final document. The tendency of project team members to be geographically dispersed, combined with scheduling considerations, places limits on face-to-face meeting opportunities. Grant developers find e-mail and electronic documents to be an efficient (i.e., cost-effective and time saving) form of interaction.
- **Recommendation 13.** Establish deadlines for yourself and others. Setting target dates to complete project tasks assists team members.

Intermediary deadlines (or milestones) contribute to the team's potential to complete the document in a timely manner. The failure to meet intermediary deadlines alerts the Principal Investigator to the need to make adjustments in the proposal development calendar.
- **Recommendation 14.** Handle each piece of paper only once. The prime concern is to eliminate unnecessary duplication of effort. A definitive plan outlining job responsibilities and the flow of information minimizes the likelihood of problems.
- **Recommendation 15.** Keep things organized. Duplication of effort can also arise out of the need to replace key documents or information that grant team members cannot locate. Files of paper and electronic resources should be organized, accessible through a standardized thesaurus, and updated regularly. Records management policies (particularly regarding the retention of files) are helpful to facilitate effective, efficient access to information.
- **Recommendation 16.** Don't fret when time is spent on activities beyond your control. Inevitably, unforeseen events will occur during the proposal development process. Success is most likely to result where team members avoid morale problems, choosing instead to employ a constructive, problem-solving approach.

In conclusion, proposal writing is a complex, time-consuming task. However, the task can be simplified and wasteful activities minimized when they are divided into manageable components.

PLANNING MEETINGS

After a decision to develop a proposal and apply for a grant, the Principal Investigator needs to prepare for a series of planning meetings. Representatives from each participating unit (libraries, departments, campuses, central offices, collaborating partner organizations) need to be invited and encouraged to attend. A directory of individuals invited to participate on the grant team along with their contact information should be compiled for use in extending invitations to the initial meeting and for distribution.

A draft proposal development calendar including key dates needs to be prepared prior to the initial meeting. The team will be empowered to decide the frequency and duration of future meetings. When the calendar has been modified to reflect the scheduled meetings, it must be made available to team members, district administrators, and partner representatives.

The Principal Investigator is encouraged to secure a consensus regarding noteworthy proposal issues, including funding agency requirements, technical specifications that need to be developed and included, the formative and summative evaluation plans, and budget components. Programmatic and financial reporting requirements and the resources necessary to accomplish them also need to be identified.

Above all, the Principal Investigator and team members must agree on the assignment of responsibilities and milestone dates. A comparative analysis of required skills and those of each team member is a necessary precondition to defining individual roles. The names and contact information (address, telephone, FAX, and e-mail) for team members and the groups they represent will be exchanged. Team members are more likely to attend future meetings if they receive reminders, agendas, and supporting documents in advance of the event.

Initial Planning Meeting

The first planning meeting will be held. The meeting convener (usually the Principal Investigator) will introduce each participant and their affiliation. Members of the group may decide to serve as the team, or they may invite others who have particular types of expertise to augment their group.

In these days of participatory and site-based management, the participants select a facilitator (or chairperson). A long-standing practice has resulted in the selection of the individual whose title and function ranks the highest. However, this approach does not guarantee either an understanding of the proposal's programmatic focus or willingness to participate in the proposal development process.

Experienced grant writers recognize that the passion embodied in the individual who initially identified the funding potential often makes that person the ideal choice to lead the team. Typically this individual serves as the Principal Investigator and takes responsibility for scheduling, coordinating, and monitoring all proposal development activities.

The initial planning meeting provides an opportunity for team members to review the funding agency documents. The Principal Investigator will deliver the completed proposal to the library administrator. It is imperative that the Principal Investigator establishes and maintains positive communication with the administrator who will sign the formal letter of transmittal and application cover sheet. If appropriate, the administrator should be invited to attend and participate in the initial planning meeting. At the very least, the Principal Investigator should periodically update the administrator regarding the team's progress. To ensure that the team members complete all required data for the grant proposal, a series of checklists is helpful. A sample checklist for the proposal development process appears in Form 1.6.

Next, the proposal team needs to review the potential funding source to determine its degree of alignment with the library's mission, services, programs, and activities. This process includes assessment of the degree of confluence between the funding entity, federal priorities disseminated by the U.S. Department of Education, and mandates issued by state departments of education.

Conceptual Design Meeting

The second proposal development meeting should focus on the drafting of a project concept. The concept will lead to the drafting of a project goal, objectives, and activities. Until the team agrees on the proposal concept, efforts are likely to remain ineffectual at best.

A group review of pertinent data describing the library's mission, programs, and services will enable team members to identify those areas most appropriate for project focus. Figure 1.2 can assist team members to summarize program ideas and activities to be included in the proposal.

Working Meetings

Proposal team members need to determine whether they will work in scheduled meetings, independently, or a combination of these environments. If team members decides to draft the proposal as a group, a series of working meetings should be scheduled at the initial meeting. The Principal Investigator distributes a calendar of the working meetings as a follow-up to the initial meeting. Ideally, working meetings will take place in an environment conducive to planning and writing. Interruptions (telephone calls, visitors, eating, and the like) should absorb a minimum of time. To keep the working meeting efficient, the Principal Investigator needs to establish an agenda and goal for the session, monitor progress, and limit the duration to a reasonable timeframe. Marathon sessions held immediately prior to the submission deadline typically do not result in a quality, fundable grant proposal.

If the team members do not produce a reasonable component of the proposal document during one or two working meetings, the Principal Investigator should be encouraged to discontinue the strategy and identify an alternative approach to draft the grant proposal document. Although working as a group often leads to creativity and the inclusion of multiple perspectives, this approach may not always be ideal. It is the Principal Investigator's job to identify the team's strengths and to modify its working structure as needed to ensure effective and efficient progress.

DECISIONS RELATING TO PROPOSAL PREPARATION

During the preliminary planning phase of a project, the team needs to make decisions related to writing, editing, and formatting the proposal. These decisions relate to the assignments of responsibility among team members. As the process continues and the proposal evolves, the potential for misunderstandings decreases if these decisions are made during the initial meeting.

Item	Notes
☐ Letter of transmittal	
☐ Executive Summary	
☐ Needs assessment	
☐ Literature review	
☐ National data	
☐ State data	
☐ Local data	
☐ Goal	
☐ Objectives	
☐ Plan of operations	
☐ Introduction	
☐ Research findings	
☐ Standards	
☐ Partners	
☐ Project management	
☐ Curriculum	
☐ Professional development	
☐ Parental involvement (as needed)	
☐ Community support	
☐ Organizations' roles	
☐ Organizations' descriptions	
☐ Communication strategies	

Item	Notes
☐ Key personnel	
☐ Principal Investigator	
☐ Team members	
☐ Job descriptions	
☐ Budget	
☐ Narrative	
☐ Justification	
☐ Evaluation	
☐ Formative	
☐ Summative	
☐ Data collection strategies	
☐ Data analysis techniques	
☐ Description of evaluator	
☐ Timeline	
☐ Alignment chart	
☐ Resumes	
☐ Sources cited	
☐ Table of Contents	

Form 1.6 Proposal Development Process Checklist

Writing and Editing Issues

Team members must make two critical decisions regarding the writing and editing of the proposal document: whether one person or a team will be responsible for these activities. Writing the proposal narrative may be assigned to team members or a single individual who may also have editing responsibilities. Alternatively, one or more team members may write the narrative while another may edit the final document.

Experienced grant seekers vary in their opinions regarding the writing and editing of a proposal document. One school of thought subscribes to writing by either a single person or a small committee (usually a subgroup of the grant development team). The other point of view supports the writing by a single individual and editing by a second person. Either approach can be successful. If the Principal Investigator has a preference, the position should be shared among group members at the initial meeting. Other team members should also make their preferences known.

When team members are not forthcoming about their preferences, conflict is likely to occur during the proposal development process. If the conflict arises at a critical juncture, valuable resources may be diverted from the collaborative effort needed to complete the document. Worse yet, the team could become dysfunctional, and the proposal might not be completed. When the team includes more than one proficient writer, there is potential for a joint writing effort (assuming the inclination of team members to expend the time and effort required). On the other hand, the team member best suited for project concept development and specific types of technical expertise (technology, staff training, professional development, and evaluation) may feel uncomfortable about having to write a portion of the narrative.

Another problem arises when several individuals contribute draft sections to a single document. While initially attractive as a way to evenly distribute the workload, final narratives tends to read unevenly and reflect differing writing styles when this approach is employed. In fact, a skilled reader may be able to identify the writing style of each individual in various sections of the proposal. Without a seamless presentation, the proposal is not likely to be funded.

If team members decide against a joint writing project, they must select an individual who will be responsible for document preparation. Once identified, the writer and team members will spend significant time meeting and discussing the proposed project.

The writer should be an excellent listener who is able to understand and convey the spirit and intent of each member's contributions. When an experienced, skilled writer participates in the proposal development process, a consistent writing style will result. Because the presentation will reflect the writer's understandings of the project, team members should review early drafts of the proposal. Team members will be encouraged to correct errors of fact, clarify components, and offer suggestions for expanding sections.

The editing function poses similar challenges. When the team includes more than one skilled editor, a potential for joint editing exists. However, the potential contributions of each editor should be carefully considered before selecting a joint editing strategy. The possibility exists for disagreements concerning work selection, punctuation, and format. To avoid discord, joint editing efforts require the preparation of a mechanism to enable editors to reach consensus.

If the team decides against joint editing, an individual editor will be selected. This individual will exercise considerable control over the presentation of the final document. Accordingly, the editor must be an objective reader and capable writer who can articulate the project and its components. Above all, the editor should not be the same individual who wrote the proposal.

Less experienced teams have the tendency to select an English teacher (or an individual who majored in English while in college) to write and edit the grant proposal. While this approach might appear logical at first sight, it makes far more sense to select a team member possessing the skills and experience directly related to proposal writing. Proposal construction requires a special type of writing; having ability in other forms of writing does not necessarily transfer over to the proposal genre.

Document Formatting Issues

Due to the level of effort required to prepare the narrative section of the grant, team members typically do not focus adequate attention on the physical layout of the document. Although the review of a proposal in a competitive environment is focused on content rather than physical format and presentation, appropriate attention to these components can mean the difference between success and failure. Therefore, grant teams need to consider formatting issues throughout the entire proposal development process.

Specific requirements set forth by the funding agency in its official announcement represent the primary formatting issues for the grant seeker to follow. These requirements typically include number of pages, spacing, margins, type size and font, and the use of particular highlighting devices (tables, charts, footnotes, and the like).

Experienced grant writers recognize the inherent advantages of preparing proposals online through the use of word processing and desktop publishing software. These capabilities enable the grant writer to work efficiently when drafting the narrative and provide ease of sending drafts to team members. The writer can print copies of the draft document "on demand" for review and comment by team members.

When the preliminary drafts are prepared electronically, formatting features can be incorporated with a minimum of effort. Regardless of the software used to draft the proposal document, team members should agree on which software packages are used. All of the team members involved in the writing and editing processes must use compatible software. This strategy enables the Team Leader to assemble the final document with minimal human intervention and data conversion.

Selected grant writers may choose to prepare a draft document in typed or handwritten form. If a team member selects one of these methods, an individual must be designated to transfer the material to the appropriate software program. Writing skills are at a premium in the drafting phase; therefore it is advisable not to discourage writers solely because they wish to prepare their portion of the document in an alternative manner.

NOTES

1. *National Research Act of 1974*, Public Law 348, *93rd Cong., 1st sess.* (July 12, 1974).

2. U.S. Department of Health & Human Services. Title 45, Public Welfare, Part 46, Protection of Human Subjects (revised January 15, 2009; effective July 14, 2009), http://www.hhs.gov/ohrp/policy/ohrpregulations.pdf (accessed August 15, 2010).

3. Russell L. Ackoff, *The Democratic Corporation: A Radical Prescription for Re-creating Corporate America and Rediscovering Success* (New York: Oxford University Press, 1994).

4. Bobby Joe Chandler, Lindley J. Stiles, and John I. Kitsuse, eds., *Education in Urban Society* (New York: Dodd, Mead, 1962).

5. Henry Mintzberg, *The Rise and Fall of Strategic Planning: Reconceiving Roles for Planning, Plans, Planners* (New York: Prentice Hall, 1994).

6. James M. Kouzes and Barry Z. Posner. *The Leadership Challenge*. 4th ed. (San Francisco: Jossey-Bass, 2007).

7. Etienne Wenger, Richard McDermott, and William M. Snyder. *Cultivating Communities of Practice: A Guide to Managing Knowledge* (Boston: Harvard Business School Press, 2002).

CHAPTER 2

Project Design

When the proposal development team completes a thorough planning process, a fundamentally sound project design is likely to result. Project design begins with consensus building, continues through the identification of ideas and concepts, and concludes with the drafting of a project goal, objectives (also called service programs), and activities. The team should take the time that is needed to make participants aware of the process.

Novice grant-seeking teams have a tendency to rush into the design stage without a clearly defined need or a projected solution. The predictable result is a disjointed array of ideas that do not adequately address target audience needs. When a group of individuals come together to write a grant proposal (also called a proposal), achieving a clear project goal may be difficult until they evolve into a team. The representatives of partner institutions must not be enabled to preoccupy themselves with "hidden agendas" rather than collaborative decision-making.

Based upon the existing feedback, the Principal Investigator must be able to determine whether the proposal development process is progressing or lagging behind the prepared timetable. If the Principal Investigator cannot refocus team efforts around a shared project goal, the participants will maintain their rigid postures on a host of issues. These "hidden agendas" may include unrelated, new services for students, faculty, and parents; involvement with emerging and experimental technologies; equipment "shopping" for pilot sites located within their agencies; and, professional development opportunities. Selected individuals may want to divide the anticipated grant funds equally among the institutions rather than share the benefits of services, programs, and opportunities that the receipt of funding will support. When a cohesive, focused grant team does not evolve from discussions about the needs that can be addressed through a grant-funded project, then the Principal Investigator is well-advised to thank individuals for their efforts, compile notes and recommendations, and continue the effort alone or with a new group.

Grant teams should avoid such situations. If team members possess a clear sense of the overall "spirit" of the proposed project, then the design process and its implementation can proceed smoothly. When a breakdown occurs in collaborative decision making, the document is unlikely to reflect the expertise possessed by individual team members. The grant team should discontinue its efforts.

NEEDS STATEMENT

The proposal is a persuasive document that articulates an identified need or problem, identifies solutions, and requests funding. Proposals can be written and submitted to government agencies, private or corporate foundations, or philanthropic individuals who share an interest in solving the need that the grant team identifies and wants to remedy or solve. Selecting the potential funding agency (also called the grantor) depends on close alignment between stated funding priorities and the goal outlined in the proposal. The grantor has the financial resources that can be used to implement the project outlined in the proposal. Writing the proposal is part of a comprehensive grant seeking process. In order to be successful, members of the grant team need to be aware of the each step in the entire process.

The six steps in the grant seeking process include the following:

- identifying or recognizing a problem or need;
- formulating an idea or solution to improve the situation or remedy the problem entirely;
- determining whether or not the proposed idea or solution furthers the organization's mission;
- designing, writing, and submitting a proposal that follows the grantor's guidelines; and
- implementing the project when funding is received.

Writing the proposal follows the critical steps of identifying a need or problem and determining how well a proposed solution aligns with the organizational mission. A well-articulated needs statement (also called the needs assessment or statement of the problem) is an essential part of a successful grant application. Without a clear explanation of the problem and its negative impact on the community that the library serves, the grantor is not likely to invest in the project. Therefore, the grantor needs to be convinced that the library can implement a unique, reasonable, sustainable solution.

The needs statement is a compelling argument with facts and statistical data that describe a problem in the community that the library has identified. In the needs statement, the grant team must convey an understanding of the problem and its impact, relating the seriousness of not taking steps to intervene and improve the situation or remedy the problem entirely. The needs statement should contain evidence that the librarian and project team have the experience and credentials to implement a successful project. Without a well-stated description of the problem to be addressed, the grantor may not be interested in the proposed solution nor convinced that the library can achieve the project goal.

Proposals focus on serving the needs of people. If the project does not deliver a service or program with a positive impact on the target audience, convincing a grantor to invest in it can be difficult or improbable. Therefore, when writing the needs statement the grant team should focus on describing the problem associated with the target population and identifying a solution to the problem.

The needs statement should begin with a definition of the problem. Citing statistical data that is provided by a credible source (e.g., state agency, federal government, local not-for-profit or community-based organization) will strengthen the needs statement. However, unless the data are relevant to the local situation, the effect will be minimal.

A description of the problem can be relatively short. However, given the critical nature of the needs statement in the proposal, the following elements should be included:

- describing the problem in the local community context;
- justifying the project to improve or remedy the problem; and
- articulating the aspect of the problem that the project will address.

Context of the Problem

This section should contain sufficient information to allow the grantor to understand the problem, identify with its impact on the target audience, and recognize the need to intervene. When the needs statement explains the local situation as part of a larger societal or organizational problem, the grantor can concur that the proposed project contributes to improving the situation. Contextualizing the problem helps the grantor to recognize the importance of the problem and the need to act. Remember that the proposed project is a solution to the identified problem. It is critical that the needs statement explain the situation and its importance so that the grantor can determine the project's value and evaluate the effectiveness of the solution.

Justification for the Project

In this section the grant team must convince the grantor that the problem is significant and merits the investment of resources. The scope of the problem and its impact on local library patrons and community residents should be stated in compelling terms. The number of people affected by the current situation, the negative impact on them, and the resulting situation in the community and the library must convince the grantor that the expenditure of financial resources and personnel is a prudent investment.

The proposal should contain a description of the approach or strategy that the library will use to implement the project. This description can be a listing of the goal(s) and objectives that comprise the project. The details of how the project will be carried out are described more fully in the proposal narrative.

Aspect to be Addressed

This section of the needs statement is a concise explanation of what aspect of the problem the project addresses so that the grantor understands the project for which funding is requested. The proposal must convince the grantor that financial support for the project is merited. A majority of societal problems cannot be resolved through a single project, but the proposed solution can be focused to better a situation for the target audience. The needs assessment should clearly state the alignment between the library's mission and implementing the proposed project to resolve the identified problem.

The Importance of a Lucid Mission Statement

A lucidly articulated project goal outlines the grant team's vision of the library's environment after successful project implementation. A considerable degree of effort is required to formulate a lucid mission statement. Inexperience or a lack of effort by team members often leads to a restatement of the grantor's guidelines. While a restatement may convey an understanding of the funding requirements, it may not reflect either the library and its partnership or the proposed project. If the mission statement lacks an understanding of the proposed project within the context of both the library's and the grantor's goals, the proposal is unlikely to be funded.

From an internal perspective, the failure to write an adequate project goal that aligns with the library's mission statement results in the wasteful expenditure of valuable resources and a continued lack of focus on the part of the proposal development team. Agreement regarding a clear, workable project goal is the preliminary step in the sequence of project design tasks. The delineation of the succeeding tasks comprises the remainder of this chapter.

PROJECT GOAL DEVELOPMENT

The project goal articulates the mission statement and should be viewed as the most important statement in the proposal. Any proposal that lacks a well-stated goal reflects a weak, disorganized planning effort.

Rather than drafting an appropriate goal statement, many proposal development teams prepare a brief statement indicating the program to be implemented, the equipment to be purchased, or the new service to be introduced. While these considerations represent important components of the final proposal, they typically relate to project objectives and activities.

When developing a goal for the proposed project, team members should consider (a) the legislative authority that empowers a government agency to fund projects with discretionary dollars, (b) the lifelong learning environment in which they work, and (c) the population intended to benefit from the proposed program or service. Government agencies at local, state, and federal levels customarily include the legislative authority in the Request for Proposal (RFP) or Request for Application (RFA).

Reading RFPs, RFAs, state guidelines, and private funding agency regulations for the administration of grant monies provides insight into the factors likely to receive highest consideration by proposal reviewers. Proposals that are responsive to stated priorities have a significantly greater chance to earn a grant award.

An effective goal statement is difficult to write. In view of the need to craft a straightforward, lucid statement, the team members should pay careful attention to work selection. The most convincing, powerful goal statements are written in the present tense and contain action verbs. An inventory of frequently employed action verbs, compiled by Donald and Patricia Orlich in *The Art of Writing Successful R & D Proposals*, is included in Table 2.1.

A simple declarative sentence can convey the project goal without confusing or misleading the reader. Such statements typically begin in the following manner: "The goal of this project is to...." If the statement cannot be written in a single, declarative sentence, team members should reconsider the project's focus.

The project focus reflects the library's environment, its patrons, and the community it serves. Therefore, proposals reflect the mission, services, and programs that are available at the library. Proposals prepared by public, school, and academic libraries have different lenses to describe problems and solutions to them. Examples of sample project goals are included in Figure 2.1.

Proposals prepared by public library teams frequently focus on bridging the digital divide, offering services to the under-represented and underserved, promoting information literacy, and supporting lifelong learning. The project may include professional development for staff so that they can better serve the target audience, public outreach programs specifically

Table 2.1 Action Verbs Often Used in Goal Statements

apply	assemble	assess
build	classify	compare
conduct	design	demonstrate
determine	develop	evaluate
examine	feed	identify
illustrate	implement	increase
install	plan	observe
prepare	produce	provide
purchase	reclaim	reduce
regulate	repair	review
select	synthesize	test
train	transport	validate

designed to interest a group of patrons, or the purchase of new resources and equipment.

When a school library leads the grant team, the focus is typically student academic achievement, needs of the learning community, enhanced instructional strategies, formal and informal professional development opportunities, increased family involvement in the learning process, and access to school library resources (e.g., key print, multimedia, and Internet tools).

Academic librarians may join with faculty colleagues to write proposals that support a student-focused project, a campus-wide initiative, or to further their personal research agendas. The project may include professional development for staff so that they can better support new curricular offerings, outreach programs specifically designed to interest a group of students, or the purchase of new technologies and resources to transform the library into a learning commons.

It is imperative that team members become familiar with the policies and public statements of their library. These documents reflect the official vision of the library's governing body (the library board, the Board of Education, the Board of Regents, or the Board of Trustees). The grant team should acquire and read the recommendations and plans developed by library task forces and committees so that they can become familiar with the vision for

Project Design 47

> The purpose of this project is to provide graduate study opportunities for Hispanic students from the rural area of Texas at Our University by strengthening the College of Education's capability to develop the three new graduate programs: MA in Education with concentration in Teaching Sciences at the Elementary Level, MA in Education with concentration in Teaching Mathematics at the Elementary Level, and Master in Sciences Plant Biotechnology.
>
> The goal of this project is to increase physical activity and healthy eating behaviors among 475 K-12 students in underserved, rural, low-income Idaho communities through evidence-based, school-level environment and policy changes that increase access to healthy foods, quality physical education, and physical activity opportunities.
>
> The goal of this project is to create a collaborative education system to accelerate college readiness among 3,612 students from preschool to high school so that the graduation rate increases from 25 percent to 75 percent by 2014.
>
> The primary goals of the project are twofold: to increase the awareness and the value of law librarianship among public librarians in Colorado while learning their current perspectives regarding law librarians and legal resources; and to collect data regarding how law librarians might provide continued instruction, training, and other support to public librarians by identifying emerging technologies and resources that are or can be used to provide legal information.

Figure 2.1 Project Goal Examples

future developments and expansions of services and programs. These groups include community members who assist library personnel in governance and management. Their collective efforts provide a blueprint of the library environment throughout the community.

THE RELATIONSHIP OF THE GOAL AND OBJECTIVES

The objectives (sometimes called service programs) further elaborate the project goal, breaking down activities into a series of desired outcomes. The following excerpt illustrates the inter-relationship between the project goal and a more focused set of objectives.

Goal: This project will prepare 50 parents to function independently and effectively as they help their 127 children achieve academic and personal potentials.

Objectives: The 50 participating parents will be able to:

1. identify two (2) "teachable moments" in daily events that occur at home;
2. structure three (3) sequential and cumulative instructional tasks in the home for each child;
3. observe each child and use checklists provided by project evaluators to monitor developmental progress;
4. use available equipment and processes at home to teach each child one (1) specific skill each week; and
5. incorporate six (6) packaged materials prepared by staff to teach specific skills during the six-month project.

The goal statement represents the strategic core of the proposal. The goal indicates precisely what the project will change and the evaluation methodologies to be used. In other words, the goal provides a basis for project evaluation. The following considerations should be kept in mind when developing a proposal goal:

- Describes the overall project, including objectives, hypotheses, and research questions.
- Frames the goal without burying it in a morass of narrative.
- Demonstrates that the goal is important, significant, and timely.
- Develops comprehensive project outcomes.
- Conveys the goal concisely in understandable words.
- Demonstrates a logical progression from the library's mission.
- Addresses the identified problem.
- States the goal so that it can be evaluated or tested.
- Demonstrates the appropriateness and importance of outcomes.
- Indicates the research findings and "best practices" that support the project.
- Justifies project outcomes as manageable and feasible.

Effective objectives employ action verbs followed by an object of the action. The objectives should designate to whom or to what the action will be addressed. A well-written project objective specifies in measurable terms a target audience and activities. The objective also indicates why the activity will occur. In most cases, further narrative will be necessary to elaborate the activities and implementation strategies. However, each objective needs to convey a major component in the proposed project. Additional information can be provided in the "procedures" section of the proposal.

The following guidelines should also be kept in mind when preparing project objectives:

- Lists specific objectives in sentences according to their order of importance.

- Details specific objectives in chronological order if the project will be implemented in phases or stages.
- Avoids confusion between objectives (ends) and methods (activities).

A good objective emphasizes what will be done and when it will be done. The supporting activities explain the strategies that will be used to achieve objectives. The following guidelines should also be kept in mind when preparing project activities:

- Keeps the objectives section relatively short.
- Uses action verbs in the infinitive form (to + verb).
- Expresses activities in measurable terms.

The objectives contain the essence of any proposal. Therefore, grant writers should not be surprised to learn that the rationale behind a funding agency's rejection of a proposal is frequently related to problems with the goal and objectives. Typical problems include:

- **Problem 1.** The project outcomes are of limited importance. In a significant number of situations, proposals do not deserve to be funded. These situations pose special problems for the grant seekers. While comments may be available from the funding agency, few individual reviewers are honest enough to inform the applicant that project objectives are insignificant or trite.
- **Problem 2.** The project outcomes are nebulous, diffuse, or unclear. Objectives and activities cannot be followed during the grant period and are not measurable.
- **Problem 3.** The project includes more objectives and activities than the budget allows. Applicant resources and requested funds are not measurable.
- **Problem 4.** The objective is never stated. In some cases, writers "talk around" an objective rather than stating it. In other instances, the objectives come across more as global purposes than specific, measurable, and achievable endeavors.
- **Problem 5.** The realism of some objectives is questionable. While significant, the proposed project cannot provide a "quick fix" to the identified problem.
- **Problem 6.** Objectives are confusing, nonspecific, not measurable, and not appropriate to support the grant goal.
- **Problem 7.** The project objectives and goal conflict. As a result, the proposal reflects confusion between the condition and the intended solution.

- **Problem 8.** Objectives are general terms and contain "activities" or "procedures." In these situations, the objectives cannot be measured, and the evaluation methodology is flawed.
- **Problem 9.** Too many objectives are included. Proposal reviewers tend to reject those projects that include an unmanageable number of objectives.
- **Problem 10.** The proposal includes too many goals. Proposal reviews cannot determine which of the stated goals can be achieved and which ones will be ignored or sacrificed.

The seriousness of potential pitfalls to be avoided during the writing of proposal objectives cannot be overemphasized. Proposal development team members need to devote special attention to writing objectives that support the project goal and provide a definite plan for its successful implementation.

CONCEPTUAL DESIGN OF THE PROJECT

After the goal and objectives are written, the grant team is ready to design the project and to identify specific activities. Certain questions merit consideration as project personnel form ideas and explore alternative approaches to accomplish project objectives.

Preliminary Checklists

The project design (or "methodology") consists of a set of procedures for implementing the objectives and activities. In other words, this section explains how the project will be conducted. Before developing the conceptual design of a project, the librarians need to address a number of questions relating to their capability to implement the project and manage grant funds. A detailed list of questions to consider in determining the grant recipient's capability to support the proposed project is included in Figure 2.2.

After the proposal development team has considered these questions, they are ready to formulate a statement of limitations by which to govern the project. Project limitations should address the extent of the project, groups or categories to be included, groups or categories to be excluded, conditions that may affect project results, and assumptions identified by the Principal Investigator or key project staff members.

Methodologies

Major methodologies include qualitative and quantitative designs. Qualitative approaches include surveys, curriculum development initiatives, and professional development programs. Quantitative approaches include case

Strategic Plan

- Does the proposed project fit the library's mission?
- Is the proposed project a high priority for the library?
- Does the proposed project have administrative support?

Resources

- How does this project impact the current allocation of library resources?
- What internal resources (technologies, office space and equipment, meeting rooms, classrooms, etc.) can the library contribute to the project?
- What internal resources can the library identify as "cost share" or "matching funds"?
- What unique features (abilities, successes, awards, previous grant management experience, location, etc.) give the library a competitive advantage in proposing the project?

Collaboration and Support

- Are the identified collaborating partners willing to participate fully?
- Can the library collaborate effectively with other institutional partners?
- Can commitments, letters of support, and endorsements be secured for the project?
- Are the library and its collaborating partners able to make the required "cost share" or "matching funds"?

Figure 2.2 Institutional Capability Checklist

studies and experimental designs. The first four categories are often referred to as "non-experimental."

Surveys

Surveys differ from experimental designs in that they attempt to measure opinions or a particular situation rather than manipulating reality, as is the case with experimental studies. A widely employed technique within the social sciences (including libraries), surveys are appropriate for collecting data regarding a particular trait or for documenting attitudes concerning a set of concepts, ideas, or programs.

In addition to a set of objectives, its key components include a data collection instrument (e.g., personal interview schedules, questionnaires) and a sample of respondents. More specifically, the survey plan generally includes determining the purpose of the study, determining the target population, determining the method of investigation, structuring the question format, writing and coding responses, planning the data analysis, determining a sample population, writing a cover letter, pre-testing the survey instrument, conducting the survey, calculating the return rate, providing a follow-up for non-respondents, processing returned data, analyzing data, compiling findings, displaying findings, making conclusions, and writing the final report.

Curriculum-Related Projects

A curriculum study design usually includes development or validation, or a combination of the two. These projects typically include a statement of objectives, description of methodology, scope and sequence of learning experiences, description of content, delineation of procedures for evaluating the effectiveness of the curriculum, and the preparation of a product. Objectives are stated from the perspective of student learning and academic achievement. In many cases, curriculum-related projects focus on the behaviors students exhibit as a result of implementation of the curriculum, translated into a rubric against which curricula are evaluated. In recent years the federal government has made grant awards available to support the adoption or implementation of tested programs as a part of school improvement initiatives.

Professional Development

Formal and informal staff training and professional development projects focus on increasing local capacities. The enhancement of instructional strategies and increased skills serve as the basis for a significant number of grant proposals.

Successful projects may include institutes to accomplish staff development tasks; outside consultants hired to train the trainer in a specific skill, software program, or instructional strategy; faculty affiliated with local institutions of higher education to deliver workshops, courses, or seminars that meet predetermined staff needs; educational technologies to disseminate new knowledge or skills; and online learning delivery systems (e.g., distance education courses for academic credit, webinars, blogs, wikis, whiteboards, and audio/video tutorial systems).

Case Studies

In order to describe and measure changes in individuals, groups, and organizations, case studies can be used. Case study methodology can be employed effectively when the project evaluation team possesses knowledge about the larger group from which the unit under study has been drawn and conducts unobtrusive observations. The research design does not include either personal bias or systematic observational bias. Case studies are most appropriate for isolating critical independent or dependent variables. In a significant number of instances, dependent variables are tested through experimental studies.

Experimental Designs

When an independent variable (i.e., characteristic, behavior, procedure, curricula) occurs and it can be associated with a dependent variable (i.e., another characteristic or observable event), an experimental design methodology is appropriate for project evaluation.

Despite the increased rigor of the statistical tests associated with experimental methods, pitfalls exist. For example, the relationship between variables is valid only when certain conditions exist. The presence of too many other independent variables may lower the degree of correlation to the extent that ensuing predictions are no better than mere chance. Furthermore, correlations rarely help determine cause and effect.

Experimental research involves the development of instruments to measure changes in behavior, the selection of subjects, random assignment of the subjects to the treatment groups (control and experimental), administering the independent variable to the experimental group, pre- and post-testing, and the analysis of results.

In recent years a comparatively new experimental technique known as *single subject design* has gained favor, particularly in the areas of contingency management and behavior modification. This method involves the use of small numbers of individuals to act as entire groups for the control and experimental phases of a study. It makes possible easy replication or duplication that is both difficult to accomplish and costly to conduct with large groups.

THE DYNAMIC PROCESS UNDERLYING PROJECT DESIGN

Laying the Groundwork for a Collaborative Effort

Regardless of the level of anticipated collaboration with partner institutions, the grant team should include institutional representatives in project planning and design meetings from the beginning. Inviting representatives from multiple institutions and organizations to discuss a proposed project does not guarantee the cohesiveness needed to develop a winning proposal. While the library administrators may consider the invited representatives to constitute a cohesive group united by a common purpose, carefully calculated strategies are required to ensure that these individuals will transcend institutional perspectives and work together in support of a shared goal.

The grant team is responsible for the development of the project concept design. Through a series of meetings, they will prepare a statement describing the problem to be addressed, proposed enhancements, systemic reform, and enhancements to current services and programs.

Each representative should participate fully in the project discussion. Suggestions, comments, and contributions from each constituency need to be acknowledged and incorporated. When the final document reflects the strengths and contributions of each partner, as well as key constituency perspectives, success and continuation following the expenditure of grant funds is significantly greater.

Steps to Prepare the Project Design

To prepare grant team members for the tasks ahead of them, the Principal Investigator should conduct a number of activities. Grant team members will find the questions included in Figure 2.3 useful to guide their discussions as they design a project. Each activity represents a strategy for exploring potential changes. The Principal Investigator is responsible for encouraging group members to participate in scheduled offerings. If any team members are unable or unwilling to participate in the pre-proposal development activities, the group may decide to change membership. The activities are designed to prepare the team as a whole and vary according to team members' experiences and expertise. Pre-proposal activities may include the following:

- discussion with colleagues;
- visits to "best practices" sites;
- participation in professional development;
- project support; and
- educational technology sessions.

Discussions with Colleagues

The project design phase typically begins with discussions among colleagues. Professional experiences, including successful grant projects implemented by colleagues in nearby libraries can provide team members with valuable insights. In some cases, elements of another project can be incorporated into the proposed design. Given the limited amount of time available to the grant team, replicating research-based, field-tested models is reasonable and worth the investment of resources (personnel, time, money).

Historically, geographic limitations precluded a site visit to learn about other projects. However, twenty-first century telecommunications technologies make virtual site visits possible.

Assessing the Need

- What is the target population?
- What are the needs/problems of the target population?
- What are the causes of the needs/problems?
- What are the major issues?
- How can the problems be measured?
- What documentation is available to support the needs?
- What does the current research in professional literature suggest?
- Do "best practices" or models from other libraries exist?

Defining the Project

- What is the project goal?
- What special approaches can be developed?
- What alternative approaches can be used?
- What is unique or innovative about the proposed project?
- What is the project's significance?
- What resources (library, collaborating partners, not-for-profit agencies) are needed to implement the project?
- What is the proposed budget?

Establishing the Library's Qualifications

- What is the library's mission?
- Does the proposed project support the library's commitment to its patrons?
- What work has the library staff completed to qualify them to undertake the project?
- Has the library managed previous grant projects successfully?
- Does the library have the capacity and resources to support the project?
- Who from the library staff will be involved in the project?
- Are internal and external partnerships negotiated?
- Do additional partnerships need to be established or strengthened?
- What are the qualifications of key project personnel?
- Will the project staff have technical assistance and guidance from experts?

Evaluating the Project

- What are the expected outcomes?
- How will the target audience be impacted?
- Who will evaluate the project?
- What data collection and evaluation methodologies will be used?
- How will the project be continued after grant funding ends?

Figure 2.3   Project Idea Development Checklist

Although virtual site visits are most easily arranged when the necessary facilities are available within the library or located at a local partnership site, inquiries may need to be directed to academic institutions, private firms, or commercial studios. The costs to conduct a virtual site visit can equal or exceed the expense of traveling to the site. A detailed comparison of the budgets required to support each option is necessary in order to determine which option best meets team members' needs and is most cost effective.

Visits to "Best Practices" Sites

Administrators, librarians, collaborating partners, and community representatives should be encouraged to solicit improvement plans from libraries recognized as leaders in their communities and across the nation (such as the Hennen American Public Library Ratings), IMLS project sites, U.S. Department of Education "Blue Ribbon" Schools, and other exemplary sites. Based on site visits and documents delineating "best practices," the grant team may identify and recommend components in need of revision. Each of these suspect components should be referred to library administrators.

Despite possible limitations relating to available resources, a visit to a site that has implemented "best practices" may be appropriate so that team members may become familiar with exemplary projects. Directors of exemplary projects are generally accustomed to scheduling visits and working with planners who express interest in replicating their efforts.

Whether or not the team decides to visit a "best practices" site, documentation and related project materials available from exemplary projects should be obtained. If a particular site is located within driving distance, a majority of team members may be able to participate in the visit. It is advisable for one of the participants to videotape the visit in order to share as much of the experience as possible with those team members not making the trip.

Participation in Professional Development

The goal of participation in professional development activities is to employ creative ways of implementing the components that ensure the successful launch of a new project. A successful professional development framework includes suggestions, recommendations, and needs identified by the professionals in the learning community.

Formal and informational sessions enable project participants to work with colleagues, regional experts, and acknowledged leaders in a given field. A series of focused professional development experiences support library efforts to build a cadre of informed librarians who are prepared to construct and deliver professional development opportunities to their colleagues.

Some teams may consider the preparation of listed topics for workshops before writing the grant proposal. However, more effective professional development frameworks combine a number of formal and informal educational formats. Opportunities include workshops, seminars, site visits, teleconferences, virtual meetings, formal graduate courses, online, and independent study.

The potential for each team member to select one or more opportunities to build a personal knowledge base benefits both the individual and the team. As a result of these learning experiences, the team member will learn new instructional strategies and assessment techniques, identify strengths and weaknesses of models, and integrate potentially valuable concepts into local services and programs.

During the planning of professional development offerings, team members need to consider the following:

- plans and implementation strategies that address academic achievement, instructional models, and professional development activities directed toward the improvement of services and programs for the target population;
- ongoing continuing education opportunities that provide district staff (administrators, teachers, school librarians, and support personnel) with the knowledge and skills they need to ensure and maintain high performance standards; and,
- local data that identify professional development and training needs as reported by district staff (administrators, teachers, school librarians, and support personnel).

Professional development activities sponsored and hosted by libraries should focus on knowledge and skills that their staff members need. Members of the library staff (administrators, librarians, support personnel, and volunteers) will benefit from opportunities that prepare them to ensure increased service to their patrons and community members. Increasing cultural diversity, evolving technologies, and access to supplemental resources (library books, online databases, and electronic materials) represent three major areas that twenty-first century proposal development teams need to incorporate into a significant majority of future projects.

Project Support

The establishment and strengthening of partnerships with local institutions, regional consortiums, state agencies, and other community-based organizations provide a number of benefits to the library. These benefits include (but are not limited to) the following:

- access to resources that the library does not own and cannot provide;
- potential to further cooperative relationships for long-term community benefits;
- increased responsiveness to community needs; and
- greater likelihood for commitment and support of library funding proposals.

As partner organizations become more directly involved with the library and its funding proposals, representatives typically prove to be more interested and willing to provide effective support and resources.

Educational Technology Sessions

Administrators, librarians, and support staff members need to understand the role of technologies in the twenty-first century environment. In their role as information professionals, librarians are appropriate advocates for the potentials and limitations of evolving technologies. With the development of technology-based instructional delivery models, librarians can evaluate and select those models that best "fit" the needs of the communities they serve.

When the library's technology plan incorporates differentiated technologies, multiple learning styles, and a diverse target population, success is more likely to occur. The technology plan addresses installation, upgrading, and maintenance issues for equipment, scheduled distribution of documentation, and local training and support systems.

Administrators play a key role through the encouragement of library personnel to master technology-based skills through self-instruction, formal graduate education, informal seminars and workshops, and other commercially available training. Continuing education can include online courses that are updated frequently to incorporate evolving capabilities and user demands. Librarians need time to learn and experiment with new resources, identify useful components, and conceptually integrate technologies into the library environment.

PROJECT MANAGEMENT

Setting policy and other administrative responsibilities fall under the auspices of the library named as the lead applicant as designated in a proposal document. However, a significant number of successful grant writers advocate the participation of each partner organization in project governance.

A project that involves the joint efforts of several institutions benefits from a representative governance framework. In order to include partner organizations, the proposal team needs to recognize the importance of designing a project Advisory Group. Formally constituted of chief administrators

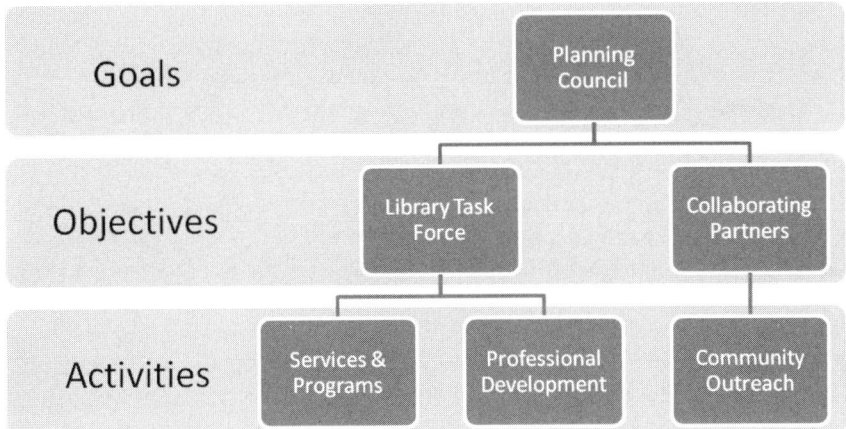

Figure 2.4 Suggested Governance Structure

(or their designees) representing the partner organizations, the Advisory Group becomes enfranchised to provide leadership and advise the applicant of record (the library and its Principal Investigator) in policy and operational matters. Members of the Advisory Group typically include Superintendents, Deans of Colleges of Education, Public Library Directors, and Chief Executive Officers of community-based organizations. A suggest project governance model is included in Figure 2.4.

In order to avoid a situation in which a single institution seizes control of a collaborative project, it is advisable to direct the grant team to design a project governance structure. Although a collaborative project governance structure possesses an advisory relationship with the library administration, its presence, combined with the active partner participation, distributes project implementation responsibilities among major stakeholders.

After a chairperson is selected, the Advisory Group should coordinate its activities with district personnel who are responsible for the component. In addition, the Advisory Group may sponsor one or more public meetings to facilitate interaction with parents, business leaders, and other community representatives. An ongoing feedback mechanism is a necessary component in the public conversation process. Announcements for meetings and comment periods should be widely distributed through the school district's official newspapers, mass media outlets (newspaper, radio, and television), and fliers distributed to students for home delivery.

Establishing an Advisory Group

The administrator of each participating institution should be invited and encouraged to serve as the official representative on the Advisory Group or to designate an individual to serve in this capacity. The importance of the Advisory

Group must be identified as an essential project component. Typically this body assumes one of the following designations: Planning Panel, Advisory Committee, Project Advisory Group, or Cooperating Institutions Council.

The body should include (at a minimum) the following representation: the chief administrative officer (library director, library dean, superintendent or designee); the project sites' administrator (department head, branch manager, principal, or designee); a professional (librarian, teacher, or school librarian) from each project site selected by his or her peers; a parent or community member from each project site selected by the appropriate constituency group; representatives of advocacy groups selected by their governing bodies; business representatives (self-selected volunteers); a higher education faculty member from each participating institution; and a representative from participating consortia. If technological innovations comprise a significant role in the proposed project, the library technology director should be encouraged and invited to join the grant team. Membership must reflect the diversity within the library community and community at-large with regard to race, language, ethnicity, gender, ability or disability, and socioeconomic status.

All Advisory Group members should be invited and encouraged to attend meetings and contribute their ideas. By means of a formal set of session minutes, members from each participating institution should assist in gathering descriptive and empirical data, identifying research-based, field-tested models and "best practices" that may be available for replication, and considering project design recommendations.

Orientation for the Advisory Group

The grant team needs to establish and maintain a positive, productive working relationship with the Advisory Group. After a grant award is made to the library, the team may want to sponsor an orientation session for Advisory Group members.

While the time and effort required to design a seminar is significant, the Advisory Group will benefit from the opportunity to learn about the project and their role and responsibilities. Guiding Advisory Group members through the proposal document will minimize misunderstandings and disagreements later in the project.

Specific topics to be covered during the orientation should include the following: identification of project partners; review of the project goal, objectives, and activities; outline of project outcomes; and, evaluation methodologies.

PARENTAL INVOLVEMENT WITH THE PROJECT

Compelling research evidence suggest that family involvement has positive effects on children's academic achievement.[1] Public library and school library media centers find that they can best serve children's needs by becoming family-centered. Professional educational organizations recognize the need for librarians and teachers to develop skills for involving families in their children's learning. In spite of reform efforts in teacher preparation programs, certification requirements do not mention family involvement, nor do school or public librarians have a requirement to work with teachers or families.[2] Field-based research to support young readers does not focus on collaborative efforts among universities, public libraries, and school library media centers.

Pre-service programs offered at higher education institutions do not routinely focus on initiatives to increase family and community involvement in children's education, nor do graduate course offerings include school librarians. Research findings published by the Colorado Department of Education's Research Library Service in several states (Colorado, Pennsylvania, New Mexico) identify the significant impact of the school libraries on academic achievement.[3]

Empowered teachers integrate research-based, technology-enriched teaching and learning tools into their standards-based classrooms. Concurrently, school librarians enrich collections of grade-level, content appropriate reading materials. These educational environments engage students and their families in learning, helping them to develop independent reading proficiency, improving individual performance on grade-level expectations, and supporting learners to achieve personal and academic success.

Staff development components can be delivered to libraries and schools that are designed to increase teachers' and librarians' use and integration of "best practices" in the learning environment; to strengthen teacher-librarian collaborative partnerships; and to involve youngsters in engaging literacy activities at home to improve reading proficiency and academic performance.

Successfully implemented, twenty-first century grant-funded projects serve as state and national models. As teachers, school library personnel, and parents develop a comprehensive professional development framework that includes informal (workshops) and formal experiences (graduate seminars), they can adopt and follow principles of professional development outlined in state[4] and federal documents.[5]

Through the use of a family involvement framework (see Table 2.2) teachers, school librarians, and adult members of the neighborhood "learning communities" can improve the teaching of reading and increase the family-child engagement in literacy activities. In concert with classroom-based learning, these activities will improve students' reading ability to meet grade-level expectations. The supportive, literacy-focused learning environment will result longitudinally in students demonstrating mastery of district expectations and meeting the U.S. Department of Education's Reading Excellence Act definition of "reading"[6] and state reading competencies for their grade levels.[7]

Table 2.2 Family Involvement Framework for Teachers

Type	Goals
General Family Involvement	To provide general information on the goals of, benefits of, and barriers to family involvement. To promote knowledge of, skills in, and positive attitudes toward involving parents.
General Family Knowledge	To promote knowledge of different families' cultural beliefs, childrearing practices, structures, and living environments. To promote an awareness of and respect for different backgrounds and lifestyles.
Home-School Communication	To provide various techniques and strategies to improve two-way communication between home and school (and/or parent and teacher).
Family Involvement in Learning Activities	To provide information on how to involve parents in their children's school, both within and outside the classroom.
Families Supporting Schools	To provide information on ways to involve parents in helping the school, both within and outside the classroom.
Schools Supporting Families	To examine how schools can support families' social, educational, and social service needs through parent education programs, parent centers, and referrals to other community or social services.
Families as Change Agents	To introduce ways to support and involve parents and families in decision making, action research, child advocacy, parent and teacher training, and development of policy, programs, and curriculum.

From *New Skills for New Schools: Preparing Teachers in Family Involvement* (Washington, D.C.: U.S. Department of Education, 1997), 21.

NOTES

1. A. Henderson and N. Berla, eds., *A New Generation of Evidence: The Family Is Critical to Student Achievement* (Washington, D.C.: Center for Law and Education, 1994).

2. Colorado State Board of Education, *Rules for the Administration of the Educator Licensing Act of 1991 (1 CCR 301-37), Certification Requirements for School Library Media Endorsement* [Online]. Available: http://www.schoollibrarymonthly.com/cert/colorado.html (accessed August 31, 2010).

3. Library Research Service, www.lrs.org (accessed August 31, 2010).

4. Colorado Staff Development Council, *CDE Professional Development Guidelines* [Online]. (1995). Available: http://www.cde.state.co.us/cdeprof/cdeprofsvc/download/pdf/pdguidelines.pdf (accessed August 15, 2010).

5. *Building Bridges: The Mission & Principles of Professional Development* (Washington, D.C.: U.S. Department of Education, 1998).

6. *U.S. Department of Education Reading Excellence Program Overview* [Online]. (1997). Available: http://www2.ed.gov/offices/OESE/REA/index.html (accessed August 31, 2010).

7. Colorado State Board of Education, Office of Standards and Assessments, *Unit of Student Assessment* (Denver: CSBE, 2009). Also available: http://www.cde.state.co.us/cdeassess/index_assess.html (accessed August 31, 2010); *National Standards,* http://www.educationworld.com/standards/national/ (accessed August 31, 2010).

CHAPTER 3

Project Narrative

The project narrative is a detailed explanation of the proposed project. Sections typically include the problem to be addressed, the proposed solution, the target audience to be served, the expected outcomes and benefits, a detailed evaluation plan, brief descriptions of key personnel, and basic descriptions of the applicant and its partner agencies. The time and effort required to draft a grant proposal provides a forum for team members to explore research-based, validated research findings; identify "best practices"; develop new ideas; better understand challenges in the learning community; and strengthen established relationships with partner groups, academic institutions, and community-based organizations.

Writing a successful grant proposal with a strong potential to be funded is within the capabilities of most librarians. Success depends on developing a well-conceived program plan (see Chapter 1); properly researching potential funding entities; focusing the proposal to fit the mutual interests of the library and the potential grantor; and putting together a comprehensive proposal package.

Grant writers need be aware of the varying types of proposals that can be requested, especially in those cases where the potential grantor designates a preference. Potential grantors may specify that requests take the form of a letter of intent, a letter proposal, or comprehensive proposal. Regardless of the type of document requested, the content does not vary significantly. Each of these proposal types is described briefly.

The *letter of intent*, generally two pages or less in length, is used when the potential grantor requests a concise thumbnail sketch of the project. This short document enables the grantor's staff to evaluate the project before requesting a comprehensive proposal. In order to be effective, the letter of intent must highlight the project goal and objectives, the anticipated outcome, staffing, timeline, and budget. The information contained in the letter of intent allows the grantor's staff to determine the extent to which the proposed project aligns with their funding interests and priorities.

The *letter proposal*, typically no more than five pages long, incorporates a description of the project, the applicant and its partnership members, and the specific request. This format is preferred by a majority of corporate and private grantors. The brief document enables the grantor's staff to evaluate projects with modest budgets (under $10,000). In order to be effective, the letter proposal must highlight the project goal and objectives, the anticipated outcomes, key personnel, timeline, and budget. The information contained in the proposal allows the grantor's staff to make a funding decision.

The comprehensive proposal is required by state and federal government agencies. Corporations and private grantors use this format for large requests (over $10,000). This format enables the applicant to include detailed information about the project, goals, objectives, outcomes, key staff, timeline, and anticipated outcomes.

PROPOSAL FUNCTIONS

Proposals serve five distinct and vital functions. These functions include serving as a sales piece, a concept paper, a plan, an agreement, and an evaluation design. Each function is described briefly.

- **Sales piece.** The grant proposal establishes a link between the applicant and the potential grantor. The grant narrative responds to the funding agency's stated interests by demonstrating that the project supports and carries out a program in keeping with the grantor's intents. The grant team may include a combined array of current and future services, programs, and activities. A lucid, insightful articulation of the relationship between these perspectives increases the applicant's chances to be awarded funding.
- **Concept paper.** A concise delineation of the proposed project in a focused concept paper underscores its importance. The broad vision employed in a concept paper encompasses a description of the problem; a proposed solution based upon research-based, validated findings; the target audience to be served; the education, credentials, and experience of key personnel; and a well-articulated evaluation plan.
- **Plan.** When the proposal is considered a plan, the document outlines activities that staff will follow to implement and evaluate the proposed project. The document includes detailed plans of action,

resource requirements, job descriptions, roles and responsibilities, evaluation methodologies and instruments, and budget information.
- **Agreement.** The grant proposal is typically incorporated into the formal award document. Consequently, elements described in the proposed project are subject to negotiation between the applicant and the grantor at the time of the award.
- **Evaluation design.** Grant proposals must include a framework to evaluate and measure project outcomes. The evaluation design includes two types of measurement: formative and summative. Summative (or product) evaluation is used to determine the extent to which the intended outcomes occurred. Formative (or process) evaluation measures the effectiveness of the project implementation, including the attainment of the project goal, objectives, and activities. A grant proposal evaluation design is incomplete without both components.

COMPONENTS OF THE PROPOSAL

The grant writing process is simplified when the team has gathered credible supporting documentation. When these documents are readily available in a proposal preparation file, the grant team will be empowered to begin the writing process and respond to potential funding opportunities as they occur. A sample listing of these documents is included in Figure 3.1.

General Information
- Mission statement for the library.
- Mission statement for each collaborating partner.
- Documentation regarding the library's goals, history, and past accomplishments.
- Geographic service area, number of residents, and number of library card holders.
- Copy of the Internal Revenue Service letter of determination for tax status.
- Copy of the State Department of Revenue letter of determination for tax status.
- Copy of the library's employer federal identification number.
- Copy of the library's employer state identification number.
- Name and affiliations of the library's governing board.
- Documentation relating to the library's last audited financial statement and current operating budget.

(continued)

(Continued)

- Compilation of present sources of restricted and unrestricted funds.
- Operational structure of the library, including geographically dispersed departments and branches.
- Descriptive data regarding educational institutions, maps illustrating location(s), including itemization of administrative centers and research units.

Specific Library Information

- Demographic data on staff, community, and patrons.
- Number of service locations and hours open.
- Census data, including population of the area, per capita income, graduation rates, educational levels of adults, languages spoken in the home, and the like.
- Number of residents by ethnicity, abilities and disabilities, gender, participation in specific programs, and, qualification in groups (low socioeconomic status, free and reduced lunch eligibility, limited English proficiency, and the like).
- Total number of librarians, paraprofessionals, support staff, and volunteers.
- Language proficiencies of library personnel.
- Level of formal education for librarians, paraprofessionals, support staff, and volunteers.
- Average years of service for library personnel.
- Scores on standardized tests for community schools.
- Total number of teachers fully credentialed, on emergency permits, or teaching outside of their specialization.
- Level of formal education for teachers, faculty, librarians, paraprofessionals, support staff, and volunteers in collaborating partner institutions and organizations.
- Teacher turnover rate.
- Per patron expenditure for the library.
- Library mill rate or level of annual government support.
- Comparison of local vs. state vs. federal funds in the library budget.
- Patron/librarian ratio.
- Awards and recognition of the library, branches, and personnel.
- Library long-range and strategic plans.
- Technologies available at the library.
- Number and types of resources (print, online, and electronic) available in the library collection.

Figure 3.1 Documents in a Proposal Preparation File

Despite a nearly universal agreement as to the components in a grant proposal, careful attention must be given to the grantor's guidelines. Although the grant team may be tempted to include supplemental materials in the appendices of the document, if the potential funding agency specifically requests that additional materials not be sent, funding may be compromised by including them. Further, strict adherence must be given to designated length limitations and formatting requirements. For instance, federal government agencies require that applications exceeding specified lengths be deemed "ineligible" and not be considered for funding.

The consequences of disregarding specific guidelines can be illustrated in the following example. A local school district's efforts encompassed four local education agencies collaborating over a three-month period to prepare a Title VII (Bilingual Education) grant proposal. Despite the input of many highly skilled personnel during the writing and documentation stages, a support staff member was delegated the key task of assembling the final document, then copying it, packaging it, and sending it off to the U.S. Department of Education immediately prior to the submission deadline.

Team members completed writing the proposal document and started to work on other assignments. They were confident that the project would receive a favorable review from the federal agency. Two months later the Principal Investigator received a letter from the agency indicating that the appendices had exceeded the specified limit, and, therefore, the entire five-year project was disqualified. Team members were devastated.

A vital aspect of the narrative involves careful adherence to a well-developed timetable. Each draft of the proposal document should play a role in the conceptualization of desired outcomes and the development of project implementation strategies. By retaining copies of all drafts generated during the writing process, team members build a frame of reference leading up to the ultimate selection of ideas and wording. The final version will represent a collaborative effort built upon the insights of participants carefully selected for their respective capabilities (see Chapter 4).

Working in a collaborative Web 2.0 document preparation environment (e.g., Google Docs, Zoho Writer, ThinkFree Online, or Writeboard) provides team members access to the document anytime from any location as it is developed. The drafting stage can proceed in a more efficient manner if the proposal components are first developed in outline form. The outlining process, in turn, can be facilitated through a careful consideration of the functions for a grant proposal. The information to be included in the narrative generally falls into a set framework of headings. Typical components include (but are not limited to) the following:

- cover sheet (face sheet);
- abstract;

- table of contents;
- introduction;
- needs assessment;
- goals, objectives, and activities;
- plan of operation;
- evaluation design and research implications;
- dissemination of findings, results, and products;
- plan for continued support (sustainability);
- budget; and
- appendices (required and/or optional).

Each of the components typically included in a comprehensive proposal document is described briefly.

Cover Sheet (Face Sheet)

The first page is typically a standardized form identifying the applicant, funding agency, requested level of support, project title, and submission date. Readers generally see the title of a proposal before anything else. The following points merit consideration when drafting the project title:

- Describe the project.
- Identify the target audience.
- Include outcomes.
- Avoid the use of acronyms.
- Make the title concise and easy to remember.
- Use an active verb.
- Reject "cute" titles.

Abstract

The abstract (or executive summary) highlights the grant proposal. Typically the abstract includes the following elements: needs assessment; goal and objectives; target audience; overview of services and programs; key personnel; evaluation methodologies; and budget. Even though the abstract appears at the beginning of the proposal, this section is optimally written after the document is complete. The abstract is typically between 250 and 500 words in length. Regardless of when the abstract is written, the writer must follow the funding agency's instructions regarding length and content. In some situations, the abstract is the only section read by the reviewer to screen applications. Therefore, an interesting, succinct abstract motivates the reviewer to read the proposal.

Table of Contents

Each section of the proposal, along with its corresponding pagination, needs to be included in the table of contents. To facilitate access to the document, headings used within the text need to be transcribed precisely in the table of contents. The table of contents should also include listings of tables, figures, forms, and other important sections of the document.

Introduction

Selected funding agencies specify that a grant application include a formal introduction. The purpose of the introduction is to present the reader with a brief description about the applicant, its partner agencies, and the environment in which the project will be implemented. Although the introduction includes "boilerplate" information, the writer needs to consider specific features that interest a particular funding agency.

The introduction is designed to assure the funding agency that the applicant is fiscally secure, efficiently managed, delivers valuable services to its target patrons and user groups, and has earned community respect. A well-crafted introduction "grabs" and interests the reader in the proposed project. The introduction may include a strong quotation or a relevant statement representing the applicant or the community.

A number of grant writers draft the introduction after the service programs (also called the project design or plan of operation) is completed. When the writer drafts the introduction after the proposal is written, the introduction conveys the importance and significance of the proposed program.

Experienced grant writers recommend that the introduction incorporate the following points:

- establish the applicant and participating partners;
- describe the applicant's history and achievements;
- convey the applicant's philosophy, purposes, and goals;
- outline the applicant's services and programs;
- identify the population served and the target audience;
- enumerate accomplishments and endorsements;
- highlight staff qualifications;
- provide credibility in related program areas;
- include information about the proposed project; and
- serve as a transition to the needs assessment.

Needs Assessment

The needs statement identifies and describes a compelling problem or need that exists and merits intervention. The needs assessment conveys the local situation, demographic data, credible statistics to demonstrate the severity of the problem, and the impact of inaction. When the needs assessment relates the applicant's mission to the funding agency's priorities, the reviewer does not doubt the need for the proposed project.

Ideally, the needs assessment is supported by documented evidence from a number of sources, including (but not limited to) government reports and statistics findings, the applicant's experience, statements from recognized experts, and findings of locally conducted empirical research. The needs assessment can include pertinent articles from professional publications, case studies, cited quotations, and statements from library patrons, students, parents, teachers, and administrators. Standardized test results, data identifying economically disadvantaged individuals in the target audience, and related demographic data contribute to the needs statement.

Experienced grant writers identify several "pitfalls" associated with the needs assessment. These concerns include (but are not limited to) the following:

- stating the need using assumptions or undocumented assertions provided as "facts" rather than validated, reliable statistics;
- using understandable statistics that do not support the identified needs;
- including comparative statistics that are not related to the local situation;
- failing to include research findings and "best practices";
- incorporating stories of people as examples;
- not limiting the needs assessment to reasonable dimensions;
- attempting to address comprehensively "all" needs or problems;
- discussing needs unmet by the proposed project;
- creating a "doom and gloom" perspective; and
- not using narrative discussions that relate national and/or state trends and statistical data to the local needs assessment.

Goals, Objectives, and Activities

The goals, objectives, and activities incorporated into the grant proposal flow from the needs assessment. Form 3.1 is a proposal idea summary worksheet.

A goal is a statement of the overall intent and outcome of the proposed project. The goal relates directly to the stated project purpose and applicant's mission statement. Experienced grant writers recommend that a proposal contain no more than three goals. Objectives are the measurable strategies that the project staff will implement to meet the goal. Well-executed objectives are specific and measurable. They include quantitative measures for outcomes and qualitative descriptions of progress. Each objective should include what will be done, by whom, to whom, by when, how,

---

State the problem: _____

_____

_____

_____

_____

Describe the library patrons:

____ Pre-school children   ____ Young adults   ____ Seniors

____ School age children   ____ Adults

Ethnicity of residents in library service area:

____ African American   ____ Latino American   ____ White

____ Asian American   ____ Native American   ____ Other

Socioeconomic factors of residents:

____ "at risk"   ____ Limited English proficient

____ English language learners   ____ poverty level

Geographic area impacted (check all that apply):

City: _____

County: _____

U.S. Census tracts:

_____

Congressional districts:

_____

Form 3.1   Proposal Development Idea Summary Worksheet

and at what performance level. Form 3.2 is a worksheet to use when drafting the project goal, objectives, and activities.

The following guidelines facilitate writing objectives:

- Address the outcomes of planned activities.
- Avoid confusing objectives with activities.
- Define the target audience or population to be served.
- Include numerical data.
- Use verbs such as *increase*, *decrease*, and/or *reduce*.
- Reflect achievable outcomes within a specified time.

```
Project goal: _____
_____
_____
_____

Project objective 1: _____
_____
_____
_____

Major activities: _____
_____
_____
_____

Project objective 2: _____
_____
_____
_____

Major activities: _____
_____
_____
_____

Project objective 3: _____
_____
_____
_____

Major activities: _____
_____
_____
_____
```

Form 3.2 Proposal Goal, Objectives, and Activities

Activities are the events that will take place during the grant period that support the achievement of objectives. Each activity contributes to attainment of projected outcomes.

Service Programs

The description of service programs is the longest section of the proposal. The grant writer needs to include a detailed plan of individual objectives, the activities that support them, and evaluation methods that will be used to measure their achievement. Each activity is described, placed on a timeline, and associated with outcomes. The service programs included relate directly to the project goal. The objectives can be attained through the execution of activities, the use of appropriate implementation strategies, and the investment of resources (personnel, time, and money). Charts, graphs, and tables enhance this section of the proposal.

Evaluation Design and Research Implications

The evaluation component focuses on measuring a project's effectiveness and efficiency. The decisions that grant team members make during the writing stage must assure the applicant and grantor that the investment is prudent. More specifically, the evaluation component enables the applicant and the grantor to determine whether or not the project achieved success through the attainment of the goal and objectives. Form 3.3 is a checklist to use during the evaluation design process.

Project evaluation includes process (formative) and outcomes (summative) components. Either a quantitative or qualitative instrument can be used for data collection. The choice depends upon the project goal, objectives, and anticipated outcomes. In selected instances, a combination (mixed design) of the two methods is appropriate.

Quantitative methods distill real-life activities into units that can be counted, measured, and manipulated statistically. Applicable data analysis techniques that allow for making inferences regarding cause and effect relationships include both descriptive statistics (averages, means, percentiles, and frequency distribution) and inferential statistics (tests, simple linear regression, and chi-square). Qualitative methods measure changes in attitudes, perceptions, understanding, and response to situations and conditions.

Experienced project evaluators recommend that a quantitative approach is appropriate to address the following types of questions:

- understanding the quantities of particular aspects of a program;
- determining if a cause-and-effect relationship occurs;
- comparing two strategies designed to achieve similar outcomes; and
- establishing numerical baselines, pre-tests, and longitudinal follow-ups.

Qualitative methods are appropriate to address the following types of questions:

- understanding the applicant and community at large to determine awareness, support, and participation in a program or service;
- gaining insight into organizational relationships that support a program or service;

Item	Notes
☐ Identify evaluation team	
☐ Internal	
☐ External	
☐ Letter of agreement	
☐ Budget	
☐ Fee	
☐ Travel	
☐ Expenses	
☐ Timeline	
☐ Design	
☐ Formative	
☐ Summative	
☐ Data collection	
☐ Focus groups	
☐ Partners	
☐ Others	

Form 3.3   Evaluation Checklist

- gathering multiple perspectives about a program or services; and
- identifying responses to indicate that the target audience benefits from the project.

The selection of a project evaluator is an essential activity during the proposal development process. When a project evaluator is identified in the proposal, the individual can participate in writing the evaluation section to ensure that the evaluation methodologies, data collection instruments, and analysis techniques measure results appropriately.

A checklist to consider when drafting the evaluation section of the proposal includes (but is not limited to) the following:

- Describe the importance of project evaluation.
- Identify the type of evaluation to be conducted and rationale for its selection.
- Include an appropriate evaluation methodology to measure the components of each objective.
- Demonstrate appropriateness of evaluation methodology.
- Indicate the steps required to replicate the project.
- Describe what information will be needed to complete the evaluation, the potential sources for it, and the instruments that will be used for its collection.
- Justify data collection instrument, analysis, and reporting activities.
- Summarize reports prepared for the grantor.
- State anticipated constraints.
- Discuss the education, credentials, and experience of the evaluator.

Dissemination of Findings, Results, and Products

Project staff members are responsible for keeping the library administrators, collaborating partners, and grantor informed about progress during the grant period. Sharing project findings, outcomes, and deliverables (the products generated during a grant period) enables the applicant and grant team to broaden local support, locate additional members of the target population, alert colleagues to new ideas, and contribute to knowledge.

Dissemination options include (but are not limited to) the following choices:

- Project web site, wiki, blog, and newsletter available to individuals, organizations in the field, and "key" decision makers who share an interest in the project.
- Workshops and seminars sponsored by the applicant to which individuals who are interested in project outcomes are invited.
- Site visits for colleagues.
- Working papers issued during the grant period that describe project findings of immediate interest to colleagues.
- Formal presentations and juried papers delivered at local, state, regional, and national conferences.
- Journal articles published in scholarly, professional, and trade journals.
- Web sites linked to the project, activities, reports, and related materials.
- Displays at state, regional, and national professional meetings and conferences.

- Demonstrations of techniques developed by the project staff and participants.
- Distribution of project reports and documents published and available commercially.
- Creation (internally or commercially) of printed, online, and electronic information packages.
- Special briefings for key state, regional, and national officials.
- Issuance of regular press releases to the mass media (print and broadcast).
- Filing of project documents with national information clearinghouses.
- Distribution of project executive summaries in print and electronic formats.

Plan for Continued Support (Sustainability)

The applicant is responsible to identify the support and resources required to continue a project after the funded period. The grantor typically requires a description of the activities that the applicant will use to continue a project. An outline for program continuation enables the applicant to demonstrate the commitment and support required to continue and incorporate a funded program into organizational operations.

Funding strategies to ensure program continuation should not rely solely on the procurement of new grants. The following questions serve as starting points for conversations regarding program continuation:

- Can the applicant incorporate project continuation costs into the library's operating budget?
- Could the program and services be supported on a fee-for-service basis?
- Does a third party have resources to subsidize services and programs?
- Might the applicant include project continuation costs in a fundraising initiative?
- Are the applicant's partner agencies or community-based organizations able to assist in supporting the continuation of project services and programs?
- Is the transfer of a portion of the project services and programs to another entity possible?

Budget

The budget reflects costs associated with project implementation. When the budget aligns with project objectives and activities, the applicant and grantor understand the costs and the anticipated allocation of resources.

A significant majority of budgets included in grant proposals have two components: a summary and a detail. The budget summary typically appears on a form supplied by the potential grantor. Columns may be included for project costs to be paid by grant funds, cash allocations to the project, and in-kind contributions from the applicant. When the grantor permits indirect costs, the total is calculated using a formula determined by the grantor or charged by the applicant.

Project costs include (but are not limited to) the following:

- salaries;
- fringe benefits (taxes, health insurance, retirement, and the like);
- office space (cost of use or rental);
- equipment purchase, use, or rental;
- software (purchase or subscription);
- resources (printed, online, and electronic);
- telecommunications (telephone, FAX, Internet access);
- postage and shipping;
- printing and photocopying;
- travel (local, regional, national);
- hotel and per diem;
- conference registrations;
- office supplies and disposables;
- stipends;
- tuition;
- professional development registration fees and materials;
- subcontractors;
- project web site design, hosting, and maintenance;
- dissemination expenses; and
- evaluation costs.

The budget summary (or narrative) is typically written after the anticipated costs are compiled. A rationale and justification must accompany budget items. Each anticipated cost should align with an objective and activity. The budget detail component summarizes the purposes of the request and includes cost calculations.

The following guidelines should be considered during budget preparation:

- Conduct research to determine prices.
- Double check math.
- Specify budget item descriptions.
- Use only whole dollar amounts.
- Round off when necessary.

Appendices

The inclusion of appendices is not uniformly required or allowed by funding agencies. Appendices provide a method for the applicant to include pertinent, supplementary information with the proposal. While appendices contain information that is not routinely read and scored by reviewers, these sections can convince reviewers to recommend funding.

In the proposal narrative each appendix needs to be identified and referenced. Typical appendices include (but are not limited to) the following:

- applicant's and collaborating partner agencies' mission statements;
- results of standardized test scores representing the target audience;
- academic achievement expectations;
- library quality reports or LibQUAL+®;
- curriculum vitae of key project staff;
- resumes of consultants for the project;
- list of the applicant's governing board members and officers;
- list of governing board members for collaborating partners;
- directory of advisory group members;
- statement of the applicant's funding sources;
- bibliography of sources consulted to draft the proposal;
- curricula for workshops, seminars, and professional development sessions that are integral parts of the project;
- letters of project commitment, support, and endorsement;
- agreements for cost share or matching funds;
- maps showing the applicant's location and service area;
- certifications;
- assurances;
- audited financial statements;
- glossary of unique terms included in the proposal;
- consortia agreements and memoranda of understandings;
- annual reports; and
- publications produced by and for the applicant.

LETTER OF TRANSMITTAL

An essential part of the proposal package, the letter of transmittal (cover letter) is typically formal and brief (no more than a single page in length). While not an official component of the proposal proper, the letter of transmittal serves as a record of the applicant's submission to the funding agency. In selected situations, the letter of transmittal serves as a reminder that a member of the funding agency provided technical assistance during proposal development.

PROPOSAL WRITING, DESIGN, AND ORGANIZATIONAL GUIDELINES

To ensure that the proposal is understandable and clear to the reviewer, experienced grant writers have an independent individual read and critique the proposal. This process ensures that the document does not contain vague statements, unclear references, and omitted sections.

The proposal's impact on reviewers is strengthened by the use of proven writing techniques. These guidelines include (but are not limited to) the following:

- Study and imitate good writers.
- Use active verbs.
- Vary sentence structure.
- Limit sentences to two commas.
- Write short, easily readable paragraphs.
- Communicate—do not strive to impress.
- Keep language clear and simple.
- Avoid flowery language, opting for short, strong words.
- Be frugal in the use of library acronyms, jargon, and buzzwords.
- Avoid "iffy" and "hopeful" statements.
- Be positive.
- Incorporate documentation (when needed).
- Avoid unsupported assumptions.
- Use spelling and grammar checking software.
- Proofread more than once.
- Employ lists to indicate steps in a sequence, materials or parts needed, items to remember, criteria for evaluation, conclusions, and recommendations.
- Follow the funding agency's instructions exactly.

Experienced grant writers strive to present the proposal in a visually attractive and appealing format. The following guidelines assist the grant writer to accomplish this task:

- Do not use fancy fonts, too may different fonts, colored paper, and other distractions.
- Use bullets to convey the message with a sense of immediacy without being wordy.
- Incorporate bold face type rather than underlining or italics as a means of emphasis.
- Leave liberal margins and spacing.
- Include charts, graphs, figures, and illustrative material when appropriate.

- Indent paragraphs five spaces to increase readability.
- Use ragged right margins.
- Limit the use of headings and subheadings to three levels.
- Unless the guidelines require an electronic submission, print the proposal on letter size, 20-pound weight paper.
- Produce the original proposal on a laser printer.
- Bind the proposal document according to the funding agency's instructions.

Complete a checklist to ensure that the entire proposal document is ready before copying. Form 3.4 is a printing checklist, and Form 3.5 is a checklist to determine that the proposal is ready to package and send to the funding agency.

Item	Notes
☐ Printer selected	
☐ Paper	
☐ Extra ink cartridge	
☐ Cover	
☐ Printing	
☐ One-sided	
☐ Two-sided	
☐ Color	
☐ Black and white	
☐ Binding	
☐ Three-ring binders	
☐ ACCO	
☐ Comb binding	
☐ Clipped	
☐ Stapled	

Item	Notes
☐ Other	
☐ Copies	
☐ Distribution list—internal	
☐ Transmitted	
☐ Extra cover sheets	

Form 3.4 Printing Checklist

Item	Notes
☐ Proposal instructions noted	
☐ Due date and time	
☐ Number of printed copies	
☐ Address	
☐ Shipping container	
☐ Delivery method	
☐ Deadline	
☐ Location	
☐ Authorized signatures	
☐ Complete proposal	

Form 3.5 Proposal Submission Checklist

CHAPTER 4

Project Personnel

Well-developed grant applications rely on qualified, experienced, prepared staff. The project staff is responsible to the library and its partners and the funding agency to implement, manage, and evaluate the proposed project. During the project concept design and proposal writing processes, the grant team will need to identify professional and support staff requirements.

The number of positions, their levels, and costs depend on the time that each individual will dedicate to the funded project. Typically, projects inlcude regular library staff members who will work with individuals hired specifically with grant funds. These individuals will be drawn from the library's professional and support ranks. It is the responsibility of the grant team to determine the number of personnel, their levels, and project responsibilities; perform, coordinate, or facilitate activities identified in the proposal as outlined in the goals and service programs; exercise stewardship of the grant funds; ensure compliance with legal requirements (federal, state, and local); comply with the grantor's and library's expectations; and prepare and submit financial and programmatic reports on a regular schedule in a timely manner.

PROJECT STAFFING REQUIREMENTS

Selecting project staff does not differ from hiring "regular" employees. The distinction between the processes is the work assignment, the time commitment, and funding sources for salaries, benefits, and associated costs. Successful project implementation and management depend upon a skillful matching of the time and effort that will be required throughout the grant period to execute the activities outlined in the narrative with project staffing levels. Although minor modifications may be possible after the project is underway, the majority of the project's personnel decisions must be made during the planning, budget development, and proposal writing stages.

Funding agencies customarily allow the applicant to identify additional personnel who are essential for project success. Experienced principal investigators and grant writers recognize the importance of naming a team that will provide project leadership and reasonable alignment with the library's regular operations. By identifying key project staff members who will work with the Principal Investigator, the grant team has the ability to invite and encourage them to participate in the development and proposal processes. When the key team members are identified, the proposal document can include highlights of their education, experience, and unique qualifications.

Novice grant teams are cautioned against identifying key project team members solely based on professional title or position held within the library. However, political overtones may influence these appointments or assignments. When grant team members are ambivalent or unable to identify key project team members, the Principal Investigator is responsible to seek resolution through discussions with library administrators.

Key project personnel share the library's mission. In a public library, the mission statement is to maintain and improve the quality of life for all citizens in the community by providing resources that enhance and contribute to individual knowledge, enlightenment, and enjoyment in the most efficient manner possible. The public library meets the needs of a diverse and growing constituency by providing services and partnering with other community organizations. School libraries share responsibilities with the teachers for all learners' academic and personal achievement; possess knowledge of the school district, its employees, policies, and "community of learners"; express a commitment to project success; and serve as advocates and ambassadors for the project. The mission of an academic library is to enhance and enrich access to the full range of information resources and services required to improve the quality of teaching, learning, research, and engagement through collaboration, resource sharing, and advocacy.

Key project positions include (but are not limited to) the Principal Investigator (or Project Director), the Project Coordinator, outside consultants, and an evaluator. If the individuals who will serve in these capacities are not identified when the application is submitted, a job description should be included in an appendix. When the applicant includes job descriptions, the positions should be described and classified in accordance with appropriate organizational parameters and compensation levels.

The size of the personnel component depends on the complexity of the project and its duration. Smaller, straightforward projects may be manageable with existing librarians and a minimal number of support staff. Routine and regular work assignments may be shifted during the project period so that the costs associated with hiring additional personnel are minimized, and funds can be allocated to the services and programs described in the proposal.

Large, complex projects require full-time management and oversight. If the Principal Investigator is a library staff member who will retain a major number of regular work assignments, then the time required for grant management can quickly exceed the hours available. When this situation arises, the grant team should seriously consider hiring a project coordinator. The number of services and programs, along with the project duration, can be used to determine how many hours a week the Project Coordinator should work. If the coordination with community partners or the reporting requirements are complex, the Project Coordinator will need sufficient time to compile data, oversee the arrangements for meetings and events, and draft narrative and financial reports for the Principal Investigator. If the grant team decides against hiring a project coordinator and support staff, the funded activities have the potential to become burdensome. This situation could result in a lack of enthusiasm and interest to carry out the project for maximum levels of success.

The library administrator can adopt guidelines to be used as the grant team is determining the level of staffing that the grantor will be asked to support. Projects that require working with a number of patrons in the delivery of services or programs frequently rely on the use of surveys (electronic, paper, or a combination of these data collection techniques), focus groups, or community conversations and meetings. Each of these activities will require significant planning, local arrangements, and follow-up. When projects involve direct interactions with college or university students, paperwork related to hiring, financial aid, and stipends can be required. Decisions about staffing may follow guidelines similar to those suggested in Table 4.1.

Requirements from the Funding Agency

Funding agencies may specify positions or time commitments as a condition to be met in the grant application. If the funding agency requires a full-time Principal Investigator, then the grant team must determine how the position will be filled. When the ideal Principal Investigator is a full-time library employee, discussions with administrators can result in the determination of how to handle the individual's routine work assignment during the grant period. The result of these conversations can be included in the proposal narrative.

Designating a current library employee to manage a complex grant project requires significant planning. If the individual holds a critical position within the library, the grant team is advised to incorporate a transition period. During these weeks when project implementation begins, the

Table 4.1 Grant Staffing Guidelines

Grant Funding Level	Library Staffing	Grant Funded Staffing	Cost Paid to Library for Project Staffing
Public Library or School Library			
Up to $10,000	Project Director Librarians Support staff		Staff time and fringe benefits
$10,001 to $25,000	Project Director Librarians	Support staff (.25 FTE)	Staff time and fringe benefits
$25,001 to $50,000	Project Director	Project Coordinator (.25 FTE) Support staff (.25 FTE)	Staff time and fringe benefits
$50,000 to $100,000	Project Director	Project Coordinator (.5 FTE) Support staff (.25 FTE)	Staff time and fringe benefits
$100,001 to $250,000	Project Director	Project Coordinator (.5 FTE) Support staff (.5 FTE)	Staff time and fringe benefits
$250,001 and greater	Project Director	Project Coordinator (1 FTE) Support staff (.5 FTE)	Staff time and fringe benefits
College or University Library			
Up to $50,000	Principal Investigator (10%)	Students	PI summer stipend; Students hourly plus fringe

Grant Funding Level	Library Staffing	Grant Funded Staffing	Cost Paid to Library for Project Staffing
$50,001 to $100,000	Principal Investigator (15% time)	Project Coordinator (.25 FTE) Students	PI summer stipend plus fringe benefits; staff salary and students hourly plus fringe benefits
$100,001 to $250,000	Principal Investigator (20% time)	Project Coordinator (.5 FTE) Students	PI summer stipend plus fringe benefits; staff salary and students hourly plus fringe benefits
$250,001 to $500,000	Principal Investigator (25% time)	Project Coordinator (1 FTE) Support staff (.5 FTE) Students	PI summer stipend plus fringe benefits; staff salary and students hourly plus fringe benefits
$500,001 to $1,000,000	Principal Investigator (35% time)	Project Coordinator (1 FTE) Support staff (1 FTE) Students	PI stipend plus fringe benefits; staff salary and students hourly plus fringe benefits
Greater than $1,000,000	Principal Investigator (50% time)	Project Coordinator (1 FTE) Support staff (1 FTE) Students	PI stipend plus fringe benefits; staff salary and students hourly plus fringe benefits

Principal Investigator can be available to work with the staff assuming "regular" work assignments for the duration of the funding period.

If the grant assignment is less than full-time, a partial reassignment may be possible within the library. The amount of time that the Principal Investigator will reallocate could be assigned to an individual hired with grant funds as a "buy-out".

Requirements from the Applicant

Library policy may require that key project positions be held by regular, full-time employees as a condition of the grant. If the library district accepts programmatic and financial responsibility for a complex project, administrators may require that the Principal Investigator work on the effort full-time. Selected libraries require that a full-time, "regular" employee manage grant projects regardless of their complexity or duration. The grant team must determine and follow library policy.

Reassigning the individual's routine work assignment during the grant period can be addressed according to the process for a funding agency required position. The result of these conversations can be included in the proposal narrative. Large, multi-year federal grants may require that the applicant specify how the Principal Investigator's work assignments will be redistributed among staff during the project period. If this element is not addressed in the proposal, reviewers are likely to question the amount of time that will actually be available for grant activities.

Project staff should be hired at parallel levels with comparable salaries. If this practice is not followed, internal problems among staff will result. Considerations in identifying project personnel include (but are not limited to) answering the following questions:

- What specific qualifications or expertise does the Principal Investigator need?
- Do key project team members have complementary qualifications?
- What education (graduate degrees) does each key staff member possess?
- Is experience an essential requirement for key personnel?
- How much time can each person commit to the project?

CAPABILITIES STATEMENTS FOR KEY PROJECT PERSONNEL

Key project staff members share the substantive responsibilities for the day-to-day activities outlined in the proposal. These individuals provide the vision and leadership that is essential to achieve project goals and objectives. The "key personnel" designation includes professional staff and non-clerical support positions.

Funding agencies allow for requests to hire additional personnel. The requested positions may include full-time and part-time employees. Critical project responsibilities may be assigned to permanent staff, provided that the time allocation is reasonable and "regular" tasks can be redirected to colleagues for the grant period.

Grant reviewers read this section of the proposal to determine whether the key personnel have the past experience and training related to the outlined activities that prepares them to manage the project and ensure success. Reviewers determine whether the grant team articulates a reasonable amount of time that each key person will allocate to project activities.

Guidelines for personnel requested in the proposal budget outline the funding agency's requirements, but customarily do not specify a level or number of positions. Each position identified in the key personnel section of the narrative has three components:

- outlined duties that relate directly to project objectives and activities;
- time allocations (routinely recorded in percentages) to project activities; and
- rationale for the time allocations in relation to the duties to be performed.

If the grant team identifies a particular individual who will be assigned to work on the project, two types of supporting information must be incorporated into the document. First, the narrative should include the individual's name, title, and responsibilities in the project—a brief description (usually one or two paragraphs) that highlights the individual's formal education, experience, and unique qualifications. Second, the appendix should include a short curriculum vita for the individual.

When the grant team includes a position that requires hiring, a detailed job description is customarily included in an appendix. The job description serves as evidence that the project planning efforts resulted in a reasonable staffing plan. Grant-funded positions can be advertised and filled according to the library's (or hiring organization's) approved process.

Each key staff person performs a critical, unique role in the project. In a public library, projects routinely include the following key personnel: Project Director, librarians, administrators (central library and branches), support staff, outside consultants and trainers, and community representatives. In a school library initiative, the project team customarily includes a Project Director, administrators (central office and campus principals), teachers (grade level leaders and department chairpersons), school librarians, support staff, and parent leaders. In an academic library, the project team generally includes the Principal Investigator, librarians, deans and chairs of one or more departments or units, support staff, outside consultants and trainers, and student representatives. Sample descriptions for typical key personnel hired with grant funds appear in Figure 4.1. Representative duties for these positions are described briefly.

Program Coordinator (To Be Hired)

This person will coordinate and ensure the successful completion of all activities taking place in the project service area. She or he will work with the Principal Investigator to develop and oversee study protocols and program evaluation activities. In addition, this person will be responsible for creating school recruitment materials (e.g., Memo of Understanding); designing and implementing a remote train-the-trainer protocol; designing and implementing quality assurance protocols for the remote service program delivery; overseeing all data collection activities; and conducting data management/analysis activities. She or he will participate in recruiting schools and will conduct literature searches to ensure the latest evidence-based practices for school nutrition and activity are integrated into the project facilitator manual.

Project Coordinator

The Project Coordinator will work with the Principal Investigator to make certain that project activities proceed smoothly, reporting requirements are met as negotiated, and project staff accountability is assured. He or she will oversee the following activities:

- coordinate and monitor the delivery of courses and professional development activities;
- develop and monitor the project budget;
- facilitate the evaluation of project activities in accordance with professional ethics and standards;
- outline project activities for the Advisory Council and librarians' community conversations;
- hire project staff;
- host and maintain the project web site;
- prepare and submit required reports to the grantor; and
- assure that the project is effectively and efficiently managed in accordance with the grantor's and library's policies and procedures.

Graduate Student (To Be Hired)

A doctoral student will be responsible for conducting literature searches, assisting with surveys/forms/protocol development, data entry, and other data analysis including qualitative analysis of key informant interviews to be conducted with students, teachers, librarians, and school administrators

Articulation Liaison

The *High School Collaborative* requires funding for a liaison during the first three years of the articulation initiative. The goals of the *High School Collaborative* are expansive and detailed; the strategic initiatives set forth require extensive coordination and support. The Articulation Liaison will be responsible for the following:

- organizing an articulation kick-off event;
- scheduling meeting times and locations for articulation work;
- facilitating and attending articulation team meetings;
- securing consultants and speakers;
- coordinating summer institutes;
- organizing and scheduling professional development sessions;
- organizing and scheduling college visits;
- enhancing the material culture of the participating schools;
- contributing to parent outreach efforts and marketing initiatives;
- increasing information sharing across the schools;
- coordinating common youth development programs; and
- preparing required documents and reports.

Figure 4.1   Typical Key Personnel Position Descriptions

Principal Investigator (or Project Director)

The Principal Investigator (or Project Director) oversees all activities, serves as the liaison among participating partner organizations, facilitates project meetings, hires (or recommends for hire) project staff, represents the project at professional meetings and conferences (as required), prepares narrative and financial reports, attends professional development and project activities, manages participating sites, and reviews project instructional materials. In essence, the Principal Investigator assumes responsibility for the achievement of the goal and objectives. The Principal Investigator provides energy and enthusiasm to the staff, participants, partner organization representatives, and community.

Typically the Principal Investigator has the following responsibilities:

- provide orientation materials to project staff and partner organizations;
- review the award notice, budget, and reporting requirements;
- serve as the liaison with the funding agency's Program Officer;
- oversee daily project operations and activities;
- hire (if appropriate) and supervise project personnel;
- authorize and document project expenditures;
- negotiate, coordinate, and document budget amendments (as needed); and
- prepare and submit programmatic and financial reports.

Support Staff

Principal Investigators rely on support staff to carry out day-to-day activities. Support staff members provide the essential work that enables key project personnel to accomplish activities and achieve objectives. Funding agencies generally allow for the hiring of support staff to facilitate project management. If funding to hire support staff is included in the budget, then a short paragraph describing the function of each position should be included in the narrative, and a comprehensive position description to be used in the hiring process should be included in an appendix.

LOCAL PERSONNEL AVAILABLE TO THE PROJECT

The project has a greater potential for success when local library administrators and staff members support the services, programs, and activities that can be undertaken with grant funds. Locally available staff members differ among types of libraries (see Table 4.2). Decisions concerning the roles that individuals may assume are based on their personal interests, participation in the project planning and proposal development processes, current work assignments, experience with similar initiatives, professional research agendas, and involvement with collaborating partners in the community.

Library Administrators

Library administrators (public library directors, school district library coordinators, and academic library deans) provide the critical link between the library and the project. Without the commitment and support from the library administrator, grant-funded programs and projects face significant implementation challenges. Grant teams that work within a library environment are advised to include specific mention of administrators' participation and contribution during the project development efforts. When administrators

Table 4.2 Local Personnel Available to the Grant Project

Grant Project Function	Setting	Sample Title in Grant Proposal
Project leader	Public Library	Project Director
	School Library	Project Director
	Academic Library	Principal Investigator
Library administrator	Public Library	Library Director
	School Library	Teacher-Librarian
	Academic Library	Dean or Director of Libraries
Project implementation	Public Library	Librarian, Reference Librarian, Programming Librarian
	School Library	Teacher-Librarian or School Librarian
	Academic Library	Reference Librarian or [Subject] Bibliographer
Instructional personnel	Public Library	Librarian
	School Library	Articulation Liaison, Teacher-Librarian, School Librarian
	Academic Library	Instructional Services Librarian or Access Services Librarian
Teaching in classroom setting	School Campus or District	Teacher or Academic Coach
	College or University	Professor

(*Continued*)

Table 4.2 (Continued)

Grant Project Function	Setting	Sample Title in Grant Proposal
Teaching in library	Public Library	Librarian
	School Library	Teacher-Librarian or School Librarian
	Academic Library	Instructional Services Librarian, Access Services Librarian, Reference Librarian
Project operations leader	Public Library	Project Coordinator
	School Library	
	Academic Library	
Project support team	Public Library	Paraprofessional, Library Assistant, Clerk, Shelver, Volunteer
	School Library	Paraprofessional, Library Assistant, Clerk, Parent Volunteer
	Academic Library	Library Technician, Graduate Assistant, Work Study Student, Intern

have the invitation and encouragement to participate with the grant team, they develop an allegiance and "ownership" of project activities.

The nature of a library administrator's job dictates how work time is allocated. While the educational leader may not be able to participate in the array of activities that a grant program may include, an administrator typically assumes the following responsibilities:

- understand the contribution of project activities to the library and community environments;

- provide support through the authorization to use resources (meeting rooms, classrooms, labs, equipment, and the like);
- support through release and professional development time for librarians and staff to participate in grant-related activities;
- review project progress and measure the impact on patrons, librarians, collaborating partners, and community residents; and
- serve as local project liaison to professional associations, sister organizations, and community representatives.

Experienced grant writers understand that unless an administrator serves as a Principal Investigator, actual participation in project management is limited. Time allocations range from 2.5 percent to 10 percent of the administrator's time. In these cases, the library may choose to estimate the dollar value to the project and include the administrator's participation as an in-kind contribution.

Librarians in Public Library and Academic Library Settings

Professional librarians possess teaching experience, library research skills, and technology proficiencies. Because they are information professionals, librarians have a unique role in the grant development process. The librarian brings a focused perspective on the needs to access resources in support of project services and programs in addition to an understanding of the print, electronic, digital, and software resources that will be required to support project activities. During the project design process, the librarian can identify and provide research studies, "best practice" models, and supporting documentation.

When professional development constitutes a component of the grant project, the librarian should participate and identify available and requested resources for colleagues, patrons, and members of the project target group. Experienced grant writers recognize the unique contributions that a librarian can make to the proposal development process. The innovative librarian will advocate for funds to purchase library resources as part of the funding request. They typically assume the following responsibilities:

- understand the relationship of project activities to available print, electronic, and digital resources;
- identify professional development activities that strengthen their collaboration with patrons;
- support project activities by enriching the library's collection;
- increase access to library materials through resource sharing; and
- share project goals, objectives, and activities individually with patrons, members of the community, and the target population.

School Librarians

Fully credentialed school librarians are usually certified classroom teachers. They possess classroom experience, library research skills, and technology proficiencies. Because they are the campus information professional, school librarians have a unique role in the grant development process.

The supportive collaboration between the teachers and the school librarian contribute to student academic achievement.[1] The school librarian brings a district or campus perspective and understands the print, electronic, digital, and software resources that will be required to support project activities. During the project design process, the school librarian can identify and provide research studies, "best practice" models, and supporting documentation.

When professional development constitutes a component of the grant project, the school librarian should participate and identify available and requested resources for teachers and students. Experienced grant writers recognize the unique contributions that a school librarian can make to the proposal development process. The innovative school librarian will incorporate a request for the purchase of library materials into the funding proposal.

While school librarians may not participate in all project activities, they should participate in all activities that classroom teachers perform since they are also teachers and have instructional components as part of their assignment. They typically assume the following responsibilities:

- understand the relationship of project activities to available print, electronic, and digital resources;
- identify professional development activities that strengthen their collaboration with teachers;
- support project activities by enriching the library collection;
- provide access to additional library materials through resource sharing; and
- share project goals, objectives, and activities individually with parents and collectively with parent-teacher organizations.

Instructional Personnel

Twenty-first century national public education policy supports a learning environment in which every child succeeds academically and personally.[2] Professional development is a requirement in a significant number of federal and state grant initiatives.

Instructional personnel (teachers in school settings and faculty at academic institutions) are critical participants in projects that involve student teaching, learning, and academic achievement. A grant team benefits through participation by instructional personnel during project conceptualization and proposal development. When they participate in the project design, teachers and faculty members can identify areas of interest that contribute to project success, introduce research-based, field-tested instructional strategies, and enhance their personal and professional skills.

Experienced grant writers recognize the demands on teachers' time. Teachers and faculty members are more likely to participate in project activities if they see a direct relationship between them and their classroom assignments. Libraries may elect to offer incentives to teachers or faculty who participate in project activities. The incentives can take many forms: "chits" to be redeemed at the end of the project, classroom enhancements (instructional materials for enrichment), priority for conference and workshop attendance, reimbursement for graduate tuition, additional computers or software for classroom use, or gift certificates to bookstores and educational materials supply stores.

While teachers or faculty may not participate in all project activities, they typically assume the following responsibilities:

- understand the relationship of project activities to the classroom and curriculum;
- select professional development activities that contribute to increased student learning and academic achievement;
- support their colleagues in project activities to enrich and enhance the campus learning environment;
- review project progress and measure the impact on students and themselves; and
- share project goals, objectives, and activities individually with colleagues, parents, and parent-teacher organizations.

The participation of instructional personnel should be described in the proposal narrative. If a teacher or faculty member has a leadership role in the project, his or her name and curriculum vita are customarily included in an appendix. However, when teachers or faculty members participate in project activities, they are not identified individually in the application.

When the school district, college, or university allocates a portion of local professional development funds to pay stipends, transportation, registration, per diem, or other expenses in support of project activities, the costs should be calculated and included as an in-kind contribution.

Parents

Principal Investigators can recruit parent leaders to assist in public library and school media center project activities. Experienced grant writers recognize that when youngsters are the target population for project activities, parental involvement is critical for success. The engagement of parents, guardians, and adult caregivers may include regular library patrons, the parent involvement coordinator for the school campus or district, a parent-teacher organization liaison, and community-based organization leaders. When parent leaders work with the grant team to develop a student-focused project, their contributions can make a critical difference. Not only can parent leaders assist with project activities, they can be critical ambassadors to other parents and advocate for student participation and support for the initiative.

Funding agencies generally allow for the support of parent leaders and organizations to facilitate project activities. Funds can be requested to acquire equipment and materials for parent organizations, materials and supplies to support their activities, and stipends to offset childcare and related expenses associated with their participation.

Innovative grant proposals include on-site childcare by licensed providers, transportation, and meals. If funding to support parent leaders is included in the budget, then a short paragraph describing their role in project activities should be included in the narrative.

NOTES

1. Keith Curry Lance, Marcia J. Rodney, and Christine Hamilton-Pennell, *How School Librarians Help Kids Achieve Standards: The Second Colorado Study* (Denver: Colorado Department of Education, 2000); Keith Curry Lance, Lynda Welborn, and Christine Hamilton-Pennell, *The Impact of School Library Media Centers on Academic Achievement* (Castle Rock, Colo: Hi Willow Research and Publishing, 1993).

2. U.S. Department of Education. *No Child Left Behind Act of 2001* (Washington, D.C.: U.S. Department of Education, 2001). Available: http://www2.ed.gov/policy/elsec/leg/esea02/index.html (accessed August 31, 2010).

CHAPTER 5

Project Evaluation

The primary focus of the evaluation section is to explain the data collection methods and instruments that will be used to monitor and evaluate the project. The data collected as part of the project will be valuable in the process to determine the success in achieving the project goal and objectives. Through a well-designed evaluation, the library can provide accountability to the grantor that the funds were a prudent investment. The library administrators and project staff can determine how well the project has been implemented, and the degree to which it delivered services and programs to the target population.

Monitoring progress as the activities are implemented enables the project team to detect problems and concerns quickly so that they can make appropriate changes. Projects rarely operate as the grant team envisions them. Sometimes the planning results in a smooth project startup with minimal problems. The project team can work with collaborating partners to launch the project activities according to the timeline outlined in the proposal. In other situations, the project team encounters setbacks, obstacles, and challenges that delay all of the planned activities. When the project is delayed, the Principal Investigator and team members have an opportunity to review the project plan to determine whether the reallocation of funds can resolve problems and allow the implementation to move forward. Regular monitoring and evaluation empowers the project team so that they can be aware of shifting circumstances, respond to them, and ensure a successful project.

Evaluation activities take two distinct yet related forms. Each evaluation component is necessary in order to secure optimal outcomes and impacts of planning and development efforts. Formative evaluation is infused through a cycle of continuous feedback and project refinement. Annual summative evaluation is essential because of the opportunity it affords the project team to examine the effectiveness of the activities and determine progress toward achieving the targets stated in the goal and objectives.

OVERVIEW OF THE EVALUATION PROCESS

Evaluation procedures describe the data to be collected with regard to each objective, the instruments to be used for data collection, and analysis techniques. The evaluation methodology is designed to assess program and project effectiveness. The Principal Investigator and grant team are responsible for selecting the individuals who will monitor and evaluate the project. They must determine if the project will be evaluated internally by library staff or externally by a subcontractor.

The applicant must agree to comply with any evaluation requirements that may be established by the grantor, including, quarterly and final progress and activity reports and financial reports of expenditures. A process/product/policy evaluation model may be used to study project impact and changes in the administration and support services provided to the target participants. Researchers may gather data for policy development regarding information access and confidentiality for future expansion.

Participating partners may evaluate project activities severally and collectively. An evaluation model uses a collaborative team comprised of the library personnel, a representative from the state department of education or state library, graduate students from a local college or university, and representatives from project libraries or schools. Through their efforts, the evaluation team will ensure that the project personnel have ownership in the evaluation as well as the benefit of members' collective expertise and experience.

EVALUATION METHODS

The applicant must design a comprehensive, appropriate evaluation plan as part of the proposal. The nature of the proposed program or project will influence the evaluation design, its complexity, data collection instruments, and analysis techniques. If the grant team members do not include a strong evaluation plan, they will be at a significant disadvantage when attempting to convince the funding agency program officers and reviewers of their ability to implement the project successfully, evaluate regular progress, and assess outcomes and results. A well-developed evaluation plan enables the applicant and its partner organizations to judge the effectiveness of the project design, the need for revisions, cost-effectiveness, continuation strategies, and potential for colleagues to replicate the project.

Experienced grant writers recognize the importance of a strong evaluation plan. If the library does not have a staff member who can design the evaluation plan, the grant team should consider working with a consultant, professional evaluator, or a faculty member from a local academic institution, research institute, or similar organization. The following guidelines provide basic guidance for the development of evaluation plans:

- Develop concrete, measurable objectives that include anticipated outcomes or results that can be evaluated.
- Explain the data collection instruments and procedures that the evaluator will use in multiple statistical tests.
- Involve the evaluator in the project design and drafting of the evaluation plan.
- Draft the evaluation plan in concert with the narrative to ensure alignment between these proposal components.
- Create a straightforward evaluation plan that measures the goal and each objective incorporated into the proposal.
- Start evaluating the program or project concurrently with the implementation.

Formative Evaluation

Formative evaluation enables the Principal Investigator, project team, key personnel, and partner organization representatives to monitor project timelines, accomplish objectives and activities and deliver professional development and training sessions. In addition, formative evaluation allows for the establishment of the support framework for participating libraries, schools, and partner community-based agencies during the funding period. Consumer reaction surveys and questionnaires can be used to measure programmatic effectiveness. Project team members should meet with principals and the Principal Investigator monthly. Public library teams will be able to study the impact of the collaboration and training and changes in library use and circulation. School-based project teams can examine curricular components and their effects on student academic achievement, teacher-school librarian collaboration, and family involvement in project activities. On college and university campuses, project team members can study the impact on faculty-librarian collaborations, changes in library use and circulation, and curricular impacts on students in the teaching and learning environment.

During the formative evaluation process, an evaluator can provide information required to refine and enhance tasks. The evaluator can review the program activities and implementation timelines, providing recommendations for improvement. Evaluation will include the identification of key "lessons learned" (problems and solutions) and the development of materials for use with the education partners based on the key lessons. Participants may be surveyed to determine the perceived value, real value, and impacts of the project.

Summative Evaluation

The summative (product) evaluation measures the effectiveness and impacts of project activities. During this phase of the evaluation project staff will summarize and analyze data, write a final report, and provide recommendations to the Principal Investigator. Team members can gather information annually to measure project activities, resource allocations, and other relevant information.

In a public library environment, the evaluators may measure higher levels of patron visits, increased numbers of reference questions and circulation of materials, growth in staff skills and collaboration among librarians and support staff, and strengthened collaborations with community-based organizations. The evaluation routinely focuses on the way libraries manage daily operations, the delivery of professional development and training to librarians and support staff, and expanded family involvement opportunities through the use of surveys, focus groups, and anonymous comments to library administrators and managers.

The project staff customarily review library documents and relevant records, including (but not limited to) newspapers, library board meeting minutes, program reports, and library web sites, blogs, wikis, and the like. Data collection may include written questionnaires and products representative of skill and standard levels attained by library staff. Information may be collected to measure the number of personnel involved in training sessions, the number of parents involved in awareness and project activities, and the number of community volunteers. The final report should describe the equitable access to tools, data, products, and information to all stakeholders.

Policy development surveys may be conducted with community residents and legislators (e.g., city council, selectmen, county commissioners) to determine their levels of satisfaction with policies regarding access to public library resources, efforts to reduce the digital divide, and professional development sessions supported by the grant. The final evaluation report to the library's administrators and its governing board, participating partner organizations, and the grantor serves as a foundation for operating guidelines and policy statements beyond the funding period.

On a school campus, the evaluators may measure higher levels of student academic achievement, growth in staff skills and collaboration among teachers, and family involvement. The evaluation routinely focuses on the way schools manage daily curricular processes, the delivery of professional development, and expanded family involvement opportunities through the use of written surveys and campus team reports.

The project staff customarily review school district documents and relevant community records, including (but not limited to) newspapers, PTA minutes, parent night/open house invitations, and school district Internet sites. Data collection may include written questionnaires and products representative of skill and standard levels attained by school staff (teachers, school librarians, administrators, support personnel, and substitutes). Information may be collected to measure the number of educators involved in training sessions, the number of parents involved in awareness and project activities, and the number of parent volunteers. The final report should describe the equitable access to tools, data, products, and information to all stakeholders.

Policy development surveys may be conducted with parents and community members to determine their level of satisfaction with policies regarding access to school library resources, teacher-school librarian collaboration, and professional development offerings funded by the grant. The final evaluation report to the school district, participating partner organizations, and the funding agency will serve as a foundation for operating guidelines and policy statements beyond the funding period.

Evaluators working on college and university campuses may measure higher numbers of student visits to the library commons, increased numbers of reference questions and circulation of materials, growth in staff skills among librarians and support staff, and strengthened collaborations with academic departments. The evaluation routinely focuses on the way libraries manage daily operations, the type and delivery of training for librarians and support staff, and the implementation of new research and reference materials. Evaluators may use surveys, focus groups, and anonymous comments to library administrators and managers.

The project staff customarily review library documents and relevant records, including (but not limited to) newspapers, library staff meeting minutes, and library web sites, blogs, wikis, and the like. Data collection may include written pre-test and post-test questionnaires from library staff members after training. The final report should describe the equitable access to tools, data, products, and information to all stakeholders.

Policy development surveys may be conducted with campus colleagues and students to determine their levels of satisfaction with policies regarding access to library resources, efforts to increase library hours and services, and professional development sessions supported by the grant. The final evaluation report to the library administrators, participating partner organizations, and the grantor serves as a foundation for operating guidelines and policy statements beyond the funding period.

THE BASICS OF EVALUATION

The importance of designing a strong evaluation plan cannot be overemphasized. Grantors require an evaluation plan so that they can assess the results of funded projects and programs. The funding agency officials need assurance that their resources have been well invested and have enabled the grantee to achieve the goal and objectives stated in the grant proposal. Library administrators need the evaluation information to determine the level of success and resources that will be required to continue a program or project after the grant period.

Novice grant writers tend to concentrate their efforts on the project goals, objectives, and activities. While these elements are critical to the creation of a well-developed document, lack of attention to the evaluation plan is a critical error. Regardless of the strength and comprehensive nature of the narrative, without a comprehensive evaluation plan with explicit data collection, statistical analysis, and reporting elements, the project is not likely to be funded. Learning that the evaluation plan is not a "last minute add-on" is a key component of success for grant development teams.

Experienced grant writers recognize that the evaluation plan is essential to secure a grant award. They follow six basic recommendations to develop an effective evaluation plan that is appropriate to the project or program. Each of the recommendations is described briefly.

- **Recommendation 1.** Review project objectives to make certain that they are concise, reasonable, and measurable. If the stated objectives do not contain measurable elements, the grant team needs to rewrite them. Until the objectives can be measured, the evaluation will not be effective. In addition to measurable elements, the objectives should contain a date by which the stated goal will be achieved. Not only does the date indicate that effort will be expended during the entire grant period, but the evaluation can measure intermediary progress for periodic progress reports. Examples of the differences between types of objectives are listed in Figure 5.1
- **Recommendation 2.** Use multiple data collection, validated instruments, and statistical measures. A well-developed project evaluation typically includes the use of several data collection instruments. These instruments may include (but are not limited to) the following: pencil-and-paper ability tests (standardized achievement tests and aptitude tests); pencil-and-paper self-reporting measures (questionnaires,

Project Evaluation 107

> **Objective 1: Underdeveloped and not measurable**
>
> To buy new library books so third-grade students will improve their reading skills.
>
> **Objective 1: Well-developed and measurable**
>
> To study the impact of a family-school-library collaboration on students' reading proficiency, so that by August 31, 2012, 2,144 learners will demonstrate an overall improvement in academic achievement and standardized test scores of third-grade students will reflect a cumulative decrease of 25 percent in the number of "unsatisfactory" and "partially proficient."
>
> **Objective 2: Underdeveloped and not measurable**
>
> To increase the number of Spanish-speaking library users.
>
> **Objective 2: Well-developed and measurable**
>
> To measure the impact of a new public computer facility developed with the Workforce Development Office, so that by June 30, 2014, an increase of 25 percent of the Spanish-speaking community residents will use library resources and information technology to prepare resumes and cover letters as part of the job-seeking process.
>
> **Objective 3: Underdeveloped and not measurable**
>
> To train librarians on best practices for working with deaf patrons, from preschool age to elderly.
>
> **Objective 3: Well-developed and measurable**
>
> To prepare 30 library staff members to effectively manage the information needs of deaf and hard of hearing patrons, so that by September 30, 2011, 90 percent of deaf and hearing impaired patrons will steadily report reliable service practices by librarians and consistent use of the library.

Figure 5.1 Differences Between Types of Project Objectives

rating scales, ranking scales, journals, and diaries); observations; interviews (face-to-face and telephone); review of project documents; and, performance tests. Examples of the different types of data collection instruments are listed in Table 5.1.

Table 5.1 Data Collection Instruments

Data Collection Techniques		Advantages	Disadvantages
Pencil-and-Paper or Electronic Ability Tests	State-required standardized, norm-referenced achievement tests	Can be administered to large groups at reasonable costs	Expensive to develop, validate, and score
	Aptitude tests	Published, standardized tests are widely available	Scores do not necessarily measure knowledge
Pencil-and-Paper or Electronic Self-Report Instruments	Questionnaires	Can be administered to large groups at reasonable costs Do not require professionals to administer	Respondents may not be truthful Potential for low, statistically unacceptable response rate May require subsequent data collection for sufficient responses
	Rating scales	Easy to complete Collects manageable, non-objective data	Respondents may be biased depending on personal interpretations of terms "Halo" effect Data may be limited by categories
	Ranking scales	Easy to complete Collects non-objective data	List may be long and difficult to rank Terms may

Data Collection Techniques		Advantages	Disadvantages
			provide discernible differences
	Semantic differentials	Easy to complete Collects non-objective data Difficult to provide politically correct, culturally sensitive and appropriate language	Difficult to score
	Q-sorts	Collects non-objective data Forces respondents to determine priorities among items	Requires elaborate instructions Suggests complex data analysis
	Diaries, journals, critical incident reports	Respondents may use their own words	Difficult to score Respondents do not complete
Observations	Standard observations	Project staff can observe first-hand, on-site	Presence of observers may change environment Reliability among respondents can be difficult to establish
	Time-sampling observations	Project staff can observe, first-hand, on-site Project staff can	Presence of observers may change environment

(Continued)

Table 5.1 (Continued)

Data Collection Techniques		Advantages	Disadvantages
		observe more frequently during project period	Reliability among respondents can be difficult to establish
Interviews	Face-to-face interviews	In-depth discussion is possible Sensitive issues may be included	Reliability among respondents can be difficult to establish High cost Require individual administration
	Telephone interviews	In-depth discussion is possible Sensitive issues may be included Less expensive than face-to-face interviews	Reliability among respondents can be difficult to establish Potential respondents may "hang up" Require significant time High cost Require individual administration
Performance tests		Parallels "real world" situation	Require individual administration May require use of adaptive technologies or alternative formats High cost

Data Collection Techniques		Advantages	Disadvantages
Document Reviews		Do not require the collection of "new" data Low cost	Documents may be difficult to obtain Data may not be reported in same format, time periods, or areas

- **Recommendation 3.** Choose an expert to evaluate the project. Experienced grant writers recognize the importance of an objective, comprehensive, multi-faceted evaluation. A recognized "rule of thumb" is to allocate approximately 10 percent of the total project budget to evaluation personnel and activities.

  Unless the Principal Investigator or a member of the grant team has an interest and the required skills to conduct the evaluation, the reasonable alternative is to identify and contract with an expert. If the grant team does not identify a project evaluator before the deadline, the narrative should contain the plan to do so. Library procedures will dictate whether the evaluator can be hired through a formal bid process or a contractual arrangement.

  Library administrators have a tendency to keep the evaluation process in-house and assign the task to a staff member. This strategy typically is less costly than hiring an outside evaluator. However, unless the identified individual has the technical research and analytical skills, interest, and time to evaluate the program or project, results can be incomplete and biased.

  Another typical practice is to contact a faculty member at the local college or university. While identifying faculty members who may be interested in overseeing the evaluation is a straightforward process, selecting the appropriate individual is more subtle and difficult. The levels of formal training in quantitative and qualitative evaluation techniques, experience, and familiarity with the content areas that are the focus of the project or program differ among faculty members. Consequently, the grant team should be prepared to invest the time required to meet with potential evaluators, review their research work and publications, and determine the "fit" between each individual, the library, its partner organizations, and the key project staff members. Only if the "fit" is evident should the "local expert" be selected to design and conduct the evaluation. When the library cannot select an evaluator during the proposal writing process, the search should continue after a grant is awarded.

- **Recommendation 4.** Write the evaluation early. Experienced grant writers understand the importance of drafting the evaluation plan as soon as the project or program goal and objectives are written. If the project evaluator is identified during the grant development process, he or she should be invited and encouraged to participate in this aspect of proposal development.

An experienced evaluator brings expertise in data collection techniques, the availability of validated instruments, the appropriateness of statistical tests to measure stated outcomes and results, and the optimal presentation formats to use in the project reports. When the evaluation plan is prepared in concert with the goal, objectives, and activities, the Principal Investigator and others (as appropriate, the grant team and/or evaluator) can align each measurable objective with a component in the evaluation plan.

If alignment is evident between the objectives and the evaluation plan, then the evaluator will be able to determine and measure success. Otherwise, the evaluator typically encounters problems in measuring success, including (but not limited to) missing or incomplete data, lack of a control group, an insufficient number of respondents, and biased responses. Sample alignment between project goals, objectives, activities, and the evaluation components are shown in Table 5.2.

Table 5.2 Sample Alignments among Project Goals, Objectives, Activities, and Evaluation Plan Components

Goal, Service Programs, Activities, Evaluation Components, and Deliverables	
Goal: To recruit and educate 10 law librarians through a comprehensive law librarianship program specifically designed to provide students with the general competencies, specialized subject training, and extensive practical experience necessary to be highly successful in this growing field.	**Service Program 1:** To integrate a formal law librarianship concentration into the LIS Program by September 2009, developing and integrating significant course offerings in law librarianship.

Goal, Service Programs, Activities, Evaluation Components, and Deliverables	
	Service Program 2: To develop and implement a focused recruitment initiative to identify 10 new law librarians who will earn their Master of Library and Information Science (MLIS) degrees from the University of Denver.
	Service Program 3: To educate and prepare 10 new law librarians who will earn their MLIS degrees from DU by June 15, 2011.
	Service Program 4: To establish a Rural and Small Practice Attorney Library Support Center so that Fellows can access, repackage, and deliver consumer legal information using an array of technologies used and preferred by attorneys.
Service Program 1: To integrate a formal law librarianship concentration into the LIS Program by September 2009, developing and integrating significant course offerings in law librarianship.	<u>Activities:</u> • Complete the design of a law librarianship curriculum of interest and significance that align with the competencies developed by AALL and ALA (see Supporting Document 4; July 1, 2008 through September 30, 2008); • Pilot new courses in law librarianship (September 1, 2008 through August 31, 2009); • Identify authoritative local, state, and national providers (print, online, and electronic formats) that emphasize issues, materials, and data of interest and relevance to law librarians (ongoing);

(*Continued*)

Table 5.2 (Continued)

Goal, Service Programs, Activities, Evaluation Components, and Deliverables
• Solicit technical assistance, curricular advisement, support, and guidance from leading law library professionals and state, regional, national, and international organizations (ongoing); and • Prepare and submit required documentation for the law librarianship concentration to the MCE Program Planning and Review Committee (PPR), the MCE deans, and the Graduate Council DU (September–October 2008). **Evaluation components:** **Intended outcome:** Courses and law librarianship concentration will be approved. **Indicator:** Approval forms signed by the PPR chairperson, MCE dean, and the Vice Provost for Graduate Studies and Research. **Data source:** Course and concentration forms. **Target:** Law librarianship courses and concentration will be added to the LIS Program. **Deliverables:** • Syllabi for five new courses in law librarianship (formative evaluation); • Resumes and CVs for adjunct faculty (formative evaluation); • Course evaluations for each course taught (formative evaluation); • DU, MCE, PPR, and LIS Program documents required to establish a

Goal, Service Programs, Activities, Evaluation Components, and Deliverables	
	new law librarianship concentration and specialized courses (formative evaluation); • Report of authoritative local, state, and national providers (print, online, and electronic formats) that emphasize issues, materials, and data of interest and relevance to law librarians (formative evaluation); • Minutes and reports from project planning team, technical assistance, curricular advisement, support, and guidance from leading law library professionals and state, regional, national, and international organizations (formative evaluation); • Continuous feedback and project refinement from outside evaluator (formative evaluation); and • Progress toward the achievement of goals and activities (summative evaluation).
Service Program 2: To develop and implement a focused recruitment initiative to identify 10 new law librarians who will earn their Master of Library and Information Science (MLIS) degrees from the University of Denver.	<u>Activities:</u> • Initiate a focused student recruitment initiative under the auspices of the MCE Office of Admissions and Enrollment Services (by September 1, 2008); • Incorporate mass media outlets (newsletters, professional association publications, and project website) to deliver MCE and LIS Program information to potential law librarianship students (August 15–November 15, 2008);

(Continued)

Table 5.2 (Continued)

Goal, Service Programs, Activities, Evaluation Components, and Deliverables	
	• Host a series of two-hour informational open house events in six selected locations (October 2008); • Solicit formal LIS Program and LLF applications (see Supporting Document 5) from potential students (by December 1, 2008); • Admit a group of 10 LIS graduate students who will serve as Law Librarian Fellows with full tuition financial support during their graduate course of study (by March 15, 2009); and • Award Law Librarian Fellowships to 10 students (by March 15, 2009). **Evaluation components:** **Intended outcome:** Recruit 10 students to law librarianship who will begin their studies Fall 2009. **Indicator 1:** Students apply to LIS Program. **Data source:** Complete application packages submitted to the Office of Graduate Studies. **Target:** 10 students will be admitted to the LIS Program with an interest in law librarianship. **Indicator 2:** Students apply for Law Librarian Fellowship. **Data source:** Tracking of student applications, including certain demographic information such as race, ethnicity, gender, and age. **Target:** Participation of students in law librarianship each year (100 percent of project goal).

Goal, Service Programs, Activities, Evaluation Components, and Deliverables	
	Intended outcome: Students begin their MLIS studies. **Indicator:** Percent of students reporting satisfaction. **Data source:** Course Evaluation Forms. Findings from evaluations of courses will be used to improve later ones. **Target:** At least 85 percent of Fellows will be satisfied or very satisfied with courses and the overall law librarianship program. **Deliverables:** • Recruitment materials for MLIS and LLF programs (formative evaluation); • Agendas, sign-in sheets, contact information, and travel reports (narrative and expenses) from open houses (formative evaluation); • LIS and LLF program applications (formative evaluation); • Admissions letters and LLF awards (formative evaluation); • Minutes and reports from project planning team, curricular advisement, and support for LLF students (formative evaluation); • Continuous feedback and project refinement from outside evaluator (formative evaluation); and • Progress toward the achievement of goals and activities (summative evaluation).
Service Program 3: To educate and prepare 10 new law librarians who will earn their MLIS degrees from DU by June 15, 2011.	**Activities:** • Deliver a 58-quarter-hour MLIS program over a 22-month period (September 1, 2009 through June 15, 2011);

(Continued)

Table 5.2 (Continued)

Goal, Service Programs, Activities, Evaluation Components, and Deliverables	
	• Provide course advisement and guidance from WLL law librarians and full-time LIS faculty to orient the Fellows into the profession and state, regional, national, and international organizations (ongoing); • Increase cultural awareness and linguistic sensitivity among the Fellows so that they are more effective in their roles as human search intermediaries for a diverse clientele (ongoing); • Facilitate mentoring for the Fellows with practicing law librarians at courts, academic institutions, and firm libraries (ongoing); • Achieve initiation and socialization of Fellows into the legal information community (ongoing); • Support and facilitate the participation of the Fellows in 660 hours of practical experience in the operation of departments and activities of WLL (six hours per week over three 10-week quarters during their first academic year (2009-2010) and 12 hours per week over three 10-week quarters in the second academic year (2010-2011; ongoing); • Support the participation of the Fellows in a minimum of 6 hours quarterly in professional development activities, including (but not limited to) workshops,

Goal, Service Programs, Activities, Evaluation Components, and Deliverables	
	seminars, and Colorado Association of Law Libraries (CoALL) and AALL meetings (ongoing); • Assist the Fellows in pursuing professional positions after graduation through assistance in resume preparation, interview techniques, and recommendations to potential employers (beginning January 1, 2011); and • Recognize Fellows' academic achievements, accomplishments, and contributions to their prospective colleagues and employers at the AALL conference in Denver (July 2010) and the MCE graduation reception (June 2011). **Evaluation components:** **Intended outcome:** Library students in law librarianship will expand their technical skills and competencies. **Indicator:** Student use of new technical skills. **Data source:** Student annual survey, beginning with a pre-survey before they begin classes. **Target:** During the first year after participation in the LIS Program, students will use two new technical skills in delivering legal information. **Deliverables:** • Course rotation, syllabi, and evaluations (formative evaluation);

(*Continued*)

Table 5.2 (Continued)

Goal, Service Programs, Activities, Evaluation Components, and Deliverables	
	• Student course work plans (formative evaluation); • Notes from weekly student meetings with Project Coordinator, monthly student progress reports, and quarterly student performance evaluations completed by appropriate WLL staff members; • Minutes and reports from project planning team, student advisements and monthly reports from the Project Coordinator (formative evaluation); • Semi-annual student LLF satisfaction survey (formative evaluation); and • Progress toward the achievement of goals and activities (summative evaluation).
Service Program 4: To establish a Rural and Small Practice Attorney Library Support Center so that Fellows can access, repackage, and deliver consumer legal information using an array of technologies used and preferred by attorneys.	**Activities:** • Conduct a cultural awareness and linguistic sensitivity session for Fellows (January 2010); • Compile bilingual (English and Spanish) lists of legal terms, cultural awareness and linguistic sensitivity resources, and administrative guides for the delivery of law library programs, services, and resources for Fellows to use in their Support Center work (January 15, 2010 through March 31, 2010); • Deliver law library support services to rural attorneys, academic and public libraries with legal collections, rural government agencies, and nongovernmental

Goal, Service Programs, Activities, Evaluation Components, and Deliverables		
		legal organizations serving diverse communities with low-income individuals and families (September 1, 2010 through June 15, 2011);
• Conduct an environmental scan to identify emerging technologies used by rural attorneys, academic and public libraries with legal collections, rural government agencies, and nongovernmental legal organizations to repackage and deliver information (April 1, 2010 through May 31, 2010);
• Compile descriptions, technical requirements, documentation, and administrative guides for rural attorneys, academic and public libraries with legal collections, rural government agencies, and nongovernmental legal organizations to use in their local communities (June 2010);
• Publish descriptions, technical requirements, documentation, and administrative guides for emerging technologies (July 2010); and
• Contribute published articles to peer-reviewed law librarianship journals highlighting the integration of emerging technologies used by rural attorneys, academic and public libraries with legal collections, rural government agencies, and nongovernmental legal organizations to repackage and deliver information to residents in diverse communities with low-income

(*Continued*)

Table 5.2 (Continued)

Goal, Service Programs, Activities, Evaluation Components, and Deliverables
individuals and families (September 2010–June 2011). **Evaluation components:** **Intended outcome A:** Fellows will access, repackage and deliver relevant legal information using an array of technologies used and preferred by rural attorneys, academic and public libraries with legal collections, rural government agencies, and nongovernmental legal organizations serving diverse communities with low-income individuals and families. **Indicator 1:** Level of use of legal resources in print, electronic, and online formats by Fellows. **Data source:** Track use of tools, i.e., database searches, print tools (reporters, treatises, etc.), and e-journals. **Target:** Use of legal resources will increase by 20 percent. **Indicator 2:** User satisfaction with availability, usability, and helpfulness of legal information. **Data source:** User survey that includes geographic location (i.e., county, community), purpose (attorney for client, public library for attorney or resident, government agency, nongovernment agency) and demographic information (i.e., race, ethnicity, gender, age, etc.). **Target:** At least 80 percent of users will report that they are satisfied or very satisfied with the availability,

Goal, Service Programs, Activities, Evaluation Components, and Deliverables		
		usability, and helpfulness of legal information.
Intended outcome B: Fellows will increase their cultural awareness related to diverse user groups.
Indicator: Fellows' scores on cultural awareness instrument.
Data source: Pre-post administration of cultural awareness instrument.
Target: Fellows' post-test scores on the cultural awareness instrument improve by at least 10 percent after they complete the training session.
Intended outcome C: Fellows will become more effective human search intermediaries for multilingual constituencies.
Indicator: User satisfaction with services provided by Fellows.
Data source: User survey that includes geographic location (i.e., county, community), purpose (attorney for client, public library for attorney or resident, government agency, nongovernment agency) and demographic information (i.e., race, ethnicity, gender, age, etc.).
Target: At least 80 percent of users will report that they are satisfied or very satisfied with the availability, usability, and helpfulness of legal information.

<u>Deliverables:</u>
• Environmental scan to identify emerging technologies used by rural attorneys, academic and public |

(Continued)

Table 5.2 (Continued)

Goal, Service Programs, Activities, Evaluation Components, and Deliverables	
	libraries with legal collections, rural government agencies, and nongovernmental legal organizations to repackage and deliver information (formative evaluation); • Publication (paper and electronic) of descriptions, technical requirements, documentation, and administrative guides for rural attorneys, academic and public libraries with legal collections, rural government agencies, and nongovernmental legal organizations to use in their local communities (formative evaluation); • Administrative handbook for the development, management, and evaluation of the Rural and Small Practice Attorney Library Support Center (Support Center; formative evaluation); • Materials from cultural awareness workshop (formative evaluation); • Bilingual (English and Spanish) lists of legal terms, cultural awareness and linguistic sensitivity resources, and administrative guides for the delivery of law library programs, services, and resources for Fellows to use in their Support Center work (formative evaluation); • Marketing materials for Support Center (formative evaluation); • Agendas, contact information, and travel reports (narrative and

Goal, Service Programs, Activities, Evaluation Components, and Deliverables	
	expenses) from Support Center (formative evaluation); • Quarterly Support Center client satisfaction surveys (formative evaluation); • Semiannual student LLF satisfaction survey with specific data about the practical component of the Support Center (formative evaluation); • Longitudinal studies of Support Center client satisfaction and student satisfaction (formative evaluation); • Notes from weekly student meetings with Project Coordinator, monthly student progress reports, quarterly student performance evaluations for the Support Service; quarterly student performance evaluations completed by appropriate WLL staff members (formative evaluation); • Minutes and reports from project planning team, student advisements, monthly reports from the Project Coordinator, and quarterly activity reports from the Support Center Coordinator (formative evaluation); • Annual use by clients subscribing to Support Center services (summative evaluation); • Annual report on Support Center budget, marketing, and client services (summative evaluation); • Articles written and submitted to peer-reviewed law librarianship journals highlighting the integration

(Continued)

Table 5.2 (Continued)

Goal, Service Programs, Activities, Evaluation Components, and Deliverables	
	of emerging technologies used by rural attorneys, academic and public libraries with legal collections, rural government agencies, and nongovernmental legal organizations to repackage and deliver information to residents in diverse communities with low-income individuals and families (formative evaluation); • Continuous feedback and project refinement from outside evaluator (formative evaluation); and • Percentage of goals and activities completed according to the project timeline (summative evaluation).

- **Recommendation 5.** Create a simple, basic evaluation plan. Effective evaluation plans produce sufficient, reliable, valid data that the evaluator can use to prepare summative and formative evaluations. The evaluation plan does not need to be complex or elaborate in order to be effective. As the project and its evaluation plan become more complex, the potential for an incomplete evaluation increases. Experienced grant writers know that the evaluation plan is intended to report the impact of the project, the achievement of objectives, and to formulate recommendations for continuation and replication. If the evaluation plan does not contribute to these ends, the grant team needs to redraft this section until the objectives are met.

    When the evaluation plan includes the use of data collection instruments, a project timeline, and statistical analysis techniques, the evaluator will compile data, perform statistical tests for data analysis, and measure the level of achievement to fulfill the goal and objectives.

- **Recommendation 6.** Begin evaluating the project when activities begin. The evaluation plan needs to begin in concert with pre-implementation activities. As soon as the library receives official notification of a grant award, the evaluator should begin work. If the evaluator will be selected after the library receives the grant award, the Principal Investigator is responsible to gather documents, data, and related materials for the evaluator's use.

Monitoring program or project progress from the beginning of the funding period is essential in order to include all activities. The concurrent monitoring of activities enables the Principal Investigator, library administrators, and key staff members to keep activities on the projected timeline. The completion of these sequential activities enables the program or project staff to make modifications as needs arise, to request budget adjustments as situations dictate, and to share progress in a timely manner with members of the library community, teachers, faculty members, librarians, administrators, support staff, parent leaders, and community-based organization leaders. An example of the timeline for a grant project appears in Table 5.3.

Selecting an Evaluator

In its role as the applicant, the library is responsible to design an evaluation and select a single evaluator or a team of evaluators. This decision may be based on the basic, straightforward evaluation requirements from the funding agency or the expertise and experience of the library staff. If library administrators do not have extensive experience working with an evaluator, straightforward guidance appears in the Office of Juvenile Justice and Delinquency Prevention Project's document *Hiring and Working with an Evaluator* (http://www.jrsa.org.jjec.about.publications.evaluator.pdf).

Funding agencies may require an applicant to subcontract the evaluation if the project is large and complex. Most grant announcements permit the applicant to identify the individual or team to conduct the evaluation. If the response time is brief, inexperienced grant writers may decide to design their own evaluation plans. Less experienced grant writers do not routinely recognize the importance of the evaluation component. Failure to include a comprehensive, statistically valid evaluation plan makes the difference between a grant award and disappointment.

Internal Evaluation Teams

An internal evaluation team brings benefits to the library. The local staff member who works as the project evaluator is acquainted with the library, its governing board members, teachers, faculty, librarians, support staff, parents, and community-based organizations. Knowledge and understanding of the library community provides an awareness of the environment into which the grant-funded initiative is implemented.

However, because of the intimate familiarity with the library, its personnel, and operations, the internal evaluator may be reluctant to identify and

Table 5.3 Grant Project Timelines

Initiatives	2009–2010	2010–2011	2011–2012	2012–2013	2013–2014
Staffing	• Hire and train liaison and provide needed resources	• Fund and support articulation liaison	• Fund and support articulation liaison		
Initiative 1	• Select articulation teams for participating schools and begin biweekly meetings • Organize articulation leadership team and begin monthly meetings • Conduct college readiness analysis	• Articulation team meetings monthly	• Articulation team meetings monthly	• Articulation team meetings quarterly	
Initiative 2	• Summer institute planning grade 11 • Summer institute	• Summer institute planning grade 4 • Summer institute	Summer institute	Summer institute	

	alignment to college readiness grades 6 and 9	implementation grade 11 • Summer institute alignment to college readiness grades 6 and 9	implementation grades 4 and 11	implementation grades 4 and 11	
Initiative 3	• Professional development for teacher leaders • Articulation-wide professional development • Professional development for school leaders	• Professional development for teacher leaders • Articulation-wide professional development • Professional development for school leaders	• Professional development for teacher leaders • Articulation-wide professional development • Professional development for school leaders	• Professional development for teacher leaders • Articulation-wide professional development • Professional development for school leaders	• Articulation-wide professional development
Initiative 4	• Arrange physical environment for college readiness	• Arrange physical environment for college readiness	• College visits for grades 4, 6, and 9	• College visits for grades 4, 6, and 9	• College visits for grades 4, 6, and 9

(Continued)

Table 5.3 (Continued)

Initiatives	2009–2010	2010–2011	2011–2012	2012–2013	2013–2014
	• Plan for common mentoring program • College visits for grades 4, 6, and 9	• Implement common mentoring program • College visits for grades 4, 6, and 9 • ACT testing at middle and high school	• ACT testing at middle and high school	• ACT testing at middle and high school	• ACT testing at middle and high school
Initiative 5		• Planning for Family Resource/Future Center at elementary and middle school • Planning for summer institute for parents	• Implement Family Resource/Future Center at elementary and middle school • Implement summer institute for parents • College visits for 150 parents from each school	• Implement summer institute for parents • College visits for 150 parents from each school • Implement family college night	• Implement summer institute for parents • College visits for 150 parents from each school

Initiative 6	• Hire consultant to assess needs and infrastructure that is needed to facilitate information sharing across the collaborative, and build collaborative network drive
Initiative 7	• Redesign Web sites of all participating schools • Design and print common marketing materials • Plan and implement kick-off event

| | • Design and print common marketing materials |

describe implementation, management, or project outcomes and results. Assigning the evaluation to a library employee may be less expensive than hiring an external evaluator. However, the internal evaluator may lack the experience and technical skills required to prepare a rigorous evaluation. If the internal evaluator is politically influenced, biased, or has a vested interest in the successes of the program or project, the evaluation report may be flawed.

External Evaluation Teams

Ideally, an evaluation team should include internal *and* external evaluators. However, there are benefits to contracting exclusively with external evaluators from outside the library. Individuals who are not involved in the library's day-to-day activities tend to be more objective during the evaluation process. Due to their independence, external evaluators can be unbiased because they have no vested interest in the success of the program or project. They bring expertise in effective approaches gained from observation and previous work on grant-funded projects and evaluations. Faculty members at local colleges and universities may agree to serve as evaluators. They understand the research methodologies, the evaluation process, and qualitative and quantitative techniques.

Networking with peers is useful to identify potential external evaluators. Teachers, school librarians, and central office administrators have opportunities to meet educational consultants, library managers, and higher education faculty members. Teachers and school librarians who enroll in graduate or postgraduate studies get acquainted with faculty who may be interested in evaluation work or know of colleagues who may be available.

PLANNING THE EVALUATION

In order to plan an effective evaluation, the grant team needs to determine how they will ensure that the library, project personnel, and collaborating partner organizations will have ownership in the evaluation and benefit from their collective expertise and experience. As they plan the evaluation, grant team members will focus on data collection and analysis. Formative evaluation needs to be infused through a cycle of continuous feedback and project refinement. Annual summative evaluation provides an overview of program or project effectiveness through a multi-method demonstration of outcomes and impacts. The evaluation plan needs to include safeguards to ensure that the data collection methods do not inhibit the intent of the program or project.

Experienced grant writers recognize the importance of a well-planned evaluation plan. They may ensure that the evaluation plan includes all of the required components by using a checklist (see Form 5.1).

Item	Notes
☐ Identify evaluation team	
☐ Internal	
☐ External	
☐ Letter of agreement with evaluator	
☐ Budget	
☐ Fee	
☐ Travel	
☐ Expenses	
☐ Timeline	
☐ Design	
☐ Formative	
☐ Summative	
☐ Data collection	
☐ Focus groups	
☐ Partners	
☐ Others	

Form 5.1   Evaluation Checklist

In addition to aligning the goal, objectives, and activities with the evaluation plan, experienced grant writers follow a number of principals:

- **Recommendation 1.** The evaluation is designed to measure the level of achievement for each objective. The grant team and evaluator need to include components to measure formative (process) and summative (outcomes or results) aspects of the program or project in the evaluation plan.

- **Recommendation 2.** Design the evaluation to suit the program or project and each objective. Each of the major evaluation designs has specific strengths that recommend its use. Major evaluation designs include the following:
  - ☐ case study (the study of a single, cohesive group);
  - ☐ a time-series design (the study to compare a group's past and current performances); and
  - ☐ a comparison group design (the measurement of the performance by an experimental group with a control group).
- **Recommendation 3.** Incorporate the use of reliable, valid data collection instruments into the evaluation plan. Results are statistically valid when the findings are compared to project objectives and education goals that have been defined by the learning community. A statistically valid outcome is not likely to occur by chance. An educationally significant outcome makes a measurable difference in meeting a specific goal.
- **Recommendation 4.** Use multiple data collection methods. Experienced grant writers and evaluators understand the importance of using professionally developed instruments to collect data. The use of these instruments is essential to measure interests, attitudes, values, and psychological states. When a single test is not available, the evaluator may determine that the use of multiple instruments will provide the desired data. If a valid data collection instrument cannot be identified, the evaluator may design a tool for use in a specific project.

Suggestions and examples of data collection instruments are available at these web sites:

IBEC, *Sample Surveys: Using Surveys For On-Going Outcome Evaluation*, http://ibec.ischool.washington.edu/static/ibeccat.aspx@subcat =outcome%20toolkit&cat=tools%20and%20resources&tri =samplesurveys.htm (accessed August 31, 2010).

Innovation Network, *Data Collection Tips: Build on What's Out There*, http://www.innonet.org/client_docs/File/Existing_instr.pdf (accessed August 31, 2010).

Roger C. Schonfeld, Donald W. King, Ann Okerson, and Eileen Gifford Fenton. *The Nonsubscription Side of Periodicals: Changes in Library Operations and Costs between Print and Electronic Formats*, Appendix B: Data Collection Instruments, http://www.clir.org/pubs/reports/pub127/appendixB.pdf (accessed August 31, 2010).

The University of Texas at Austin, Information Architecture Group, *Empirical Data Collection Instrument*, http://www.ischool.utexas.edu/

~iag/projects/.../empiricaldatacollection.doc (accessed August 31, 2010).

- **Recommendation 5.** Establish causality in the evaluation design for important issues or large-scale studies. If the evaluator is measuring a "cause and effect" situation, scientific evidence gathered through empirical research and the use of more than one analysis technique is recommended. Establishing its merits is critical when a program or project includes a large group of participants or significant costs.
- **Recommendation 6.** Collect data as unobtrusively as possible. The evaluator is cautioned to select data collection instruments that require participants to spend reasonable, limited amounts of time and resources to respond. When data collection includes specific identifiable data (name, address, Social Security number, etc.) regarding youngsters under the age of 18 years, the evaluator and Principal Investigator share the responsibility of providing the library with written evidence that appropriate precautions and privacy protections are taken.
- **Recommendation 7.** Determine the need to use a representative sample, its size, and composition. If the use of an entire population is too large for a program or project, the evaluator may choose to determine the size and use a statistically significant sample.
- **Recommendation 8.** Analyze data through the use of techniques that are technically sound and suited to the data and its quality. The evaluator is responsible for the selection of the statistical tests that will be used to analyze data. Reliable data can be analyzed using a number of standard statistical tests. Twenty-first century evaluators typically perform data analysis using statistical software (such as the *Statistical Packages for the Social Sciences*© or *SPSS*©). Specific statistical tests can be identified in a basic text or on the Internet. Useful Internet sites include (but are not limited to) the following:

    Vassar Stats: Website for Statistical Computation, http://faculty.vassar.edu/lowry/VassarStats.html (accessed August 31, 2010).

    The Prism Guide to Interpreting Statistical Results, http://www.graphpad.com/articles/interpret/principles/stat_principles.htm (accessed August 31, 2010).

    SPSS, Inc., http://www.spss.com (accessed August 31, 2010).

- **Recommendation 9.** Interpret data analysis in terms of the goal and objectives so that it is meaningful to both the layperson and the professional. The evaluator is responsible for the presentation of data

analysis in project reports. The formal reports need to include analytical discussions, discussions of the analysis techniques, and summaries of technical data. Executive project summaries may include interpretations of the data without detailed explanations.
- **Recommendation 10.** Offer recommendations when asked specifically to do so, and limit comments to those aspects addressed in the project goal and objectives. Evaluations do not customarily include recommendations. However, when the evaluator is asked to do so, a brief narrative describing modifications, enhancements, changes, and suggestions for improvement may be included. The evaluator needs to be cautious to avoid statements that are not favorable to the school district, the project staff members, or the funding agency.

ANALYZING EVALUATION DATA

Experienced evaluators use standard processes to analyze data. Comprehensive, rigorous evaluations enable the grantor and the grantee to measure program or project success. In addition to an objective report of the activities that took place during the grant period, the evaluation typically serves as part of the justification to extend or continue a program or project.

In order to conduct an objective evaluation, an experienced evaluator relies on the collection of reliable data, the use of standardized statistical techniques, and the drafting of a formal report for review by the library administrators, project staff members, and the funding agency's program office. An experienced evaluator will follow four basic steps to conduct the evaluation process:

- pilot testing–to determine whether the data collection instrument enables the project staff to gather the requested information in a manageable form that can be analyzed efficiently and accurately;
- conducting the analysis–to perform the statistical tests efficiently so that the results are significant and reliable;
- interpreting the results–to measure the level to which outcomes and results meet the stated objectives; and
- making recommendations (if requested to do so)–to suggest modifications, enhancements, and additions to the program or project to increase the level of success.

Useful Internet sites include (but are not limited to) the following:

DLESE, *Find a Resource*, http://www.dlese.org/library/query.do?q=evaluation+data+analysis&s=0 (accessed August 31, 2010).

Free Management Library^{SM}, *Basic Guide to Program Evaluation*, http://www.managementhelp.org/evaluatn/fnl_eval.htm (accessed August 31, 2010).

The University of Texas at Austin, Instructional Assessment Resources, Evaluate Programs: Analyzing Interview Data, http://www.utexas.edu/academic/ctl/assessment/iar/programs/report/interview-Analysis.php (accessed August 31, 2010).

WRITING THE EVALUATION REPORT

Writing the evaluation report is the final component of implementing and managing a grant-funded project. The evaluation serves as the official document that reports the activities, achievements, level of success, data, and findings of the program or project. Experienced grant writers and evaluators recognize the importance of a concise, accurate, and objective evaluation document. Whether the project was evaluated quantitatively, qualitatively, or with a mixed design, the evaluator is responsible for drafting a document that communicates project activities to the library, project staff, library personnel, collaborating partners, and community-based organization representatives.

Effective evaluation documents typically contain an executive summary, a formative (process) overview, and a summative overview that includes five sections: introduction, evaluation design and sampling, data collection, data analysis, and findings. Each of these components is described briefly.

Executive Summary

This separate but related report includes the significant components of the evaluation document. The purpose of this document is to share the program or project and its goal, objectives, and findings with readers who are not familiar with the initiative. The Executive Summary can be posted on the library's web site, the project web page, and linked to on sites maintained by partner organizations. Paper copies of the Executive Summary are typically more widely disseminated than the evaluation report.

Formative Evaluation

This portion of the evaluation presents an overview of the process by which the program or project was implemented and managed. Process evaluation monitors project timelines, the accomplishment of objectives and activities, and the related activities scheduled during the grant period.

Summative Evaluation

This portion of the evaluation presents an overview of the program or project, measurements of the level of success in achieving the stated goal and objectives, and findings that were identified through the data collection and analysis processes. This portion is typically the lengthiest component of the evaluation report. The following five components comprise the summative evaluation:

Introduction

In this section the evaluator presents a brief description of the program or project that is the subject of the report. The needs assessment, funding sources, goal, and objectives should be included.

Evaluation Design and Sampling

In this section the evaluator describes the evaluation design, sampling activities that were used, and limitations that were encountered during the process. Experienced evaluators identify and explain the rationale for each component in the research design.

Justification for sampling, stratification, and grouping of program or project participants is an important aspect of this section. A detailed discussion of the procedures used to determine the size, composition, and representative nature of the sample is essential.

Data Collection

In this section the evaluator describes each of the data collection instruments used, the rationale for its inclusion, and the data that was gathered. Copies of each data collection instrument should be included in an appendix unless prohibited by copyright protection.

Information that describes the pilot testing, validity, and reliability of the data collection instruments needs to be included. In addition, the evaluator typically describes the individuals who administered the data collection instruments, the manner in which the administration occurred, and the method used to record the data. If data collection instruments were deemed "invalid" or "missing" in the data analysis, an explanation should be provided.

An experienced evaluator will describe all evaluation activities and the places (classrooms, library, meetings, etc.) in which they took place.

Data Analysis

The evaluator will describe each of the statistical tests, the data that were analyzed, and the results. The individual statistical tests used in the data analysis typically include a justification and explanation. Charts, graphs, and related visual presentations typically enable the evaluator to include complicated data in an understandable format.

Findings

In this section the evaluator describes the program or project results or outcomes. Through a concise narrative, the evaluator is able to convey the positive impacts and identify negative aspects of the program or project. The evaluation includes statements that inform library administrators and governing board members, enabling them to make policy decisions.

Typically an evaluation report contains both positive and negative elements. Experienced evaluators report the evaluation limitations and findings for each objective. The degree to which the project activities contributed to the achievement of stated measurements is noted. When the stated objectives were not met, the evaluator will provide an explanation and detail the process by which the determination was made.

Recommendations are included when the library or the grantor requests that the evaluator identify them. Otherwise, recommendations are not typically included in an evaluation report.

Useful Internet sites to assist novice grant writers as they are learning to write evaluation plans include (but are not limited to) the following:

> Cherokee Preservation Foundation, *Grant Work Plan*, www.cherokeepreservationfdn.org/grantapp09/2009Grant-Work-Plan.doc (accessed August 31, 2010).
>
> Eastern Michigan University, Office of Research Development, *Fine-Tuning the Evaluation Section of the Grant Proposal*, http://www.ord.emich.edu/publications/publications_subdir/handbook/handbook_subdir/7evaluation.html (accessed August 31, 2010).
>
> Institute of Museum and Library Services, *Outcome Based Evaluation Webography*, http://www.imls.gov/applicants/learning.shtm (accessed August 31, 2010).
>
> National Network of Libraries of Medicine, *Guide 6: Define an Evaluation Plan Up Front*, http://nnlm.gov/outreach/community/evaluation.html (accessed August 31, 2010).

CHAPTER 6

Budget Development

Budget preparation is critical in the grant preparation process. The budget represents the projected actual expenses that are essential to implement, manage, and evaluate the proposed project. Grant budgets must support the goals of the project and be allowable under proposal guidelines, governing regulations from the appropriate Office of Management and Budget (OMB)[1] Circular, and the library's institutional policies for expenditures and financial management.

In 1988, Congress reinstituted the Cost Accounting Standards Board (CASB) as a permanent and independent board assigned to the Office of Federal Procurement Policy (OFPP) in the Office of Management and Budget (OMB).[2] CASB has exclusive authority to make, promulgate, amend, and rescind cost accounting standards and regulations. The OFPP Administrator (who serves as the CASB Chairman) ensures that no agency regulation is inconsistent with cost accounting standards (CAS). Costs subject to CAS cannot be subject to other agency regulations that differ in the measurement, assignment, and allocation of costs.

Cost principals that govern the budget development process differ among types of organizations. Colleges and universities follow the principles in OMB Circular A-21, *Cost Principles for Educational Institutions*.[3] Public libraries that operate as part of city or county governments or as library districts follow the provisions set forth in OMB Circular A-87, *Cost Principles for State, Local, and Indian Tribal Governments*.[4] Libraries that are established and operate as not-for-profit organizations are subject to the regulations outlined in OMB Circular A-122, *Cost Principles for Non-Profit Organizations*.[5]

Experienced grant writers recognize the importance of allocating resources to achieve the project goal and benefit each of the collaborating partners. Novice grant writers may misunderstand the budget and approach the activity as "dividing up the pie." After the grant team identifies the maximum dollar award amount, they may be tempted to divide funds equally among the applicant and partner organizations. Proportioning the funds rather than investing them in order to implement a successful project is quickly evident to grant reviewers. This strategy is almost never funded.

Grant funding agencies employ staff and outside readers who see a significant number of proposals and budgets during a submission period. Consequently, these individuals understand project costs and are proficient at identifying unrealistic budgets.

THE ROLE OF THE BUDGET

The budget section delineates the anticipated project expenses in four main categories: personnel, operations, facilities and administrative costs, and cost share (in-kind or cash matches). Budgeting requires the grant team to have the ability to identify expenses, understand local expenditure guidelines and regulations, and perform basic mathematical calculations. Success is directly related to devoting sufficient time to gather baseline cost data and to calculate project expenses carefully over the grant period.

Grant writers are cautioned to avoid overestimating or under-estimating budgetary needs. Grant funds are never intended to supplant or replace local funds. If a request is accompanied by an insufficient budget that does not appear to be adequate to support the outlined objectives and activities, reviewers may determine that the grant team has not fully developed the project. When the request reflects the maximum award and expenses are not succinctly justified, reviewers may conclude that the applicant is attempting to secure funds with the grant award to replace unavailable local monies. If the expenses do not align closely with the project goals, service programs, and activities, the reviewers may begin to wonder how carefully the grant team prepared the application. Items in the budget which have not been mentioned in the narrative automatically cause reviewers to ask probing questions.

Expenditures must relate directly to the scope of work included in the project. The grant team is cautioned to align each item in the budget to a specific activity. Reading the project objectives and activities aloud during the budget development process enables the grant team to identify and include comprehensive costs. After the grant team identifies the anticipated expenses, actual costs must be calculated in compliance with the applicant's and grantor's guidelines and procedures. Each item needs to be listed clearly and placed in the budget categories specified by the grantor.

Table 6.1 provides a framework for the alignment between project goal, objectives, activities, and expenditures. The grantor's accountability

Table 6.1 Worksheet to Align Project Goal, Objectives, Activities, and Expenditures

Major Goal and Objectives	Description of Evaluation to Measure Attainment of Goals, Objectives, Activities, Deliverables	Costs
Goal:	The success of program outcomes resulting from the objectives presented in this application will be demonstrated by:	
Objective 1:	Activities: • Evaluation components: • Deliverables: •	Personnel: Operating: Facilities: Cost share:
Objective 2:	Activities: • Evaluation components: • Deliverables: •	Personnel: Operating: Facilities: Cost share:
Objective 3:	Activities: • Evaluation components: • Deliverables: •	Personnel: Operating: Facilities: Cost share:

requirements can be met through the alignment of costs with project implementation, management, and evaluation components. A well-prepared budget also reflects the applicant's recognition of stewardship with the grantor's funds.

BUDGET PREPARATION

The budget is a plan for expending project funds in specified cost categories. Government agencies and a significant number of private funding bodies (foundations, corporations, and the like) provide budget forms or require specific formats. Most libraries use internal formulas and forms to calculate expenditures. Staff members in the finance or accounting department can work with administrators, librarians, and the grant team as they develop the project budget. Finance directors and their staff members can provide cost figures required by the parent organization (e.g., county, city, school district, college, university, and the like) to calculate expenses, and in-kind contributions (cash match and cost share contributions).

Ground Rules for Budget Preparation

Experienced grant writers rely on templates to develop budgets. The following recommendations will assist the grant team to formulate a budget within library guidelines that supports the proposed project.

- **Recommendation 1.** Review the grantor's guidelines at least twice prior to budget development. The guidelines provide specific information regarding allowable and non-allowable expenses, budget forms, and indirect costs rates (if and when applicable).
- **Recommendation 2.** Determine cost estimates as soon as the project objectives, services, programs, and activities are identified. Cost estimates must be realistic and allow for reasonable annual increases.
- **Recommendation 3.** Keep copies of written estimates, budget calculations, and negotiated costs for the grant.
- **Recommendation 4.** Prepare a list of expenses by categories on the forms provided by the grantor. The library finance director can provide rates for commonly needed items.
- **Recommendation 5.** Round off costs up to the nearest dollar.
- **Recommendation 6.** Include inflation factors for multi-year project budgets. The library finance director can provide approved rates for budget planning.
- **Recommendation 7.** Align budget expenses with the stated objectives, services, programs, and activities. The budget justification explains the need for direct costs and must be consistent with the proposal narrative. Costs that do not align with the narrative should be eliminated.
- **Recommendation 8.** Calculate costs for release time, stipends, substitute pay teachers, and librarians at library rates. The library administrator and finance director can provide the approved rates for budget planning.
- **Recommendation 9.** Estimate the evaluation cost at 10 percent of the total grant expenses. If the grant team determines that an outside evaluator will be hired, determine whether the individual will collaborate with the grant team or be hired through a competitive process after funding is awarded.

- **Recommendation 10.** Submit a draft budget to the library finance director for review. Ideally, the final budget should be submitted with the proposal at least two weeks before the submission deadline to allow for review. This timeframe allows the grant team to make changes and correct minor data entry errors before the proposal is submitted.

Identify the Costs

Expenses associated with the grant budget can be grouped in five domains: direct costs, indirect costs, cost sharing, matching funds, and in-kind contributions. Each of these categories is discussed briefly.

Direct costs are those expenses that can be specifically identified with a project or program. General direct costs items include the following categories: personnel (full-time, part-time, temporary, and students); fringe benefits; equipment (office, computers, technologies, and specialized devices); consultants; travel (local, out-of-district, regional, state, and national); communications (telephone, FAX, and Internet access); postage and shipping; printing and copying; office supplies; disposables; instructional materials; software; and other services and subcontracts as needed.

Indirect costs are incurred by the library through common activity and therefore cannot be specifically identified with a particular project or program. General categories which comprise indirect costs include the following:

- plant operation and maintenance (utilities, janitorial services, building maintenance, and repairs, etc.);
- use of buildings (classrooms, laboratories, computer labs, library media centers, and the like) and equipment;
- project management and accounting;
- library expenses; and
- general administrative expenses.

Funding agencies generally allow projects to include a proportionate share of indirect costs. The grant team must be certain that the grantor allows the inclusion of indirect costs. If indirect costs are allowed, the team should understand the manner in which they are calculated, the limit that can be charged in the proposal, and any other imposed limits or restrictions.

A library may negotiate an indirect cost rate with a federal department or agency. Full recovery of this rate is essential to the parent organization's financial stability. The finance director can provide the negotiated indirect cost rate and documentation indicating the period for which the rate is valid. If a funding agency will not allow charging the full indirect cost rate, the unallowable portion may be eligible as a cost sharing expense.

Cost sharing distinctions must be made between requirements stated in the request for proposal or request for application and what the applicant offers in hopes of persuading reviewers to recommend a project for funding. While cost sharing is routinely associated with colleges and universities, public and school libraries need to be aware of the federal requirements when entering into a partnership for the purposes of research. Documentation for cost sharing must be carefully calculated and recorded. Without careful attention to the detailed records required for cost share, the grantor may not allow selected entries.

Congress and federal agencies do not set a uniform percentage for cost sharing. Experienced grant writers use a 5 percent contribution of total costs as an acceptable minimum. Individual federal agencies may require significantly higher cost sharing. Cost sharing is subject to the same stringent audit requirements as the sponsor's funds.

Matching funds may be required or allowed in grant budgets. The library's finance director can provide local guidelines and restrictions for the calculation of matching funds. Matching funds include cash from non-federal sources or commitments using non-cash commodities. Calculations of non-cash matches may include a percentage of time allocated by full-time personnel; the use of equipment or disposables; or related items.

In order to be eligible as matching funds, the outlay of cash or use of commodities must be expended on project activities during the funding period. Cash matches are frequently required by funding agencies for equipment acquisition programs. The exact dollar value of the matching expenditures must be reported after the fact. Typically these funds are provided by the applicant and partner organizations.

In-kind contributions are donations of time, services, or goods made by a donor to help support the operations or services provided by the library and its partner organizations. In-kind contributions do not include cash. Therefore, the donor retains a degree of control over the donation. Because of this "relationship," the library is well advised to keep the donor informed about the manner in which the donation is used.

The grant team may consider "in-kind" contributions to be interchangeable with "matching," but the term customarily refers to costs borne by an external organization. The library and its partners can benefit from encouraging local businesses and community-based organizations to support a grant project.

Local firms and organizations can support a grant project by donating their services or offering them at a reduced fee. Donations may include the printing and distribution of publicity, hosting a grant event, underwriting the honorarium for a speaker or performer, providing food or beverages, or supplying decorations for a celebratory event.

Experienced grant writers rely on guidelines to accept in-kind contributions. The following recommendations will assist the grant team to determine the acceptance and calculation of in-kind contributions.

- **Recommendation 1.** Acknowledge each in-kind contribution for the grant project. Send the donor a thank you letter and include documentation in a grant proposal appendix.
- **Recommendation 2.** Decline in-kind contributions that do not comply with library policy. The library and grant team should not feel obligated to accept every donation that is offered.
- **Recommendation 3.** Build relationships and community support through in-kind contributions. Do not consider an in-kind contribution to be a one-time donation. Use the opportunity to build a continuing relationship between the library, its partner organizations, and the community.
- **Recommendation 4.** Calculate the value of in-kind contributions in terms of "fair market value." Maintain a journal of in-kind contributions and include a copy in a grant proposal appendix.
- **Recommendation 5.** Estimate the dollar value of in-kind contributions from volunteers and board members. The library and each of the partner organizations need to calculate these contributions for the grant project.

Drafting the Budget

Drafting the budget requires the grant team to decide on the level of resources for each budget category. Grantors and federal agencies provide the blank forms on which the budget must be recorded. Experienced grant writers recognize the importance of preparing a comprehensive, mathematically accurate budget. Although they may prepare the budget using the library's internal forms, the final application must contain the forms provided by and/or required by the grantor.

Accounting software simplifies the budget preparation process. While the final forms may not be available electronically for completion, using software with formulae to perform calculations (e.g., Microsoft Excel) shortens the time required to enter and modify data. Linked spreadsheets enable the data entry process to be minimized and calculations over multiple years to be performed automatically. The calculations provide the grant team with correct totals that can be transferred to the required forms. Additionally, the financial data can be transferred to word processing software (like Microsoft Word) to prepare the budget justification document without rekeying the data.

Worksheets facilitate drafting a grant budget. The grant team can review the following categories and answer the questions as they complete each category. Tables 6.2, 6.3, and 6.4 provide sample budget worksheets for public, school, and academic libraries respectively.

Table 6.2 Budget Worksheet for a Public Library

Budget Category	Funds Requested	Local match		Project Total
		Cash 15%	In-kind 10% +	
Personnel				
Salaries				
Benefits				
Operating				
Contract services				
Telephone/Data				
Software				
Supplies				
Printing				
Postage				
Travel				
Project Evaluation Costs				
Technology				
Computer equipment				
Other equipment				
Telecommunications installation				
Capital expenditures				
Books				
Other				
Totals	$	$	$	$

Table 6.3 Sample Budget Worksheet for a School Library

Budget Category	Funds Requested	Local Match (In-kind)	Project Total
1. Salaries and Wages			
Project Director			
Coordinator of Staff Development			
Secretary			
SUBTOTAL			
2. Fringe Benefits (0%)			
SUBTOTAL			
PERSONNEL TOTAL			
3. Professional Development			
Keynote trainers/speakers (honoraria)			
Travel (airfare) From: To: (# people × # trips)			
Lodging (# people × # nights × rate per night)			
Per diem (# people × # days × rate per day)			
Meeting space rental			
Teacher stipends			
Food			
Computer use and connectivity during training			
Training materials			
Teacher Mini-Grants			

(*Continued*)

Table 6.3 (Continued)

Budget Category	Funds Requested	Local Match (In-kind)	Project Total
PROFESSIONAL DEVELOPMENT TOTAL			
4. Equipment			
Computers for full-time project staff			
Printer for full-time project staff			
EQUIPMENT TOTAL			
5. Project Management			
Mileage (# miles × GSA rate)			
Per diem (# people × # days × rate per day)			
Lodging (# people × # nights × rate per night)			
Conference registration			
Office space			
Furniture			
Software			
Photocopying and printing			
Consumable office supplies			
Telecommunications (phone, FAX, Internet)			
Postage and shipping			
Project Web site design and maintenance			

Budget Category	Funds Requested	Local Match (In-kind)	Project Total
PROJECT MANAGEMENT TOTAL			
6. Project Evaluation			
Evaluation team members' fees			
Travel (airfare or mileage)			
Lodging (# people × # nights × rate per night)			
Per diem (# people × # days × rate per day)			
Data collection forms (design and printing)			
Data analysis			
Dissemination			
PROJECT EVALUATION TOTAL			
GRAND TOTAL			

Personnel

Consider the number and qualifications of staff required to implement, manage, and evaluate the project. Staff requirements can be determined by answering the following questions:

- Who will serve as the Project Director (or Principal Investigator)?
- Will additional professional staff be hired?
- Can library staff be assigned to work with the project?
- Are graduate students or volunteers available to work on the project?
- How many support staff members are required?

Table 6.4 Budget Worksheet for an Academic Library

Unit:			
Project Title:			
Project Period:			
Budget Category	Funds Requested	Cost Share	Project Total
1. Salaries and Wages (full-time employees)			
Principal Investigator			
• Academic Year (9 months)			
• Summer Stipend (3 months)			
Faculty			
• Academic Year (9 months)			
• Summer Stipend (3 months)			
Staff			
SUBTOTAL			
2. Student workers			
Graduate Assistantship Stipends			
• Academic Year (9 months)			
• Summer Stipend (3 months)			
Work Study			
Hourly student employees			
3. Fringe Benefits (% for full-time employees)			
Faculty			

Unit:			
Project Title:			
Project Period:			
Budget Category	Funds Requested	Cost Share	Project Total
Staff			
Graduate assistants			
Work Study			
Hourly student employees			
SUBTOTAL			
4. Travel			
Domestic travel			
Travel (airfare) From: To: (# people × # trips)			
Taxis and shuttle OR car rental			
Lodging (# people × # nights × rate per night)			
Per diem (# people × # days × rate per day)			
Mileage (# miles × GSA rate)			
Conference registration			
International travel			
Travel (airfare) From: To: (# people × # trips)			
Taxis and shuttle OR car rental			

(*Continued*)

Table 6.4 (Continued)

Unit:			
Project Title:			
Project Period:			
Budget Category	Funds Requested	Cost Share	Project Total
Lodging (# people × # nights × rate per night)			
Per diem (# people × # days × rate per day)			
Mileage (# miles × GSA rate)			
Conference registration			
TRAVEL TOTAL			
5. Equipment ($5,000 or more per unit; itemize)			
Computers for full-time project staff			
Printer for full-time project staff			
EQUIPMENT TOTAL			
6. Project Management			
Mileage (# miles × GSA rate)			
Office space			
Furniture			
Software			
Photocopying and printing			
Consumable office supplies			
Telecommunications (phone, FAX, Internet)			

Unit:			
Project Title:			
Project Period:			
Budget Category	Funds Requested	Cost Share	Project Total
Postage and shipping			
Project Web site design and maintenance			
PROJECT MANAGEMENT TOTAL			
7. Project Evaluation			
Evaluation team members' fees			
Travel (airfare or mileage)			
Lodging (# people × # nights × rate per night)			
Per diem (# people × # days × rate per day)			
Data collection forms (design and printing)			
Data analysis			
Dissemination			
PROJECT EVALUATION TOTAL			
8. Other direct costs			
Sub-awards or subcontracts (attach detailed budget)			
Consultants (attach CV and detailed budget)			

(*Continued*)

156　Librarian's Handbook for Seeking, Writing, and Managing Grants

Table 6.4　(Continued)

Unit:			
Project Title:			
Project Period:			
Budget Category	Funds Requested	Cost Share	Project Total
Construction or remodeling (attach detailed budget)			
Participant incentives (attach detailed budget)			
Student tuition (# credit hours × # hours × # students)			
TOTAL OTHER DIRECT COSTS			
9. Indirect costs (Use federally negotiated rate)			
Base (MTDC = total direct costs − equipment costing $5,000+ per unit − student tuition − participant costs)			
IDC rate (total MTDC × rate)			
INDIRECT COST			
GRAND TOTAL			

Determine the time allotment for each position. Consider the following questions:

- What is the planned timeframe for each objective?
- Does the funding agency require full-time project staff? If so, who?
- Will library and partner organization staff have sufficient time to invest in the project?

Grant team members need to understand "buzzwords" related to the personnel section of the budget. Time is frequently identified as "full-time equivalents" (FTEs) and is recorded as a decimal. A 1.00 FTE means that the total

Table 6.5 Personnel Effort and Cost Calculations

Name	Role	Rate	Effort	Total
Salazar	Project director	$60,000	15%	$9,000
Meltzer	Project coordinator	$42,000	100%	$42,000
Richardson	Secretary	$35,000	25%	$8,750
Chevalier	Graduate assistant	$12,000	50%	$6,000
				$65,750

amount of paid service is the equivalent of one person working full-time, 40 hours a week for 12 months. Any figure less than 1.00 indicates that the staff member will devote the stated proportion of a full-time equivalent to the task or project. Sometimes the funding agency's requirements ask the applicant to designate the "percent of time" to be allocated to a task or project. For example, a half-time employee position is expressed as 50 percent or .50 FTE. Table 6.5 shows personnel effort and cost calculations.

The grant budget can be calculated by following these guidelines:

- include the names of key personnel;
- append job descriptions for new grant-funded positions;
- pay rates must follow library compensation scales;
- follow library rates to calculate costs for release time, stipends, and substitute pay; and
- specify realistic percentages of the time and effort to be expended by each named individual or position on the project.

Fringe Benefits

Fringe benefits cover the employer's contributions to federal and state governments (e.g., taxes, unemployment insurance, Social Security contributions). This category also includes insurances (health and dental) and retirement programs. Table 6.6 shows personnel effort and cost calculations with fringe benefits.

The grant budget can be calculated by following these guidelines:

- calculate fringe benefits at the rates used by the library for employees;

Table 6.6 Personnel Effort and Cost Calculations with Fringe Benefits

Name	Role	Rate	Effort	Total
Salazar	Project director	$60,000	15%	$9,000
Meltzer	Project coordinator	$42,000	100%	$42,000
Richardson	Secretary	$35,000	25%	$8,750
Chevalier	Graduate assistant	$12,000	50%	$6,000
				$65,750
Name	Employee category	Fringe Benefit Rate	Total	Fringe Benefit Total
Salazar	Appointed faculty	32%	$9,000	$2,880
Meltzer	Non-appointed	24%	$42,000	$10,080
Richardson	Staff	24%	$8,750	$2,100
Chevalier	Student	3%	$6,000	$180
			$65,750	$15,240

- include health insurance, life insurance, disability insurance, retirement plan premiums, Social Security, Medicare, and unemployment insurance; and
- pro-rate fringe benefit rates for part-time employees.

Equipment

The purchase of equipment is a challenge for grant teams. The potential to acquire expensive, specialized equipment under the guise of "grant-related" can be tempting. However, the majority of funding proposals cannot be considered as opportunities to purchase, upgrade, or replace capital equipment. Exceptions to this guideline require the equipment to be essential for the implementation of a project.

The grant budget can be calculated by following these guidelines:

- identify the acquisition cost of "equipment" (federal government minimum is $5,000) and "useful life" (federal government requires one year or more) allowed by the library and the funding agency;
- negotiate with the finance director to determine the acquisition cost and useful life rates to be used;
- itemize equipment required for the project with estimated costs;
- understand the library purchasing process and bidding requirements; and
- document the bidding process and retain bids as part of grant reporting.

Consultants

Hiring a consultant to perform major tasks or to sell a packaged, comprehensive solution to an identified problem is a temptation for novice grant writers. An authority on the program area, a local college or university faculty member, or a noted expert may add "punch" to the application, but they should be included only after careful consideration. A consultant is not an employee and works under the Internal Revenue Service definitions for independent contractor (self-employed).[6] The library is responsible for classifying outside consultants correctly and following the rules of engagement when working with them.[7]

While the majority of funding agencies allow these types of expenses, the grant team should consider available options to bring expertise and technical assistance to the project staff and participants. The library and its partners are advised to identify potential individuals and strategies to share research-based models, "best practices," and "communities of practice" with the project sites.

The grant budget can be calculated by following these guidelines:

- identify individuals who will provide consulting and/or technical assistance to the project;
- contact the consultant(s) to determine the level of interest in affiliation with the proposed project;
- secure a written commitment and curriculum vita from consultants who will work on the project;
- understand the library guidelines for hiring consultants;
- determine whether the consultant's fees will include expenses and travel;
- negotiate the consultant's fees, expenses, and travel; and
- document the hiring and contracting process as part of grant reporting.

Travel

Travel to visit project sites, bring together advisory groups, and attend conferences is a routine grant request. While the majority of funding agencies allow these types of expenses, the grant team should calculate the frequency and time required for staff to travel for grant-related purposes. The library and its partners are advised to identify project sites and to review the calendar of meetings (advisory group, staff, parent leaders, and community representatives).

Per diem, lodging, and mileage travel costs are generally calculated according to the provisions of the General Services Administration (GSA).[8] Air travel is subject to the Fly America Act.[9] Enacted in 1974, the Fly America Act mandates the use of U.S. flag air carriers for federally funded international travel. Since its enactment, innumerable changes have taken place in the airline industry. Because of this evolution, the Fly America Act and the federal travel regulations promulgated under the act have been revised to allow travelers more flexibility while remaining in compliance with the law. Table 6.7 includes a sample worksheet to calculate travel for a grant proposal.

Table 6.7 Travel Cost Calculations

Budget category	Funds Requested	Cost Share	Total Cost
Salazar travel (Denver, CO – San Antonio, TX [RT])			
Travel (airfare)	$316	0	$316
Taxis and shuttle	$50	$50	$100
Lodging (1 person × 3 nights × $106 rate per night)	$318	0	$318
Per diem (1 person × 3 days × $66 rate per day)	$198	0	$198
Mileage (50 miles × $ .50 [GSA rate])	$25	0	$25
Parking at airport ($10 × 3 days)	$30	0	$30
Conference registration	0	$250	$250
Totals	$937	$300	$1,237

Budget Development

The grant budget can be calculated by following these guidelines:

- understand the library guidelines for out-of-area and out-of-state travel;
- identify individuals (project staff, participants, partner organization representatives, parents, teachers, librarians, administrators, and others) who will travel as part of project activities;
- estimate the cost of local travel using the library mileage allowance and per diem (if allowed);
- determine the number of individuals, the number of days, mode of transportation, and per diem for out-of-district travel; and
- review the funding agency's guidelines in order to include costs for required meetings.

Communications

The grant team must estimate expenses attributed to the oral, written, and electronic communication among the project staff, participants, partner organization representatives, parents, teachers, librarians, administrators, and others. Funding agencies typically allow these expenses and the grant team should calculate them carefully. The library and its partners are advised to identify project sites, the types of communications to be used during the project period, and the numbers of individuals with whom communication is envisioned (advisory group, staff, parent leaders, and community representatives). Communications expenses include telephone, facsimile, Internet access, courier services, postage, and shipping (commercial carriers). These costs are calculated according to library costs or lists of approved expenses.

The grant budget can be calculated by following these guidelines:

- identify all costs related to project implementation, management, and evaluation;
- estimate costs using library costs as guidelines;
- determine the costs associated with web site presence, development, and maintenance for the project; and
- include telephone, Internet connectivity and access charges, facsimile, and written communication costs (paper, envelopes, courier service, postage, and shipping).

Supplies and Materials

The grant team must estimate expenses associated with supplies and materials. Funding agencies typically allow these expenses and the grant team should calculate them carefully. The library and its partners are advised to identify project sites, the types of supplies and materials needed during the project period, and the numbers of individuals for whom these items need to be purchased. Supplies and materials include paper (white, colored, and special use), writing implements (pens, pencils, markers, and the like), computer and printer supplies (ink cartridges–black and color, flash drives, and similar items), professional development and workshop training materials, and participant materials. These costs are calculated according to library rules, vendors' catalogs, and lists of approved expenses.

The grant budget can be calculated by following these guidelines:

- understand limits imposed by the library and/or funding agency regarding the purchase of disposables for project use;
- determine the types and prices for disposable supplies (paper, pens, pencils, computer supplies (ink cartridges);
- include student materials (workbooks, CDs, DVDs); and
- consider the costs to acquire software (single user and networked versions) along with training and documentation.

Other

The grant team must consider miscellaneous expenses. Funding agencies typically allow these expenses when adequate explanation and justification accompany the request. The grant team needs to calculate these costs carefully by following these guidelines:

- determine expenses allowed by the library and funding agency;
- verify legal and audit requirements from the funding agency and include the costs (if allowed);
- identify the costs for services to be purchased from the library (computing, maintenance and support for equipment, custodial services, transportation services, media services, data gathering and analysis, and the like);
- calculate one-time expenses (conference registrations, workshops, teacher and librarian graduate school tuition, and the like);
- identify outside services to be purchased from commercial vendors (equipment rental, admissions for field trips, and the like); and
- include stipends to be paid to participating community-based organizations, parent leaders, and others.

Budget requests customarily include a justification narrative. The budget narrative is a brief explanation of each item, its importance to project implementation, and its relationship to a specific objective or activity. If the grant team is unable to justify an item, the cost should be eliminated from the request. Reasonableness and justification should be the attributes that are readily apparent in the budget presentation.

Reviewing the Budget

Grant applications cannot be submitted without the signature of an administrator. The library administrator (or designee) is empowered to sign a grant application. When the grant application is submitted, the proposal presents the library's offer to implement, manage, and evaluate the project. If the proposal is selected for a grant award, the application is routinely incorporated into the binding agreement between the library and the grantor.

The legal considerations associated with a funded grant proposal necessitate consultation with and review by library administrators prior to submission. The library administrator's involvement during proposal development work provides a forum for discussions as the project concept evolves into a finished proposal. However, the Principal Investigator assumes the responsibility to compile the draft proposal document, schedule a meeting with the administrator, and review the project. Experienced grant writers recognize the opportunity for administrators to offer suggestions and modifications. The grant team should respond to these ideas and incorporate them into the finished document.

Time considerations require advance scheduling of a meeting with library administrators. Experienced grant writers learn the number of days in advance that meetings need to be scheduled. An alternative approach is to schedule the meeting as soon as the grant team receives authorization to pursue the funding opportunity. Scheduling a meeting at least a week before the submission deadline provides the flexibility that may be needed. Library administrators maintain busy calendars, and scheduling well in advance of a deadline serves the grant team well.

ADDITIONAL BUDGETING CONSIDERATIONS

The Influence of Funding Agencies on Budget Formatting

Government agencies supply detailed instructions and blank forms on which applicants must submit grant proposals. Federal and state government agencies require applications to be submitted electronically.

The budget justification form customarily takes a narrative form. Each line item within the budget categories is explained briefly. The explanations should convince the reviewer that the expense is essential to successful project implementation, management, and evaluation.

Private funding agencies and corporate foundations may allow a generalized line-item format that parallels expense categories. The applicant has more flexibility to formulate a budget. Regardless of the budget format that the funding agency requires, the grant team must respond directly to the requirements.

Budget Adjustments and Amendments

After the funding agency makes a grant award, the library and its partners need to implement the project according to the proposed plan. Neither library administrators nor the Principal Investigator can make significant changes in the project budget without approval in writing from the grantor.

Shifting monies from one category to another is a budget adjustment. Funding agencies customarily allow the grantee (the library) to shift funds within specified limitations without written authorization. This limit customarily ranges from 10 to 20 percent of the budget category.

If the grantee wants to reallocate a larger portion of funds, the grantor must agree to a budget amendment. This time-consuming process requires a formal, written request from the grantee (library administrator or other official) to the program officer at the funding agency. The amended budget should clearly identify the categories from which funds were subtracted and increased. Copies of the written request and authorization must be maintained in the grant's financial files.

Subcontracts

Subcontracting enables the grantee (library) to enter into a formal arrangement with another entity (organization or individual) to provide a particular product or service identified in the proposal. The subcontractor serves as an agent of the grantee and must honor all terms and conditions the grantor imposes on the grantee. The purpose of the subcontract document is to establish those requirements contractually.

Upon receipt of the grant award, the library administrator and Principal Investigator should meet and discuss the subcontract requirements. After confirming the cost, time period, scope of work, billing processes, reporting timelines and formats, an appropriate subcontract instrument, and special needs of the project, a determination can be made regarding the applicability of the library's bidding process requirements. If required, the library's approved process must be used. If a formal bid is not required, the finance director (or a designee) will write and mail the subcontract. The subcontract advises that a purchase order will follow. The subcontractor is asked to identify the appropriate vendor name and site and then sign and return the agreement.

The primary contractor bears responsibility for ensuring that the subcontractor follows the stated terms. Formal subcontracts include cost reimbursement and the fixed price types. Each type is described briefly.

Cost Reimbursement

The subcontractor agrees to perform services for a stated period, up to an established dollar amount. This type of subcontract is used when the work cannot be clearly specified or defined. Reimbursement is predicated on the grantor's agreement to allow reimbursement for the costs incurred. The cost reimbursement agreement is useful for basic research. The Principal Investigator is responsible for monitoring work progress and reporting by the subcontractor.

Fixed Price

The subcontractor agrees to perform specified services for a predetermined, fixed amount of money. The fixed price subcontract is the simplest and most frequently used subcontract. When more than one vendor or provider is available, the fixed price subcontract frequently results in the optimal price. The fixed price subcontract can be used when the statement of work can be clearly specified.

The grantee (library) should require subcontractors to provide final invoices within 30 days of project conclusion. The Principal Investigator is responsible for requesting and maintaining a record of the subcontractor's expenses. Reports and invoices from the subcontractor need to be filed and maintained for inclusion in reports to the funding agency.

NOTES

1. *Office of Management and Budget*, http://www.whitehouse.gov/omb/ (accessed August 31, 2010).

2. Federal Aviation Administration, *Cost Accounting Standards, 14.2.2, The Cost Accounting Standards Board*, http://fast.faa.gov/archive/v1198/pguide/98-30c14.htm (accessed August 31, 2010); *Cost Accounting Standards*, http://en.wikipedia.org/wiki/Cost_Accounting_Standards (accessed August 31, 2010).

3. Office of Management and Budget, *Circular A-21*, http://www.whitehouse.gov/omb/circulars_a021_2004/ (accessed August 31, 2010).

4. Office of Management and Budget, *Circular A-87*, http://www.whitehouse.gov/omb/circulars_a087_2004/ (accessed August 31, 2010).

5. Office of Management and Budget, *Circular A-122*, http://www.whitehouse.gov/omb/circulars_a122_2004/ (accessed August 31, 2010).

6. Internal Revenue Service, *Independent Contractor (Self-Employed) or Employee?* http://www.irs.gov/businesses/small/article/0,id=99921,00.html (accessed August 31, 2010).

7. Columbia Business School Alumni, *Rules of Engagement*, http://www7.gsb.columbia.edu/alumni/careers/news/Rules-Engagement (accessed August 31, 2010).

8. U.S. General Services Administration, *Per Diem Rates*, http://www.gsa.gov/portal/category/21287 (accessed August 31, 2010); U.S. General Services Administration, *Meals and Incidental Expenses (M&IE) Breakdown*, http://www.gsa.gov/portal/content/101518 (accessed August 31, 2010).

9. *Fly America Act*, Title 49 of the United States Code, Subtitle VII, Part A, subpart I, Chapter 401, 40118 - Government-Financed Air Transportation, http://frwebgate.access.gpo.gov/cgi-bin/usc.cgi?ACTION=RETRIEVE&FILE=$$xa$$busc49.wais&start=5502594&SIZE=12823&TYPE=TEXT (accessed August 31, 2010).

CHAPTER 7

Appendices

Appendices contain additional, detailed information that amplifies the narrative and budget. The funding agency's guidelines may list required appendices, limit the materials that can be submitted in the appendices, or leave the decision to the grant writer. In addition to submitting the required appendices, the grant team may identify relevant material that is appropriate to include in optional appendices.

Regardless of the rationale for including materials in an appendix, correct references from the narrative, clarity of presentation, relevance to the project objectives and activities, and detailed statistical data are essential. The titles for each appendix should be listed in the table of contents. Because they are referenced in the text, the order of appendices (especially those that are optional) should parallel the flow of the narrative.

THE ROLES OF APPENDICES

Materials become part of the appendices for three main reasons. First, the funding agency requires that specific information be included in an appendix rather than in the narrative. Second, the narrative contains a reference to nonessential materials that the grant team wants to include as a way of persuading reviewers and program officers that the project is worthy and ready for funding. Third, the narrative length limitation does not allow for the inclusion of all the information the grant team wants to share with the potential grantor.

Typical materials that appear in appendices include grant compliances (required by the funding agency); demographic data; community resources; profiles of participating partner organizations; curriculum vitae for key project personnel; job descriptions for grant-funded positions; lists of relevant curricula standards; benchmarks; test scores that reflect students' academic achievement levels; compilations of curricular standards or competencies that will be used in project activities; literature reviews; descriptions of "best practices" and research-based, field-tested models; letters of commitment; statements of support; and, a bibliography of resources consulted during the grant preparation process. Each type of material is described briefly.

GRANT COMPLIANCES AND ASSURANCES

Federal and state grant application packets routinely require that the grant team include copies of compliances and assurances. These documents are included as part of the official contract between the grantor and the applicant. Grant compliances and assurances cite specific federal laws, rules, and regulations pertaining to the project. These forms must be completed, signed by the library administrator (or a designee), and submitted as part of the application. Signing these documents indicates that the library agrees to comply with their requirements and provisions. Reviewers do not score the compliances and assurances. However, failure to include the required forms in the proposal packet results in disqualification.

Federal grants awarded by the U.S. Department of Education are subject to Education Department General Administrative Regulations (EDGAR).[1] Application packets may contain the following:

- Assurances–Non-Construction Programs (Standard Form 424B rev. 7-97);[2]
- Certifications Regarding Lobbying (ED 80-013);[3]
- Disclosure of Lobbying Activities (LLL form; 0348-0046);[4]
- General Education Provision Act (GEPA) Provision 427[5] and reauthorized by the *No Child Left Behind Act of 2001*;[6]
- Intergovernmental Review of Federal Programs for applications that are subject to the requirements of Executive Order 12372 of July 14, 1982;[7]
- Budget Information, Non-Construction Programs (ED Form 524);[8]
- Non-Discrimination (Title IV of the *Civil Rights Act of 1964*,[9] Section 504 of the *Rehabilitation Act of 1973*,[10] as amended, Title IX of the Education Amendments of 1972,[11] and the *Age Discrimination in Employment Act of 1975*,[12] as amended);
- Drug-Free Workplace Act of 1988;[13] and
- Survey of Ensuring Equal Opportunity for Applicants.[14]

Federal grants awarded by the Institute of Museums and Library Services (IMLS) require that applicants submit certifications regarding federal debt status, debarment and suspension, nondiscrimination, and a drug-free workplace. Applicants requesting more than $100,000 in grant funds must also certify regarding lobbying activities and may be required to submit a "Disclosure of Lobbying Activities" form. Some applicants will be required to certify that they will comply with other federal statutes that pertain to their particular situation. In addition to a significant number of the forms listed above, IMLS application packets may contain the following:

- Assurance of Audits of States, Local Governments, and Non-Profit Organizations in accordance with OMB Circular A-133;[15]
- Native American Human Remains and Associated Funerary Objects;[16]
- Assurance of compliance with Section 106 of the *National Historic Preservation Act of 1966* (as amended)[17] for historic properties and the *Archaeological and Historic Preservation Act of 1974* for archaeological guidance;[18]
- Environmental protections as outlined in the *National Environmental Policy Act of 1969* (as amended); Executive Orders 11514, 11738, 11990, 12608, 11988 (as amended); the *Coastal Zone Management Act of 1972* (as amended); State (Clean Air) Implementation Plans under section 176(c) of the *Clean Air Act of 1955* (as amended); *Safe Drinking Water Act of 1974* (as amended); the *Endangered Species Act of 1973* (as amended); the *Wild and Scenic Rivers Act of 1968* (as amended); the *Flood Disaster Protection Act of 1973* (as amended);[19] and
- Research on human and animal subjects in compliance with the *Laboratory and Animal Welfare Act of 1966*, animal welfare regulations, rules, and provisions for animal treatment.[20]

Private foundations customarily require that the applicant provide evidence of eligibility for funding. The library needs to provide a copy of its letter of determination as a 501(c) (3) status from the Internal Revenue Service.[21] Libraries are part of larger organizations and may be associated with government agencies and departments (e.g., town, city, county, state). The library may need to make certain that its application goes through an organization that is tax exempt for the federal and local governments. For this reason, libraries may apply for grant funding through the Friends of the Library organization. The library may also need to submit a copy of the last audited financial statement as part of the application process for one or more years. The financial statements provide impartial, third-party evidence that the entity is a *bona fide* organization with a history of sound financial management.

DEMOGRAPHIC DATA AND COMMUNITY DESCRIPTIONS

Demographic data enables the library to represent accurately the descriptive information about patrons and residents of the communities in which they are located. Data included in this appendix must be accurate, clearly presented, easy to read, and supportive of the proposal program or project.

The demographic data should reflect community information including (but not limited to) population; number of households; family median income levels; poverty levels; languages spoken at home; educational levels; ages of residents; and, birth rates. In the case of school libraries, the demographic data should include student grade levels, ethnic representations, and qualifications for the federal free and reduced-price lunch program.

Academic libraries submit data including (but not limited to) student population at the undergraduate and graduate levels; ethnic representations; number of domestic students of color; number of international students and countries of citizenship; the number of traditional and non-traditional students; and retention rates.

Federal demographic information is compiled, analyzed, and published by the U.S. Bureau of the Census every 10 years. Findings for the latest (2010) and earlier census takings are available in the *U.S. Statistical Abstracts* and on the Internet.[22] Each state government maintains demographic data that can be accessed from its home page.[23] Sample demographic information appears in Tables 7.1 and 7.2.

PROFILES OF PARTICIPATING INSTITUTIONS

Grant projects that rely on effective collaborative efforts among partner organizations need to convey the unique contributions from each entity. In order to convey this information, the narrative customarily includes a brief description of the collaborative effort, an overview of project management, the identification of key representatives, and brief statements regarding the responsibilities and contributions of each partner. The appendix should contain a one-page description for each participating partner organization.

The funding agency may suggest or require information describing each partner. A sample document may be included in the application packet.

CURRICULUM VITAE AND JOB DESCRIPTIONS

Funding agencies routinely ask the applicant to include a brief curriculum vita for each of the key project personnel. The format may not be specified, but a length limit may be given. The purpose of these documents is to provide evidence that key project personnel have the knowledge, skills, and

Table 7.1 University Student Demographic Data

	University Student Profile			
	Undergraduate Students		Graduate Students	
	#	%	#	%
Total Enrollment	1,259	100.0	581	100.0
Gender				
• Male Students	680	54.0	239	41.1
• Female Students	579	46.0	342	58.9
Ethnicity				
• Hispanic	588	46.7	224	38.6
• White	549	43.6	306	52.7
• Other	122	9.7	51	8.7
• All Minorities	701	55.7	257	44.2
Low Income Students	755	60.0	293	50.5
First Generation Post-secondary Students	818	65.0	299	51.5
Degrees Awarded	220		146	

experience to implement and manage the project. The grantor may decide whether to fund a project based on the strength of the key personnel.

Ask each key project staff person who is identified by name in the narrative to submit a current curriculum vita (or resume). If a length is specified, ask the individual to shorten the document. Shortening an individual's curriculum vita without specific permission is an invasion of intellectual property and academic freedom.

If time permits, the Principal Investigator or library may specify a format for use by all of the key personnel. While the use of a standardized format is not required, the appendix will reflect a uniformity that otherwise cannot be achieved easily.

Table 7.2 Family Economic and Demographic Data

Indicator	Baca County	Bent County	Kiowa County	Las Animas County	Prowers County	SE BOCES Region Total
Total Population	4,525	5,796	1,757	15,685	13,858	41,621
Population under 18	1,136	1,493	449	4,013	4,240	11,331
Median Family Income (All Families)	$23,054	$22,325	$26,779	$20,844	$23,931	$23,387
Median Family Income (Female-Headed)	$12,625	$11,771	$13,750	$11,042	$10,678	$11,973
Adult Literacy Rate	68%	63%	85%	59%	78%	71%
Adult Educational Level (HS or Greater)	67%	59%	60%	53%	59%	60%
Children in Poverty	242	350	52	1,144	1,127	2,915
Children at Risk	21.1%	25.8	10.7	33.4	27.3	23.7

Source: *KidsCount in Colorado!*

When the library requests support for a grant-funded position for which an individual will be hired, draft and include a representative job description. Each requested position should be mentioned in the narrative with a reference to a complete job description in the named appendix.

Job descriptions demonstrate the responsibilities and duties for the position, educational requirements, experience, technical skills, and competencies. Whenever possible, use job descriptions that the library's Human Resources Office has approved.

A private foundation may request a list of the governing board members, their affiliations, and years of service on the board. This information should be accompanied with a brief explanation of the type of board (e.g., governing, advisory) and its level of involvement with library operations and the grant project. Specific descriptions of the board members and their involvement demonstrate that they are active in the community, have the contacts to support major initiatives, and are highly regarded and respected leaders.

STANDARDS, BENCHMARKS, AND ACADEMIC ACHIEVEMENT

Significant attention to student academic achievement is ascribed to federal, state, and private grant awards. All of the states that have adopted academic standards distribute them in print and electronic form.[24] In order to convince the funding agency that the proposed project will increase student academic achievement, the grant team needs to include three major components.

First, the affected state curriculum standards need to be cited in the narrative. Without identifying the specific standards at the appropriate grade levels, the proposal will be vague and non-specific.

Second, the grant team should locate the specific standards addressed by the grant project and cite them in the narrative. The actual text may be included in an appendix. Experienced grant writers may also provide a chart or other graphic to show the correlation between standards, project objectives, and activities.

Third, a longitudinal overview of the "gap" between expectations and students' actual academic achievement on standardized tests should be included in the narrative. Specific, detailed data may be included in an appendix. Experienced grant writers recognize the importance of acquiring and maintaining these data in electronic form over a period of years to show changes and trends over time. Examples of these three components appear in Table 7.3.

LITERATURE REVIEW, "BEST PRACTICES," AND MODELS

Experienced grant writers recognize the importance of justifying the project implementation strategy. As part of the proposal drafting process,

Table 7.3 Standards, Benchmarks, and Academic Achievement Data

Current Colorado Model Content Standards: Science	
Standard 1	Students apply the processes of scientific investigation and design, conduct, communicate about, and evaluate such investigations.
Standard 2	Physical Science: Students know and understand common properties, forms, and changes in matter and energy. *(Focus: Physics and Chemistry)*
Standard 3	Life Science: Students know and understand the characteristics and structure of living things, the processes of life, and how living things interact with each other and their environment. *(Focus: Biology—Anatomy, Physiology, Botany, Zoology, Ecology)*
Standard 4	Earth and Space Science: Students know and understand the processes and interactions of Earth's systems and the structure and dynamics of Earth and other objects in space. *(Focus: Geology, Meteorology, Astronomy, Oceanography)*
Standard 5	Students understand that the nature of science involves a particular way of building knowledge and making meaning of the natural world.
Colorado Model Content Standard #1 for Science: Benchmarks for Grades 6–12	
Benchmark 1	Grades 6–8: ask questions and state hypotheses that lead to different types of scientific investigations

Colorado Model Content Standard #1 for Science: Benchmarks for Grades 6–12	
	(for example: experimentation, collecting specimens, constructing models, researching scientific literature) **Grades 9–12:** ask questions and state hypotheses using prior scientific knowledge to help design and guide development and implementation of a scientific investigation
Benchmark 2	**Grades 6–8:** use appropriate tools, technologies and metric measurements to gather and organize data, and report results **Grades 9–12:** select and use appropriate technologies to gather, process, and analyze data, and to report information related to an investigation
Benchmark 3	**Grades 6–8:** interpret and evaluate data in order to formulate logical conclusions **Grades 9–12:** identify major sources of error or uncertainty within an investigation *(for example: particular measuring devices and experimental procedures)*
Benchmark 4	**Grades 6–8:** demonstrate that scientific ideas are used to explain previous observations and to predict future events *(for example:*

(Continued)

Table 7.3 (Continued)

Colorado Model Content Standard #1 for Science: Benchmarks for Grades 6–12	
	plate tectonics and future earthquake activity)
	Grades 9–12: recognize and analyze alternative explanations and models
Benchmark 5	**Grades 6–8:** identify and evaluate alternative explanations and procedures
	Grades 9–12: construct and revise scientific explanations and models, using evidence, logic, and experiments that include identifying and controlling variables
Benchmark 6	**Grades 6–8:** communicate results of their investigations in appropriate ways *(for example: written reports, graphic displays, oral presentations)*
	Grades 9–12: communicate and evaluate scientific thinking that leads to particular conclusions

Alignment of STEM Learning Outcomes & Colorado Model Content Standards in Science	
STEM Learning Outcomes	**Colorado Model Content Standard #4 for Science: Benchmarks for Grades 6–12**
Understanding the geographic variation of physical, ecologic,	**Grades 6–8:** natural processes shape the Earth's surface

Alignment of STEM Learning Outcomes & Colorado Model Content Standards in Science	
STEM Learning Outcomes	**Colorado Model Content Standard #4 for Science: Benchmarks for Grades 6–12**
cultural, and economic phenomena around the world.	*(for example: landslides, weathering, erosion, mountain building, volcanic activity)* **Grades 9–12:** the feasibility of predicting and controlling natural events can be evaluated *(for example: earthquakes, floods, landslides)* **Grades 6–8:** major geological events such as earthquakes, volcanic eruptions, and mountain building are associated with plate boundaries and attributed to plate motions **Grades 9–12:** the atmosphere has a current structure and composition and has evolved over geologic time *(for example: effects of volcanic activity and the change of life forms)*
Understanding what a satellite image is, how different satellites measure different phenomena, and how these images need to be spatially referenced.	**Grades 6–8:** technology is needed to explore space *(for example: telescopes, spectroscopes, spacecraft, life support systems)* **Grades 9–12:** the scales of size and separation of components of the solar system are complex

(Continued)

Table 7.3 (Continued)

Alignment of STEM Learning Outcomes & Colorado Model Content Standards in Science	
STEM Learning Outcomes	**Colorado Model Content Standard #4 for Science: Benchmarks for Grades 6–12**
Understanding the geographic variation of physical, ecologic, cultural, and economic phenomena around the world.	**Grades 6–8:** models can be used to predict change *(for example: computer simulation, video sequence, stream table)*
	Grades 9–12: graphs, equations or other models are used to analyze systems involving change and constancy *(for example: comparing the geologic time scale to shorter timeframe, exponential growth, a mathematical expression for gas behavior; constructing a closed ecosystem such as an aquarium)*
	Grades 9–12: scientific knowledge changes and accumulates over time; usually the changes that take place are small modifications of prior knowledge but major shifts in the scientific view of how the world works do occur.
Understanding what a satellite image is, how different satellites measure different phenomena, and how these images need to be spatially referenced.	**Grades 6–8:** scientific knowledge changes as new knowledge is acquired and previous ideas are modified *(for example: through space exploration)*
	Grades 6–8: there are interrelationships among science, technology, and human activity that affect the world
	Grades 9–12: print and visual media can be evaluated for scientific evidence, bias, or opinion

(Continued)

Alignment of STEM Learning Outcomes & Colorado Model Content Standards in Science	
STEM Learning Outcomes	Colorado Model Content Standard #4 for Science: Benchmarks for Grades 6–12
	Grades 9–12: interrelationships among science, technology and human activity lead to further discoveries that impact the world in positive and negative ways

Source: Colorado Department of Education, Office of Standards and Assessments, *Colorado K-12 Academic Standards in Science,* 2007.

the Principal Investigator should require grant team members to conduct a literature search to identify and evaluate "best practices" and researched-based, field-tested models. The grant team members can work with library administrators to select the appropriate project implementation strategies and evaluation methodologies.

Evidence of this research should be included in the introduction to the implementation strategy (see Chapter 3) and the evaluation section (see Chapter 5). Lack of this information may cause the program officer and reviewers to question the manner and process that the library used to design the project.

LETTERS OF COMMITMENT AND LETTERS OF SUPPORT

Letters from the chief executive officers of participating partners, community representatives, and other appropriate individuals can strengthen a proposal. However, letters that identify the applicant and include identified specific support and "good wishes" do not necessarily need to be sent with the application. Such statements do not reflect an understanding or level of active participation in the proposed program or project.

Letters of commitment that outline specific contributions and activities from the sender in support of the proposal provide compelling evidence of a collaborative effort. Unique cash, in-kind, and matching contributions need to be mentioned. Consequently, each of these letters will be individualized and unique to the proposal.

Letters of support are general in nature and do not necessarily include collaborative statements. These letters indicate awareness of the proposed program or project and convey generalized support. The value of these statements is significantly less than letters of commitment.

BIBLIOGRAPHY OF RESOURCES CONSULTED

Experienced grant writers recognize the importance of citing the sources for statistical data, standardized test score reports, and other documents that are mentioned in the proposal narrative. The grant team may use printed, electronic, and online resources published by the school district, state department of education, U.S. Department of Education, the U.S. Bureau of the Census, and other government agencies.

Grant team members may be asked to submit a list of the resources consulted during the research, design, and drafting stages of the grant proposal. Compiling a single list as the final bibliography strengthens the proposal.

NOTES

1. U.S. Department of Education. *Education Department General Administrative Regulations* (EDGAR), Title 34, Code of Federal Regulations (CFR), Parts 74–86 and 97-99, December 2008 ed., http://www2.ed.gov/policy/fund/reg/edgarReg/edgar.html (accessed August 31, 2010).

2. U.S. Department of Education. *Assurances—Non-Construction Programs*, OMB Approval No. 0348-0040, http://www2.ed.gov/programs/8003/assurancessf424b.pdf (accessed August 31, 2010).

3. U.S. Department of Education. *Certification Regarding Lobbying*, http://www2.ed.gov/fund/grant/apply/appforms/ed80-013.pdf (accessed August 31, 2010).

4. U.S. Department of Education. *Disclosure of Lobbying Activities*, OMB Approval No. 0348-0046, http://www2.ed.gov/fund/grant/apply/appforms/sflll.pdf (accessed August 31, 2010).

5. U.S. Department of Education. Section 427 of GEPA, OMB Control No. 1894-0005 (Exp. 01/31/2011), http://www2.ed.gov/fund/grant/apply/appforms/gepa427.pdf (accessed August 31, 2010).

6. U.S. Department of Education. *No Child Left Behind Act of 2001*, http://www2.ed.gov/policy/elsec/leg/esea02/index.html (accessed August 31, 2010); U.S. Department of Education. *Reauthorization of the Elementary and Secondary Education Act*, http://www2.ed.gov/policy/elsec/leg/blueprint/index.html (accessed August 31, 2010).

7. The National Archives. Executive Order 12372 of July 14, 1982, *Intergovernmental Review of Federal Programs*, http://www.archives.gov/federal-register/codification/executive-order/12372.html (accessed August 31, 2010); U.S. Department of Education. *Application for Federal Assistance*, SF-424, OMB Number 4040-0004, Expiration Date March 31, 2012, http://www2.ed.gov/fund/grant/apply/appforms/sf424CoreForm.pdf (accessed August 31, 2010).

8. U.S. Department of Education. *Budget Information, Non-Construction Programs*, OMB Control Number 1894-0008, Expiration Date February 28, 2011, http://www2.ed.gov/fund/grant/apply/appforms/ed524.pdf (accessed August 31, 2010).

9. U.S. Department of Justice. Civil Rights Division. *Title VI of the Civil Rights Act of 1964*, 42 USC § 2000d, http://www.justice.gov/crt/about/edu/ (accessed August 31, 2010).

10. U.S. Department of Housing and Urban Development. *Section 504 of the Rehabilitation Act of 1973*, http://www.hud.gov/offices/fheo/disabilities/sect504.cfm (accessed August 31, 2010).

11. U.S. Department of Justice. Civil Rights Division. *Title IX of the Education Amendments of 1972*, http://www.justice.gov/crt/about/cor/coord/titleix.php (accessed August 31, 2010).

12. U.S. Department of Labor, *Age Discrimination Act of 1975*, http://www.dol.gov/oasam/regs/statutes/age_act.htm (accessed August 31, 2010).

13. U.S. Department of Labor. *Drug-Free Workplace Act of 1988*, http://www.dol.gov/elaws/asp/drugfree/screen4.htm (accessed August 31, 2010).

14. U.S. Department of Education, *Survey of Ensuring Equal Opportunity for Applicants*, OMB Number 1894-0010, Expires May 31, 2012, http://www2.ed.gov/fund/grant/apply/appforms/surveyeonensuringequalopp.pdf (accessed August 31, 2010).

15. Office of Management and Budget. *Circular A-133, Audits of States, Local Governments, and Non-Profit Organizations*, http://georgewbush-whitehouse.archives.gov/omb/circulars/a133/a133.html (accessed August 31, 2010).

16. U.S. Department of the Interior. National Park Service. *Native American Graves Protection and Repatriation Act of 1990*, http://www.nps.gov/history/nagpra/mandates/25USC3001etseq.htm (accessed August 31, 2010).

17. Advisory Council on Historic Preservation. *The National Historic Preservation Act of 1966*, as amended, http://www.achp.gov/nhpa.html (accessed August 31, 2010); Advisory Council on Historic Preservation. *Working with Section 106*, http://www.achp.gov/work106.html (accessed August 31, 2010).

18. U.S. Department of the Interior. National Park Service. *Archaeological and Historic Preservation Act of 1974*, http://www.thecre.com/fedlaw/legal13/archpreserv.htm (accessed August 31, 2010).

19. The National Archives. Executive Orders Disposition Tables Index, http://www.archives.gov/federal-register/executive-orders/disposition.html (accessed August 31, 2010); Environmental Protection Agency. *The National Environmental Policy Act of 1969*, as amended, http://ceq.hss.doe.gov/nepa/regs/nepa/nepaeqia.htm (accessed August 31, 2010); U.S. Department of the Interior. National Park Service. *Coastal Zone Management Act of 1972*, as amended, http://www.nps.gov/history/local-law/fhpl_cstlzonemngmt.pdf (accessed August 31, 2010); Environmental Protection Agency. *History of the Clean Air Act*, http://www.epa.gov/air/caa/caa_history.html (accessed August 31, 2010); Environmental Protection Agency. *Safe Drinking Water Act of 1974*, http://water.epa.gov/lawsregs/rulesregs/sdwa/index.cfm (accessed August 31, 2010); Environmental Protection Agency. *Summary of the Endangered Species Act*, http://www.epa.gov/lawsregs/laws/esa.html (accessed August 31, 2010); Wild and Scenic Rivers Council. *Wild & Scenic Rivers Act*, http://www.rivers.gov/publications/wsr-act.pdf (accessed August 31, 2010); Federal Deposit Insurance Corporation, Flood Disaster Protection Act of 1973, as amended, http://www.fdic.gov/regulations/laws/rules/6500-3600.html (accessed August 31, 2010).

20. U.S. Department of Agriculture, National Agricultural Library. *Animal Welfare Act of 1966*, as amended, http://awic.nal.usda.gov/nal_display/index.php?info_center=3&tax_level=3&tax_subject=182&topic_id=1118&level3_id=6735&level4_id=0&level5_id=0&placement_default=0 (accessed August 31, 2010).

21. Internal Revenue Service. *Exempt Organizations—Private Letter Rulings and Determination Letters*, http://www.irs.gov/charities/charitable/article/0,,id=123213,00.html (accessed August 31, 2010).

22. U.S. Census Bureau. *Census Bureau Home Page*, http://www.census.gov/ (accessed August 31, 2010); U.S. Bureau of the Census. *Census 2010: It's in Our Hands*, http://www.census.gov/compendia/statab/2010/2010edition.html (accessed August 31, 2010); U.S. Census Bureau, *The 2010 Statistical Abstract*, http://www.census.gov/compendia/statab/2010edition.html (accessed August 31, 2010); U.S. Census Bureau, *The 2010 Statistical Abstract: Earlier Editions*, http://www.census.gov/compendia/statab/past_years.html (accessed August 31, 2010).

23. U.S. Census Bureau, *The 2010 Statistical Abstract: State Abstracts*, http://www.census.gov/compendia/statab/st_abstracts.html (accessed August 31, 2010).

24. U.S. Department of Education. *Standards and Assessments Peer Review Guidance: Information and Examples for Meeting Requirements of the No Child Left Behind Act of 2001*, http://www2.ed.gov/policy/elsec/guid/saaprguidance.pdf (accessed August 31, 2010); U.S. Department of Education. *Lead & Manage My School*, http://www2.ed.gov/admins/lead/account/saa.html (accessed August 31, 2010).

PART 2
Implementation and Management

CHAPTER 8

After the Proposal

After your proposal is submitted, the grant team may fall into a post-project development malaise. The experienced grant writer keeps the following points in mind while awaiting a decision from the funding agency.

The time between proposal submission and award notification varies from a few weeks to many months. In the case of state and federal grants, the average wait is approximately four months. The proposal guidelines include an estimated timeline. The grant award may be made after the announced date for a number of reasons.

The funding agency may receive more proposals than had been anticipated. In such situations, the number of available reviewers may not be sufficient and additional readers will need to be recruited. Training new reviewers requires time that may not be included in the announcement. A thorough review process requires significant time, especially if the applications are lengthy. Multi-year grants are complex and detailed. These documents require that reviewers spend several hours reading and scoring each grant proposal.

Problems and delays beyond the funding agency's control may occur. Panelists may become unavailable, receive summons for jury duty, suffer family crises, or have accidents. During the mid-1990s, in early 2003, and again in 2010, winter blizzards forced federal officials to close their Washington, D.C. offices for several days, thus putting all activities behind schedule.

In short, the waiting time prior to notification remains an estimated rather than a firm date. Government agencies customarily make grant awards prior to the end of the current fiscal year. If the awards are not announced prior to that date, appropriated funds may revert back to the general fund and no awards can be made.

ACTIVITIES BETWEEN THE SUBMISSION AND DECISION

If the library has a grants office, rely on them to monitor the post-submission process. This office may be in close contact with the potential grantor for proposals and activities that are not related to a specific program or project. The period between the submission and the award announcements represents a good time for the grant team to reflect on the implications of both success and failure. Related questions may include:

- What will we do if the grant is not funded?
- Where else might we request funding or "shop" the product?
- What will we do if we are funded?
- Who will handle the immediate responsibilities required to accept the grant?
- Will the key project personnel be available?
- What will be required of the Project Director?
- What can we accomplish while we await a decision?

Refrain from contacting the funding agency unless a program officer calls the library to request additional information. After the release of the request for application through the deadline for submitting the proposal, the funding agency cannot answer questions. When a written process to submit questions and receive answers is available, make use of it as the need arises. Recognize that the funding agency may compile questions until a specified date, prepare written responses, and send them out to all potential grantees simultaneously. The process may take more time that the grant team allows to receive the answer to an inquiry.

The grant award notification process may be specific and varies among funding agencies. Generally, the grantor notifies the library administrator or Principal Investigator by email, a telephone call, or an award letter. When this situation occurs, the Principal Investigator is responsible to contact the library administrator, representatives of collaborating partner organizations, and the grant team members. Notification from the library director's office to the Principal Investigator and others depends on local practices.

Whether the grant application is funded or not, the scores and comments from each reviewer can be obtained in writing from the program officer. Government agencies are required by law to forward this information to applicants and do so without waiting for a formal request. Such feedback is likely to prove beneficial in future efforts to secure grant funding.

STRATEGIES FOR SUCCESSFUL GRANT RECIPIENTS

Celebrate when your proposal is funded. Hard work deserves to be rewarded. Everyone involved in the grant development effort needs to realize that writing the proposal represents a first stage.

When the library administrator or designated official signs the proposal, the signatories execute a legal and binding contract to implement, manage, and evaluate the program or project. It is imperative to begin the implementation on time so that the objectives can be achieved according to the timeline, and reports will be submitted on time.

One recent story serves as an illustration of the negative consequences of implementing a grant-funded project. A few days after a library administrator received notification of a grant award, additional documentation from the grantor surfaced in his daily mail. He filed it with a copy of the proposal and promptly got busy handling other administrative duties. Four months later, the library director received a letter from the grantor indicating that a quarterly report was overdue. An embarrassed library director opened his file drawer and discovered that those hastily filed papers were instructions and forms for the quarterly grant reports.

The following checklist will prove useful for the Principal Investigator to avoid difficulties and problems during the initial program or project implementation:

- Meet the program officers who will handle program and financial issues and establish a rapport with them.
- Verify the grant award dollar amount.
- Review the reporting schedule for the project period.
- Understand the method of payment that the grantor will use and the required financial forms.
- Determine the dates on which payments will be sent from the grantor to the library.
- Submit a letter of acknowledgement and acceptance.
- Modify the objectives and activities to reflect a reduction by the grantor in the budget.
- Submit a written notice of changes in the objectives and activities that are reflected in a reduced budget.
- Consult with key project personnel and central office administrators to make project modifications or budget reductions.
- Convene a project meeting to transfer responsibility for the implementation, management, and evaluation from the central office and key project personnel.

The Principal Investigator is responsible for revising the project starting and ending dates as appropriate. Working with the library grants officer for assistance can make the process less stressful, especially for a first-time Principal Investigator.

Project implementation should begin within 30 days. The Principal Investigator is responsible to take the following steps:

- Send a thank-you letter to members of the grant team and partner organization representatives.
- Ask the library director to inform the governing board about the grant award.
- Work with the Human Resources Department, prepare the paperwork required to post, advertise, and hire employees for grant-funded positions.
- Publicize the award with the library and the community.
- Identify the office space, furniture, and equipment that key project staff will occupy, making arrangements for project staff to occupy the space and begin their work as soon as possible.
- Prepare requisitions to order project materials and supplies.
- Work with the finance director to prepare the required documents for formal bids.
- Be prepared to attend the library board meeting to answer questions about the project and the items to be purchased through the bid process.
- Set up subcontracting arrangements, if necessary, conducting inquiries to ascertain whether potential subcontractors can perform up to the library's expectations.
- Establish project administrative procedures, timelines, and reporting schedules.
- Meet with advisory committee members, project staff, and the evaluator to review the goal, objectives, activities, and evaluation methodologies.
- Review project duties and responsibilities with staff members.
- Establish a schedule for project staff to transition from the "regular" duties to the project.
- Discuss the transition period, project documentation, and the evaluation of activities and personnel with principals, key personnel, and project staff.
- Alert project staff and the library community of the importance that open communication and meaningful conversations have on the project.
- Remind everyone that the project implementation, management, and evaluation will occur according to the plans set forth in the proposal.

A majority of librarians do not have experience as active project participants handling funds, following grant procedures, or directing funded programs. The Principal Investigator needs to schedule a meeting with the library finance director to discuss the procedures and guidelines for managing grant funds. Prior to the meeting, the Principal Investigator should send the finance director a complete copy of the proposal, notes for award negotiations, and a list of the reporting schedule.

A typical grant-funded project may encompass a complex array of activities. The project cannot begin officially until all of the acceptances are completed and the binding contract has been received from the grantor. Financial procedures will be new to most first-time grantees. Project participants need to review and discuss business procedures so that they are confident and understand the library's procedures and the grantor's reporting requirements. These activities are part of the grant management process and are described in detail in Part 2.

STRATEGIES FOR ORGANIZATIONS FAILING TO OBTAIN GRANT FUNDING

Grant seekers who are active in the grant development process for any appreciable length of time will experience disappointment. An experienced grant writer observed, "The only people I know who have a 100 percent success rate are those who have written just one proposal and had the good fortune to receive funding!"

As unfair as it might seem to proposal writers, good proposals do not always attract money. In some cases, the funding agency does not have sufficient funds to award money to each fundable proposal. When a grant seeker receives notification that a project will not be funded, the news should not be taken personally, cause feelings of rejection, or convince an individual to give up.

Focus should be placed on the importance of learning from non-funded proposals. The proposal writing process is a growth experience. Librarians, teachers, faculty members, community partner organization representatives, and administrators can benefit from the process and enhance their skills so that they will learn to write stronger proposals and obtain funding in the future.

When a non-award notice arrives from the grantor, the grant seeker should review the reasons cited in the letter. When the funding agency announces grant awards, contact the program officers assigned to your project to obtain reviewers' scores and comments. This information provides insight into the proposal's strengths and weaknesses.

Meet with the grant team to review the scores and reviewers' comments. The Principal Investigator can facilitate a discussion focused on ways to rewrite and strengthen the proposal components that received low scores. Consider reconvening the grant team when they can review and study funded proposals from the competition. Identifying weaknesses in a proposal provides a learning experience that can assist team members to prepare stronger grant proposals in the future.

POOR GRANTMANSHIP PRACTICES

Success as a grant writer depends, in part, on an ability to develop writing skills. Poor writing, presentation, and packaging practices do not contribute to success. Several practices detract from the merits of a well-developed grant proposal.

The Narrative

Librarians possess sophisticated information seeking and retrieval skills. They can provide accurate information to describe the potential funding agency, its interests, and past funding patterns. Submitting a well-written proposal to the appropriate potential grantor is essential for success.

Experienced grant writers study submission guidelines and requirements carefully. Failure to follow them can result in rejection. Successful grant writers will study and review guidelines several times before drafting the proposal. They have personal techniques to identify and remember the grantor's guidelines. Keeping track of the requirements is essential, and they differ from one grantor to another. Suggestions for this aspect of grant development appear in Chapter 1.

The use of jargon, "fifty-cent words," and terms intended to impress the reader weaken rather than strengthen a proposal. Readers may become confused when the narrative contains specialized terms. When librarians use language that only they are likely to understand or "buzz words," reviewers become annoyed.

A needs assessment filled with more problems or deficiencies than a single grant can address can cause concern among grant reviewers and program officers. One program officer observed, "If a library sends me a proposal that tries to address every problem through one program, I know they haven't spent enough time planning. If I can't see where my money will make a real impact, then I'll move on to the next proposal."

Reviewers do not award high scores to proposals that annoy them. One of the most frequent mistakes that novice grant writers make is to read a few journal articles and paraphrase them in the proposal. Not only can experienced program officers and reviewers identify this practice, they interpret the technique negatively.

Numerous errors in spelling, grammar, or punctuation are likely to turn a reviewer's attention away from the narrative. The importance of proofreading can't be overemphasized; after proofing the proposal personally, assign someone the responsibility to double-check the document.

Fonts that are small, ornate, or varied detract from the proposal. Grant guidelines may include specification for the font, size, and spacing; these requirements must be followed. Unusual fonts can cause reader eyestrain. Olde English is beautiful, but the eyes rapidly tire after reading more than a few words. Small print also causes the reader to engage in skimming, thereby increasing the likelihood of missing key points. Complicated, hard-to-understand passages are not scored high and can cause proposals to be rejected. Economical, straightforward language conveys information effectively. In addition, alternative forms of presenting information (graphs, charts, timetables, and the like) can be effective to present statistical and detailed information.

If a proposal fails to convey clarity of purpose, reviewers are unlikely to recommend it for a grant award. For instance, the authors came across one that included the following goal: "... to provide an outstanding, state-of-the-art program where students achieve academically." Such statements leave the reviewer wondering, "What is the real purpose of the program? What is the project goal?" Vague wording seriously compromises a proposal.

Funding agencies require or prefer collaborative projects. Grantors providing resources to libraries want assurance that patrons, community members, businesses, non-profit organizations, and institutions of higher education will contribute to the proposed activities and support them. A major trend that began in the late 1990s has been a requirement by selected funding agencies to include written commitment letters as part of the proposal.

Failure to describe project management experience and capabilities generally results in a non-funded proposal. The library's previous grant success can be a critical factor for the reviewers to consider. A Principal Investigator who has managed grant projects in the past has an advantage over novice counterparts. However, novice grant writers and the Principal Investigator can provide evidence of skills and capabilities by describing their previous achievements and assignments.

The Budget

The budget must align with the project. If the reviewer identifies a substantial expense that was not mentioned in the narrative, the score for this section of the proposal will reflect the discrepancy. An astute reviewer or program officer will easily detect non-aligned or misaligned expenses.

Reviewers will detect a "padded" budget. Novice grant writers may fail to do an effective job of research and overestimate or "guess" at project costs. At best, the program officer or reviewer will think the writer is lazy; at worst, the writer will be perceived as dishonest. In both cases, the proposal is unlikely to be funded.

Incorrect budget computations indicate a lack of attention to detail. Twenty-first century computers have a built-in calculator. When the Principal Investigator does not use a calculator, the finance director needs to check the budget for completeness and accuracy.

The Details

The growing trend in the twenty-first century is for grant proposals to be submitted electronically. However, if the funding agency requests that submissions be printed on paper, the document should not employ fancy bindings or colored paper, but should be printed on white paper and stapled in the upper left corner. One corporate foundation official admitted that he actually required proposals to follow an A-C-B, rather than the usual A-B-C format. He instructed his secretary to check each proposal when it arrived and to discard those that did not follow his prescribed format. His rationale was that anyone who didn't follow his instructions probably wouldn't handle his money wisely.

A primary reason for funding agencies to require a specific format, length, and components is to facilitate an equitable review process. Each reviewer follows the guidelines and scores the proposal according to a rubric. When an applicant does not follow the proscribed format, the reviewer may become frustrated and score the proposal low or deem it to be "nonresponsive."

Proposals that exceed a pre-established page limit are not funded. In fact, some organizations check the number of pages as proposals arrive. One program officer stated, "If it says I want 25 pages, I stop reading when I've read 25 pages. If I haven't read a complete proposal by then, the applicant can forget about receiving a grant from us." Federal reviewers are not required to read more than the specified limit of pages or the appendices.

Missing assurances, compliances, and signatures routinely result in the rejection of a proposal. Missing components convey a lack of attention to detail and indicate that key personnel may be careless. If the applicant overlooks simple things, like numbering pages or defining acronyms and specific terms, the reviewers might suspect that project personnel would not pay attention to the details of the proposed program. Lack of a signature may also indicate that the library administrator was not aware of the proposal or its submission. In order to make sure that a proposal is complete, compile a checklist prior to drafting the proposal.

Deadlines are non-negotiable. Upon receipt of the application packet, the Principal Investigator and grant team members should circle the deadline and mark it on their calendars. They need to develop a realistic timeline immediately in order to complete the proposal in advance of the deadline. Some funding agencies require that proposals arrive at their offices by

5:00 p.m. local time on the deadline date. Others require that the proposal be sent in a package with a date supplied by a commercial carrier before the deadline date and time.

RESUBMITTING THE PROPOSAL

In the event that the Principal Investigator and library officials believe that their proposal has merit, they may decide to resubmit. They may decide to incorporate reviewers' comments into the proposal and resubmit it to the same funding agency. Experienced grant writers recognize the potential to receive funding on the second submission of a proposal. One National Endowment for the Humanities staff member recently noted that almost 90 percent of resubmissions are funded. At the same time, the probability of success may increase when additional sources accompany a resubmission.

Grant writers need to remember that no matter how well the proposal is written and packaged, factors outside of their control may play a role in their failure to get funded. Funding agencies have limited monies to award. In addition, grantors often strive for geographical balance in funding.

If the proposal is not resubmitted to the same funding agency, the program officer may be able to recommend other sources. In some cases, the program officer may offer to contact colleagues on your behalf.

As a final resort, you can explore the possibility of obtaining other sources of funding. Parent-teacher organizations, community-based organizations, and friends groups can be helpful in raising money and community awareness of the project's potential impact. Philanthropists with a professed interest in the project's stated goals may provide assistance. If the proposal has merit, don't give up!

CHAPTER 9

Implementing the Project

Congratulations! Your project has been funded. You did your homework, chose a great team, planned well, and wrote a winning proposal. While it may seem like the end of a long road, receiving funding is only a first step.

Implementing and managing a funded project require substantial effort and major commitments of time and resources. Management includes activities such as overseeing project implementation, planning and organization, hiring and managing personnel, marketing, record-keeping, financial oversight, accounting, reporting, and evaluation. Management also often includes a fair amount of political positioning, deal-making, and outright wrangling within an organization. Luckily, most organizations have protocols and procedures in place to aid in many management functions. Some may even have a person or office to provide assistance.

The Principal Investigator (Project Director) is ultimately responsible for overseeing all aspects of the project or program. Successful grant management begins with this individual. Effective Principal Investigators possess excellent communication skills, attention to detail, and the drive to ensure that all project obligations are met on time and as promised. Effective Principal Investigators are also leaders. They lead by example and know how to build a team. However, they also know that they cannot do the job alone, and they delegate responsibility to meet the demands of competing obligations.

GETTING STARTED: CELEBRATE, PRAISE, AND COMMUNICATE

Winning a grant is a major accomplishment. Planning and drafting a funded proposal is no small task. Receiving funding for an important project is a feather in your cap, a boon for your organization, and an opportunity for your stakeholders.

Moving forward at a steady pace is critical to a project's long-term success. Adopting a forward-thinking mindset from the start creates a healthy work ethic and positive work environment. With this in mind, project implementation should begin soon after the award letter is received. Depending on the organization, implementation may include activities like accepting the grant, filing paperwork, setting up accounts, and notifying partners. These often tedious tasks will undoubtedly take some time to complete. If your library has not received a number of grants in the past, the Principal Investigator will need time to establish the project, conduct initial meetings, and begin the implementation of activities, programs, and services. Handling these important details in a timely manner will allow the real work of the project to begin on schedule.

But before even these initial activities, it is important to celebrate, praise, and communicate. Regardless of whether an organization publically acknowledges the accomplishment, it is critical for the Principal Investigator to recognize the tireless hours, unrewarded efforts, and hard work the project team performed over the pre-award period. Significant awards (i.e., those exceeding $250,000) frequently require months or years of planning, working with library colleagues and community representatives, and designing a comprehensive project that addresses an identified need. The project team is comprised of the people who put in the extra effort to craft a winning proposal. Before moving ahead with any implementation tasks, they deserve recognition and should be rewarded with praise. Rewarding team members may include:

- informing team members about the award before anyone else;
- organizing an informal get-together or luncheon;
- publically recognizing team members at a staff meeting or through a departmental email;
- organizing an official celebration;
- highlighting team members in a newsletter, web site, or blog; and/or
- formally recognizing the accomplishment in personnel files or performance tracking.

In library organizations, there are many ways to acknowledge a team's hard work. Certainly, everyone would appreciate a big raise or a year-end bonus. Unfortunately, at most institutions the financial situation or organizational structure will not allow for monetary rewards. Fortunately, there are many ways to reward your team. After many hours of hard work over months or years, the Principal Investigator knows the individual members on the team best. Sometimes a sincere thank you is all that is needed. Be creative. The important thing to remember is that successful grant writing is a team effort. If you reward your team now, they will continue to reward you in the future with their hard work and input.

Once you have told your team, you must then tell *everyone else*! It is imperative to make everyone in your organization fully aware of your project from the beginning. All new projects affect the library organization in some way. Workloads may increase or duties may be shifted. Sometimes projects championed by others are put on hold or take a backseat to new endeavors. Because some change is inevitable, the members of your organization deserve to know about your project immediately. Failing to inform your colleagues could lead to resentment within the library staff at a time when you would expect only praise. Failing to inform your colleagues throughout the library organization could also lead to organizational roadblocks throughout the course of your project. By informing everyone, the Principal Investigator is taking appropriate steps to avoid hard feelings, turf struggles, and disagreements over the course of the project.

This early stage is also your opportunity to begin the public promotion of your project. Depending on the size of the award or type of grant, national and local news media may be interested in reporting the story. At the very least you will want to notify the members of your local community. Because publicity and marketing are often critical components of successful grant management, a full section of this chapter is devoted to these issues. For now, just remember that you will only receive your award once. Take advantage of the excitement by getting the word out as widely as possible.

Notifying Partners

In today's competitive funding environment, developing a strong network of partners is the cornerstone of good grant planning and management. Grant writing (and grant winning) is a collaborative endeavor that requires a wide array of associations both within and outside of your organization. In the planning stage, formal and informal partners are identified. These are the people and organizations that will help fulfill project obligations. A partnership network is also the group that will provide the support and collaboration needed to sustain projects and develop future proposals.

Maintaining good relationships with project partners is critical to successful grant management. Positive relationships and goodwill are fostered through good communication. Keeping partners well informed at all stages of project development and implementation ensures that all parties understand their obligations. Good communication also creates fertile ground for collaboration and advancement.

Formal partners are those with whom a written partnership agreement exists (see Form 9.1). A partnership agreement defines the relationship between the partner and the project. In most cases, formal partners are legally bound to fulfill their pledged obligations. Because of the legal nature

1. Applicant Organization:

2. Partner Organization Name:

3. List the Partner's key roles and responsibilities in the project:

- Solicit technical assistance, program advisement, support, and guidance from library professionals and state, regional, national, and international organizations.
- Participate in a focused target audience recruitment initiative and host open houses.
- Incorporate mass media outlets (newsletters, professional association publications, and project web site) to deliver grant project information to the patron and community.
- Increase cultural awareness and linguistic sensitivity among the project team.
- Facilitate mentoring for project team and patrons (as needed).
- Support organization representatives in professional development activities.
- Recognize project team achievements, accomplishments, and contributions to their prospective colleagues and employers.
- Deliver library support services to academic, special, and public libraries with collections, government agencies, and nongovernmental organizations serving diverse communities.
- Conduct an environmental scan to identify emerging technologies used by rural attorneys, academic and public libraries with legal collections, rural government agencies, and nongovernmental legal organizations to repackage and deliver information.
- Compile and publish descriptions, technical requirements, documentation, and administrative guides for colleagues in community organizations, academic, special, and public libraries to use in their local communities.
- Attend the quarterly Project Advisory Council meeting.

We, the undersigned Partner organization, agree to the following:

- We will carry out the activities described above and in the Application Narrative.
- We will use any federal funds we receive from Applicant organization in accordance with applicable Federal laws and regulations as set forth in the program guidelines and the terms and conditions of the grant award.

> - We assure that our facilities and programs comply with the applicable Federal requirements and laws as set forth in the program guidelines.
>
> ___
> Signature of Partner Authorizing Representative/Official Date
> ___
> Name and Title of Partner Authorizing Representative/Official (Type or Print)

Form 9.1 Sample Partnership Statement

of this type of partnership, formal partners should be notified formally. In other words, they should receive written notification from an authorized agent of the grantee's institution. It is also good practice to kindly remind partners of their obligations under the partnership agreement. For formal partners this should be done in writing and, if possible, in person. A significant period of time may have passed since the partnership was agreed upon, key personnel may have changed, or the partner may have temporarily set aside the project for other priorities. Reminding formal partners of their obligations at the outset will help avoid any misunderstanding when it comes time for them to fulfill their obligations. Doing so in writing documents the formal nature of the relationship and provides proof of the partner's knowledge of their obligations.

Informal partners are all of those other networks that support a project or program. Informal partners may be community members or association leaders who were recruited to refine ideas, local politicians or religious figures, community activists, or members of other departments in your organization. By definition, relationships with informal partners are casual and agreements are often oral. While informal partners need not receive formal notification, it is advisable to notify them of your success as soon as practical. Informal partners may be contacted by phone or in person; or you may consider hosting a luncheon or social hour to thank them for their support and inform them of how they can help the project move forward.

Accepting the Award

Both the grantor and grantee may have a prescribed procedure for accepting an award. The Principal Investigator must understand the grantor's requirements as well as those of his or her own institution. Depending upon organization size and type, the Principal Investigator may or may not be responsible for negotiating and accepting the award. Most organizations will have a grants office or financial administrator to perform these duties. Regardless of the organizational infrastructure, the Principal Investigator is responsible for ensuring that the proper procedure is followed. If the Principal Investigator and the grant team did their homework before submitting the proposal, each individual on the project team will already have a well-developed rapport with the officials and administrators. Follow up with these individuals is important to ensure that all grant requirements are met.

Review Project Award Information and Documents Provided by the Grantor

When the library's authorized agent or official signs the acceptance document, a formal commitment to implement, manage, and evaluate the project or program exists. It is imperative to begin the implementation on time so that the objectives can be achieved according to the timeline, and reports are submitted on time.

The following checklist will prove useful for the Principal Investigator to avoid difficulties and problems during initial program and project implementation.

- Meet the program officers who will handle program and financial issues to establish a rapport with them.
- Verify the grant award dollar amount.
- Review the reporting schedule for the entire project period.
- Understand the method of payment that the grantor will use and the required financial forms.
- Determine the dates on which payments will be sent from the grantor to the grantee.
- Submit a letter of acknowledgement and acceptance or other acceptance procedure designated by the grantor.
- Modify the objectives and activities to reflect a reduction (if needed) and submit written notice of changes in objective and activities.
- Consult with key project personnel and central library administrators when making project modifications or budget reductions.
- Revise the project starting and ending dates as appropriate.
- Consult the grants office or officer for assistance.
- Convene a project meeting to transfer responsibility for the implementation, management, and evaluation to key personnel.

THE PROJECT HANDOFF

Navigating administrative minutiae may consume the first several weeks of a grant-funded project or program. Set-up often involves a great deal of paperwork, many meetings, and significant time. Generally, the Principal Investigator is responsible for completing all set-up tasks. However, some institutions may have a program office or officer who can provide assistance.

Bringing together the library representatives from administration, human resources, the physical plant, and the grant team can provide a continuity of information and a transparent approach to launching a successful project. Questions can be answered to everyone's satisfaction and clarifications about internal library procedures, parent organization processes, and grantor requirements can be addressed. While preparing for a handoff meeting can be a challenge, facilitating all the necessary steps can make the transition from a grant application to a grant implementation environment more seamless and less problematic. Typical set-up considerations, tasks, and topics to be covered in the handoff meeting appear in Form 9.2.

Acceptance Paperwork

Most organizations will have an office or high level official designated to negotiate and accept grant awards. In smaller organizations, the Principal Investigator may be responsible for some negotiation and acceptance duties. Regardless of whether the grant team leader or some other official does the negotiation, the Principal Investigator should keep good records of all acceptance communications and paperwork. If records are not automatically provided, the Principal Investigator should request copies to complete his or her file.

Internal Accounts and Fiscal Paperwork

Project set-up generally requires the creation of numerous internal accounts. Generally, each account will require a different set of paperwork. Examples of typical set-up paperwork include human resources payroll, eligibility to work documents, benefits forms, copier accounts, telephone service, long distance codes, spending accounts, and purchasing cards. Meticulous recordkeeping practices are important. Copies of all account records and paperwork should be maintained by the Principal Investigator or another responsible individual.

STAFFING AND TRAINING

Grant-funded projects often require the work of people beyond the library staff and members of the grant team. When the project is complex, grant budgets customarily include funds to hire full-time and part-time employees. Hiring is a time-consuming process. Major hiring activities include drafting position descriptions, posting notices, interviewing, and completing paperwork required by the human resources department. Staffing a grant-funded project may also include redefining or shifting the duties and job responsibilities of current employees.

Activity	Timeframe	Notes and Comments
☐ Determine start-up period	6 to 8 weeks	
☐ Review partnership agreements and subcontracts		Request subcontracts
☐ Financial requirements		
☐ Grant account set up	6 to 8 weeks	Budget Officer
☐ Signature authorizations form		PI – submit to Budget Officer
☐ Hand-off meeting		
☐ Invite library administrators		
☐ Invite Budget Officer		
☐ Invite partner representatives		
☐ Reporting dates established		Set by grantor
☐ Draft narrative and financials		Allow 2 weeks for internal review
☐ Final narrative and financials		Allow 2 weeks for internal review
☐ Project personnel	4 to 6 weeks	
☐ Notify Human Resources about positions to fill		
☐ Position descriptions (complete final drafts)		
☐ Salary & benefits		
☐ Hiring committee		
☐ Follow library hiring process		

Activity	Timeframe	Notes and Comments
☐ Work space	2 to 3 weeks	Work with facilities manager
☐ Work space/keys/supplies		
☐ Equipment (computer/printer/other)		
☐ Phone/long distance code		
☐ Credit or purchasing card (if applicable)		
☐ U.S. mail		
☐ Project presence (web, brochures, flyers, etc.)		
☐ Review programmatic impact	12 weeks	
☐ Student recruitment		

Form 9.2   Project Handoff Meeting Topics

New initiatives require professional development and training for library personnel. Grant-funded projects are no different. New employees need to be oriented to institutional policies and procedures, computer systems, and essential job duties. For current staff, training may include accounting and coding for grant funds, information about data collection or reporting requirements, or information about the creation of project deliverables. In addition to requirements within the library, selected parent organizations (e.g., cities, counties, school districts, colleges, and universities) may have set orientation requirements and training procedures that must be followed. Others may leave training decisions up to the department or unit. Technology training in the use of new software or equipment may need to be negotiated with the vendor or a hired consultant if there are no qualified or knowledgeable individuals at the parent organization.

Hiring Project Personnel

In a well-developed grant proposal, the professional and support staff requirements for the project have already been identified. Key project personnel, such as the Principal Investigator, are often identified by name in the grant proposal, along with a detailed description of their relevant qualifications and educational backgrounds. Most likely, the proposed budget also includes a calculation of the amount of time each of these individuals is projected to spend on grant activities and the costs associated with their participation. As a result, if the grant team has already identified all the participants under the grant (and they are still all available at the time of the grant award), hiring any additional project staff may not be warranted.

It is not uncommon, however, for some staff (often those individuals who carry out the day-to-day activities) to be selected and hired after the grant has been awarded. Again, in a well-developed grant proposal, the funding for such positions would have been included in the grant budget, even though no specific individual was identified. In this case, the grant team must be prepared to proceed quickly with the selection and hiring process as soon as the team is notified of the grant award. A checklist for hiring project staff appears in Form 9.3.

Steps to Take	Timeframe	Notes and Comments
Step #1: identify funded position(s)	1 week	
☐ Review position description (modify as needed)		
☐ Determine salary range		
☐ Identify internal and external advertising sites		
Step #2: set-up hiring process	2 to 6 weeks	Coordinate with Human Resources
☐ Secure approval to post position(s)		
☐ Finalize position description		
☐ Determine closing date		

Steps to Take	Timeframe	Notes & Comments
☐ Post position(s)	2 to 4 weeks	Work with Payroll Clerk
Step #3: work with hiring committee		
☐ Review applications		
☐ Develop interview questions		
☐ Interview candidates		
☐ Check references	1 week	Work with Payroll Clerk
☐ Recommend applicant for hire		Coordinate with Human Resources
☐ Send letters to applicants not selected		Work with Payroll Clerk
Step #4: complete HR paperwork to hire		Work with Payroll Clerk
☐ Conduct background check		
☐ Complete HR forms		
☐ I-9 form		
☐ W-4 form		
☐ Grant account		
☐ Notify employee of start date		
☐ Schedule orientation attendance		
☐ Attend supervisor's training (Project Director)		
☐ Notify library administrators & grantor (as applicable)		

Form 9.3 Steps To Take For Hiring Project Staff

In many ways, hiring staff under a grant is no different than hiring staff under any other circumstances. There are some important distinctions, however. Since the grant is for a specific period of time, any positions that are funded solely under the grant are time-limited or temporary. More importantly, since grant funds must be used only for activities and expenditures authorized under the terms and conditions of the grant, job duties and functions of grant staff must align with the goals and objectives of the project. Thus, grant staff may have less flexibility in their job duties and responsibilities than other similar staff positions in the organization. The Principal Investigator must ensure that others in the organization understand the role and any limitations imposed upon grant-funded staff and ensure that they only perform duties that are authorized under the grant when grant funds are used to compensate them for their time. Finally, there may be more accountability associated with grant-funded positions than the organization is accustomed to, and the need to document the person's actual working activities and expenditures for the funding agency through interim and final reports, timesheets, and other accounting measures may seem daunting at first. Often the granting agency has very specific instructions and guidelines regarding the way in which such activities and expenditures must be documented. The importance of learning about and complying with any such requirements cannot be overstated.

There are times when the grant team might find itself in the position of having to hire someone unexpectedly. Given the time lapse between grant proposal submission and grant award notification, a key project staff member may no longer be available to work on the grant. The grant team might also need to hire someone new if it becomes apparent that there is a need to hire additional staff that were not identified in the grant proposal or grant budget. In these situations, the granting agency may need to be contacted before any new hiring occurs. Customarily, any significant changes to a grant project in its programmatic scope, key personnel, or budget will need to be approved by the granting agency.

Project personnel will be hired according to the library's affirmative action policies. Libraries and their parent organizations seek to attain the following when hiring so members of traditionally under-represented groups are represented in the pool of candidates:

- the achievement of a workforce with adequate representation of ethnic minorities, women, the disabled, disabled veterans, and veterans of the Vietnam era;
- the elimination of discrimination in employment on the basis of race, color, religion, national origin, sex, sexual orientation, marital status, pregnancy, age, disability, disabled veterans, or Vietnam era veterans status;

- the maintenance of genuine equality of opportunity by ensuring that reasonable requirements and the merits of the individual are the sole criteria for appointment, retention, and advancement of employees;
- the maintenance of salary equity among employees; and
- the provision of opportunities for employees from under-represented groups as well as other employees to improve their qualifications for advancement.

Applications for positions and hiring for the project will use the procedures that the library uses to fill regular staff vacancies. An applicant will submit an application (frequently using an online system located within the library or parent organization's web site), a minimum of three letters of reference, a resume, and official transcript to the chair of the Selection Committee. The Selection Committee reviews all applications, identifies qualified individuals, checks references, and schedules interviews. Recommendations for hiring are forwarded to the library administrator. When a candidate accepts a position, the human resources director sends the formal employment contract, explains required pre-employment paperwork (background check, verification of eligibility to work in the United States, etc.) and benefits (insurances, retirement, vacation allowances, sick leave, etc.), sets a starting date, and schedules new employee orientation.

Employees, Consultants, and Volunteers

The time between the grant proposal submission and the grant award notification may be months. One positive aspect of this downtime is the availability of additional time to reflect on all staff qualifications and the experience needed to implement the grant. This is an excellent time for current staff members to review their project duties and responsibilities, especially if there is still the opportunity to define duties and responsibilities of yet to-be-hired project staff members and make any necessary adjustments.

If the library organization is hiring a new employee, the grant budget will need to be reviewed to determine whether there is funding for a full- or part-time position and whether the position has any fringe benefits associated with it. How will the person be compensated? Will the employee be paid a salary or an hourly wage? In addition, because all grants are time-limited, what will be the length of the new employee's term of employment under the grant? Does the work of the project require a six-month commitment on the part of the new employee or longer? Whoever is hired must understand all the terms and conditions of his or her employment under the grant and expectations must be clear. Most organizations will have a human resources department that can help with some of these important decisions.

If the library hires a consultant rather than an employee, it is important to review the grant award to determine whether there are any restrictions regarding the percentage of the budget that can be used to hire consultants or subcontractors. A consultant is an individual who has been brought into the project to provide expert advice in a particular area. Customarily, the consultant must be written into the budget of the grant in order to be paid from project funding. Typically, a consultant does not receive fringe benefits, but is paid under a contract for specific services during a specific period of time. It will generally be necessary to draft some kind of Request for Proposal (or RFP) for the services and expertise that is needed. The RFP can then be sent to consulting firms or individuals with known expertise in the grant area of focus. A checklist of the steps to hire a subcontractor or consultant appears in Form 9.4.

Steps to Take	Timeframe	Notes and Comments
Step #1: include roles in final proposal		
☐ Determine required costs		
☐ Verify Budget Officer of indirect cost rate for subcontractors		
Step #2: request permission	2 to 4 weeks	
☐ Review partnership agreements (as applicable)		
☐ Identify tasks, deliverables, and schedule for completion		
☐ Complete library form		
☐ Secure library administrator's approval		
☐ Submit to library administrator for approval		
☐ Receive signed approval		
Step #3: establish project calendar		
☐ Determine invoice dates		
☐ Identify payment dates		

Implementing the Project 209

Steps to Take	Timeframe	Notes and Comments
☐ Schedule dates for deliverables		
☐ Verify dates reports due to Project Director		
☐ Schedule evaluation activities		
Step #4: modify (as required)		

Form 9.4   Steps to Take for Hiring Subcontractors and Consultants

Finding an experienced, skillful consultant can be time-consuming, and the ideal time to identify and seek out appropriate consultants is during the development of the grant proposal. Getting referrals from colleagues who have used particular consultants in the past can be extremely helpful.

An often overlooked potential worker is the volunteer. Although it is time-consuming to train volunteer workers and develop meaningful work for them, it may be an ideal option depending upon the nature of the activities under the grant. If the library is already set up to work with them, volunteers may be well-suited to assist with specific short-term activities funded under the grant.

Developing Position Descriptions

It is important to develop specific position (or job) descriptions for each grant-funded position. Often job descriptions are developed through the grant proposal planning process and become part of the grant proposal itself. The positions needed for a successful grant may include full-time employees and part-time contributions from current employees. When a current employee is assigned to grant activities, arrangements should be made to ensure that regular assignments will be handled by other workers.

For each position, the grant team must determine what types of skills and experiences are essential and create a job description that outlines the functions as they relate to the goals and objectives of the grant. Job descriptions routinely include the following components:

- job title;
- essential functions of the job, including any physical requirements;
- salary or hourly wage;

- preferred and required qualifications and/or experience, technical skills, and educational requirements;
- status (part-time or full-time);
- benefited or non-benefited; and
- start and end date (if temporary).

As with any decisions regarding potential employees, the library's human resources department should be consulted so that their staff members can assist with the development of job descriptions. Requirements for grant-funded positions should parallel those of current employees so that compensation and benefits can be comparable. There may be a job description template that must be used or boilerplate language that must be incorporated into each job description for your organization.

The Principal Investigator is responsible for all project activities, financial management, and reporting to the library administrators and to the grantor. Members of the grant-funded team who will be hired can be described in the personnel section of the application narrative; if allowed, job descriptions should be included in an appendix. Typical grant project staffing may include a Principal Investigator, full-time coordinator (see Table 9.1), professional library staff, technology specialist (see Table 9.2), and paraprofessional support.

Table 9.1   Position Description for Project Coordinator

Job Title: Project Coordinator
Position Number:
Department: Library
Supervisor:
Salary Range:

I. Required Qualifications

Education: MLIS required; second graduate degree or PhD preferred
Experience: Library experience preferred. Community outreach experience. Ability to troubleshoot desktop applications. Supervisory experience. Excellent research skills.
Licenses and/ Certifications:
Special Knowledge, Skills, and Abilities: Excellent communication and interpersonal skills; strong analytic and problem-solving skills; ability to work in a team environment; and flexibility in response to changing circumstances. Current awareness of new trends and issues in the legal community.
A. Language Skills: Proficiency in the English language is needed, and working knowledge of one or more foreign languages is preferred. Must be able to communicate with diplomacy and tact, both in person and on the telephone.

B. Mathematical Skills: Strong math skills are needed to design management tools using spreadsheets and database applications.
C. Reasoning Ability: Must be able to work independently, effectively, and confidentially using tact and excellent judgment. Analytical skills are required for decision making. Must be able to analyze and organize work and set priorities.
D. Other Skills and Abilities: Must be able to interact with all members of the library user and practitioner communities as needed. Must be detail-oriented, with an extremely high accuracy rate in all work done.
E. Physical Demands: Must be able to sit at and use a PC for extended periods of time and move and/or lift boxes up to 25 lbs.
F. Work Environment: The work environment is a varied one. This position will work in the library, public libraries, county libraries, and at community partner sites.
Other requirements or factors:

II. Specific Duties

* Coordinate with the library and project partners to ensure readiness and thorough preparation for implementation of project activities. (40%)
* Participate in recruitment process for target population. (10%)
* Maintain and track project databases. (20%)
* Participate in planning, setting timelines, action plans, and implementation of program. (20%)
* Plan and oversee special events to promote the project. (10%)

Advertising the Position

In addition to the job application form, the grant team needs to determine if any other required documentation must be part of the application materials. Other materials may include cover letters, resumes (or curriculum vitae), a list of references (personal and professional), and writing samples. Requesting a cover letter has become a standard practice because the document can provide an opportunity for applicants to state their interests in the project and reflects applicants' writing style and language proficiencies.

The grant team might also want to consider the locations for posting the position. The library may have requirements for internal postings and a period during which only current employees may apply. Even if there is no organizational policy requiring an internal posting, the grant team should

Table 9.2   Position Description for Technology Support Specialist

Job Title: Technology Support Specialist
Position Number:
Department: Library
Supervisor:
Salary Range:

The Technology Support Specialist will assist the project team with acquiring, installing, and testing the new technology; will support library and staff training and the library mini-lab.

I. Required Qualifications

Education: BS in computer science, information technology, or closely related field required; MLIS or MS preferred
Experience: Five years IT experience, focus on online and communications technology; two years project and/or personnel management; Library experience preferred. Ability to troubleshoot desktop applications.
Licenses and Certifications:
Special Knowledge, Skills, and Abilities: Excellent communication and interpersonal skills; strong analytic and problem-solving skills; ability to work in a team environment; and flexibility in response to changing circumstances. Current awareness of new trends and issues in the legal community.
A. Language Skills: Proficiency in the English language is needed. Must be able to communicate with diplomacy and tact, both in person and on the telephone.
B. Mathematical Skills: Strong math skills are needed to design management tools using spreadsheets and database applications.
C. Reasoning Ability: Must be able to work independently, effectively, and confidentially, using tact and excellent judgment. Analytical skills are required for decision making. Must be able to analyze and organize work and set priorities.
D. Other Skills and Abilities: Must be able to interact with all members of the library user and practitioner communities as needed. Must be detail-oriented, with an extremely high accuracy rate in all work done.
E. Physical Demands: Must be able to sit at and use a PC for extended periods of time and move and/or lift boxes up to 25 lbs.
F. Work Environment: The work environment is a varied one. This position will work in the library, public libraries, county libraries, and at community partner sites.
Other requirements or factors:

> **II. Specific Duties**
>
> - Troubleshoot new systems and software during pilot and prior to institutionalization. (35%)
> - Work closely with the Instructional Designer in the design, development, and pilots of the technology and network infrastructure. (25%)
> - Work with the Technology Department to install new hardware, software, and equipment. (20%)
> - Support library and staff training (with Instructional Designer) and library mini-lab. (15%)
> - Assist in evaluating project. (5%)

consider the advantages of inviting applications from library colleagues before going public with the position announcement. Hiring from within can be a great morale booster, as it sends a message to the library community that current employees are valued and eligible for advancement.

Given the work that has gone into the development of the grant proposal, the grant team may be in a better position than the human resources department to know where to advertise the position. A public announcement can be made on the library web site, the statewide and regional library job line, the American Library Association's ALA JobList,[1] web sites, professional journals or newsletters (in print or electronic), blogs, and listservs to which potential applicants may subscribe. When the grant involves a partnership with other organizations, representatives may have appropriate means to distribute and advertise the position as well. Often it is the library's current employees, colleagues, or the local community of practice who are the best resources for identifying potential new employees.

The Interview Process

It is important for the grant team to determine the structure of the interview process in advance of conducting any interviews. The grant team will need to determine how it wants to go about sorting through the applications. Will there be a selection committee? How will consensus be reached regarding whom to interview and how many?

Once applicants have been selected for interviewing and prior to the actual interviews, the grant team should distribute the applicants' materials (the application, resume, cover letter, etc.) to members of the interview team. Each member of the interview team should become familiar with the materials prior to the interview. When it is apparent to an applicant that the team has read his or her cover letter and application, it speaks well for the organization and the interview process.

In addition to drafting the interview questions in advance, the grant team should also determine what information will be disclosed about the hiring process to each applicant. What is the timeframe for making a decision? How will applicants be notified? The applicants will appreciate knowing any information that the library and interviewers can share about the hiring process. Finally it is helpful to identify an organization contact person for each applicant at the time of the interview. Often applicants have legitimate reasons for needing to notify the organization of relevant changes in their situation.

If possible, it is best to have the same people interview all applicants. The interviewers need to reach consensus in ranking the applicants so that they agree who is the top candidate. It is important to request the applicant's permission to check references and to make sure the applicant knows that any offer is contingent upon the reference check and any other background checks required by the library or the grantor.

Developing Interview Questions

If any of the selection committee members or interviewers has not had the opportunity to interview applicants before, it is important to ensure that each interviewer is familiar with the kinds of questions that are appropriate to ask. Each interviewer should be familiar with the basic legal do's and don'ts regarding interviewing, and someone with expertise in employment law should review the questions before the interviews occur.

Library administrators and their human resources office staff are fully aware of the federal and state laws that ensure applicants are treated equitably and not discriminated against during the hiring process on the basis of age,[2] disability,[3] national origin,[4] pregnancy,[5] race,[6] religion,[7] or sex;[8] and are not subjected to sexual harassment.[9] The requirements of these laws can seem intimidating and confusing at first glance (see Table 9.3). Making the applicant feel comfortable during the interview is essential for everyone (see Table 9.4). One of the distinct advantages of the information age is the wealth of online information that is directly available from the web sites of federal and state agencies that enforce these laws and regulations. Through frequently asked questions sections (FAQs) many common questions are answered clearly and succinctly. Although there are many books and articles published that are related to employment law, most libraries that take the time to explore them are surprised to learn how helpful the actual government sites can be. Of course there is no substitute for discussing a specific issue with the human resources department and the library's attorney if legal advice is necessary. Becoming familiar with these sites is highly recommended.

Table 9.3   Overview of Federal Equal Employment Statutes

The Age Discrimination in Employment Act of 1967 (ADEA) protects individuals who are 40 years of age or older from employment discrimination based on age. The ADEA's protections apply to both employees and job applicants. Under the ADEA, it is unlawful to discriminate against a person because of his/her age with respect to any term, condition, or privilege of employment, including hiring, firing, promotion, layoff, compensation, benefits, job assignments, and training.

Title I of the *Americans with Disabilities Act of 1990* prohibits private employers, state and local governments, employment agencies, and labor unions from discriminating against qualified individuals with disabilities in job application procedures, hiring, firing, advancement, compensation, job training, and other terms, conditions, and privileges of employment.

Title VII of the *Civil Rights Act of 1964* prohibits discrimination on the basis of nationality. Whether an employee or job applicant's ancestry is Mexican, Ukrainian, Filipino, Arab, Native American, or any other nationality, he or she is entitled to the same employment opportunities as anyone else.

The *Pregnancy Discrimination Act* is an amendment to *Title VII of the Civil Rights Act of 1964*. Discrimination on the basis of pregnancy, childbirth, or related medical conditions constitutes unlawful sex discrimination under Title VII. Women who are pregnant or affected by related conditions must be treated in the same manner as other applicants or employees with similar abilities or limitations.

Title VII of the Civil Rights Act of 1964

- Prohibits discrimination on the basis of race. Equal employment opportunity cannot be denied any person because of his/her racial group or perceived racial group, his/her race-linked characteristics (e.g., hair texture, color, facial features), or because of his/her marriage to or association with someone of a particular race or color. Title VII also prohibits employment decisions based on stereotypes and assumptions about abilities, traits, or the performance of individuals of certain racial groups. Title VII's prohibitions apply regardless of whether the discrimination is directed at Whites, Blacks, Asians, Latinos, Arabs, Native Americans, Native Hawaiians and Pacific Islanders, multiracial individuals, or persons of any other race, color, or ethnicity.

- Prohibits employers from discriminating against individuals because of their religion in hiring, firing, and other terms and conditions of employment.
- Prohibits discrimination on the basis of sex. It is unlawful to discriminate against any employee or applicant for employment because of his/her sex in regard to hiring, termination, promotion, compensation, job training, or any other term, condition, or privilege of employment. Title VII also prohibits employment decisions based on stereotypes and assumptions about abilities, traits, or the performance of individuals on the basis of sex. Title VII prohibits both intentional discrimination and neutral job policies that disproportionately exclude individuals on the basis of sex and that are not job related.
- Prohibits sexual harassment. Unwelcome sexual advances, requests for sexual favors, and other verbal or physical conduct of a sexual nature constitute sexual harassment when this conduct explicitly or implicitly affects an individual's employment, unreasonably interferes with an individual's work performance, or creates an intimidating, hostile, or offensive work environment.

Table 9.4   Tips for Making the Interview as Painless as Possible

- Be an informed interviewer. Do your homework and review all the applicant's materials before the interview.
- Make arrangements in advance for the interview room, chairs, table, etc. Make any reasonable accommodations that have been requested in advance.
- Make the applicant feel welcome and as comfortable as possible. Offer water (or something) to drink.
- Introduce the interview team to the applicant.
- Explain upfront how the interview will be conducted. When, for example, will the applicant have the opportunity to ask any questions he or she may have?
- Provide the applicant with the name of a contact person before he or she leaves the interview.
- Offer any details you can about the next steps in the hiring process.
- Thank the applicant for applying for the position.

One of the best places to begin is with The United States Equal Employment Opportunity Commission (EEOC).[10] Among many other duties, the EEOC has the responsibility for ensuring that applicants are not discriminated against during the hiring process. Generally, questions that are not directly job-related should be avoided in the interview as they may be perceived to be discriminatory. Although these laws may not technically apply to an individual library (most of the EEOC requirements apply to employers of 15 or more employees), it is highly recommended that interview questions steer clear of the areas identified above that are generally deemed to be unrelated to the job in question.

The interview questions should be drafted in advance of the interviews, and it is recommended that all applicants be asked the same questions. Because interviews are conducted by a team, members should decide in advance who will ask each question. Rotating this responsibility among interviewers gives the applicant the opportunity to interact with as many potential coworkers as possible. A couple of open-ended questions at the end of the interview will give the applicant the opportunity to explain in his or her own words anything else they would like to say or to ask any remaining questions regarding the position. The applicant may want to expand upon or clarify an earlier answer. Remember, the goal of the interview is to secure an appropriate match between the qualifications and desires of the applicant and the needs of the organization. Sample interview questions appear in Table 9.5.

After the Hiring Decision Is Made

After an offer of employment has been given and accepted, the Principal Investigator is responsible for notifying and thanking other applicants who were not hired, particularly those who were interviewed for the position.

Table 9.5   Sample Program Coordinator Interview Questions

Why are you interested in the program coordinator position?
What qualities will you bring to this position?
How do you envision beginning the outreach process during this initial start up time/year?
What qualities should the project coordinator possess and why?
Tell us about a time something didn't work or go the way you thought it would and how you handled that?
How would you handle potential conflict that may arise with library patrons or grant team members?

Taking the time to thank all applicants, even through a form letter, builds goodwill towards the library.

As soon as possible, meet with the new staff member and provide him or her with as much information as possible about the grant. Put the new employee's position clearly into the context of the goals and objectives of the grant. Include him or her as part of the team as much as possible, as the success of the grant project ultimately depends upon everyone doing their job well.

SETTING UP THE PROJECT OFFICE

All projects and programs need space in which to operate. Space considerations may include assigning or acquiring office space, reserving conference and/or workspace, and reserving space for special events.

In addition to space, team members will need office furniture and storage space for project records and deliverables. Acquiring a sufficient number of desks, chairs, tables, file cabinets, and smaller pieces of furniture may require requesting existing resources from the parent organization, arranging for items to be moved, and/or purchasing items not available through other sources.

Almost all project staff require the use of computers, printers, telephones, a fax machine, and a copier. Some projects may also require the use of specialized equipment such as digital scanners, video cameras, and recording equipment. Be sure to follow any special rules when purchasing equipment. For example, some organizations may only allow computer purchases through a named distributor. Grantors may also have special rules concerning equipment purchases. If installation and maintenance are not provided by the library, then the Principal Investigator may need to contract for those services.

Project staff members will want to use at least one or two types of software. When considering software choices, preference should be given to familiar applications and those that team members are most likely to use. Project teams will increase productivity through the use of office applications software (e.g., word processing, accounting, database, email, and calendar). New software must be compatible with the applications already in use within the library environment. If the Principal Investigator or team members are unsure, a consultation with an IT staff member or systems librarian can lead to the selection of reasonable software solutions.

Some projects may require the creation of external accounts with suppliers and vendors. Be sure to check with your organization to find out if special permission is required before setting up any external accounts. Also be sure to find out if your organization already has an account with the vendor you want to use.

ANNOUNCING THE GRANT AWARD

It is important to notify all partners and key supporters immediately of the grant award. Under most circumstances, a quick personal phone call is best, followed up by a more formal announcement as soon as possible. This is the first post-award opportunity to thank partners and supporters and to share enthusiasm for the project once again.

Beginning with the official announcement of the grant award, it is crucial that the grant team begins to coordinate a consistent image and message for all its activities related to the grant project. The goal is to build recognition and create visibility for the grant project. Even the best projects can languish without effective promotion. When distributing any promotional information regarding the grant award, remember to check whether the granting agency requires the acknowledgement of the granting agency through the use of its logo or a boilerplate statement when distributing such information.

Internal Promotion of the Grant Award

In the initial flurry of activity related to the grant award, it is easy to overlook the importance of effectively managing the internal promotion of the newly funded project. By effectively using the library's web site, wikis, blogs, email system, and other tools for communicating, the grant team can keep the library's leadership abreast of the grant project and its activities, enhancing the value of the project with administrators and managers. In addition, keeping others in the loop about the project, particularly through the use of collaborative tools, will often lead to unexpected benefits in the form of helpful ideas, suggestions, and useful comments from colleagues. Most importantly, effective communication lessens the opportunity for conflicts of interests or perceived conflicts of interest to arise among the various departments or activities of the library.

Traditional Ways of Promoting the Grant Project

While there are many new technology-based options for promoting or marketing the grant project, some of which are described below, it is appropriate to issue a traditional press release and/or a radio public service announcement. Some granting agencies give guidance regarding how to promote their grant awards. For example, the Institute of Museum and Library Services provides assistance with outreach efforts for its grantees and has made a *Grantee Communications Kit* available on its web site.[11] The kit includes a sample news release, a sample radio public service announcement, and other tips to generate publicity, many of which are universally applicable.

The use of promotional items is another traditional way to market grant projects or activities. For years libraries across the country have been extremely creative in promoting their services and programs through the use of free, promotional items. Librarians attending a conference or training or event often receive a "free" promotional gift. This strategy can be a powerful marketing tool for grant funded projects. However, if grant funds are used to purchase such items, it is important to make sure that the grantor permits this use of grant funds. Items may include such things as magnets, postcards or note cards, coffee mugs, paper weights, business cards, window decals, mini posters, bookmarks, buttons, badges, T-shirts, caps or other apparel, tote bags, stickers, pencils and pens, and bracelets or wristbands. The potential for any item to be transformed into an interesting promotional item for the grant project is limited only by the grant team's imagination and budget.

Web Sites and Other Electronic Publications

In the digital environment of the twenty-first century, there are numerous ways to promote a grant project without much cost. The library's web site is a good place to begin experimenting with and refining the message and image the grant team wants to convey about the project. This often means working collaboratively with internal personnel who are responsible for maintaining and updating the web site. In order to ensure that any published information is accurate and consistent with the grant team's message, it is worth the effort to provide coworkers with the exact language regarding the grant project that is to be published. If this is not feasible, request the opportunity to preview or review any information that is to be published about the grant project by other individuals within your organization before it is made public. This will ensure compliance with the grant requirements and control the look and feel of the way information is communicated about the project.

In addition to creating a presence on the library's web site, consider the possibility of creating a professional looking brochure or flyer regarding your project. Attractive flyers or brochures can be easily created using tools such as Microsoft Publisher[12] or similar applications.[13] The brochure or flyer can then be emailed (or mailed) to unlimited numbers of people and organizations quickly and at little to no cost. Getting the word out through the use of electronic newsletters and articles, email discussion groups or listservs, and other forms of online communication is quite easy and effective.

Online Surveys

An often overlooked way of marketing the grant project is through the development and distribution of an online survey. A survey can be a very useful tool in collecting important data quickly regarding what project stakeholders think. Online surveys can also be an effective way to evaluate the success of the grant project or its activities at various stages of the project.

There are many online survey tools on the market today that provide easy interfaces for creating surveys and automatically generate reports from the collected data.[14] Most companies offer a free version for very basic surveys and more advanced packages for more complex surveys at various costs. In selecting survey software, look for some degree of creative freedom in question format and design and one that provides enough tools to analyze the results. In most cases, the software will allow recipients to complete the survey online by simply clicking on a link to the survey from an email that has been sent to them by the grant team.

Promoting the Grant Project Using Social Media

The way in which organizations get the word out about their activities and programs has dramatically changed over the past 10 years. Web 2.0 technologies have altered the way librarians and their user communities think about communicating. Although the use of social media for marketing is fairly recent, it is here to stay. Social media has been defined as "[p]articipatory online media where news, photos, videos, and podcasts are made public via social media websites through submission."[15] Connecting large numbers of individuals to the goals, objectives, and activities of the grant project is now possible in ways that were not even contemplated a few years ago.

Blogs. One of the easiest ways to enter into social media marketing is through the use of a blog. A blog is often described as an online diary "that others can comment on."[16] It is the ability of others to view and comment on the diary or journal that makes it participatory. The creation of a blog about the grant project—whether it is posted on the library's web site or elsewhere—will create additional visibility for the project. One of the advantages of a blog over some other forms of social media is that it allows the creator to retain the ability to self-select the information he or she wants to share about the project. At the same time, however, the creator gets the benefit of learning from and listening to individuals who are interested enough to share their thoughts about the project.

Before developing a blog, it may be worthwhile to get a general idea of the blogosphere by visiting such blog search sites as Technorati and Google Blog Search.[17] When the grant team is ready to create its own blog, free and open source software exist for blog development.[18] As with the use of all social networking tools, blogs must be kept current or they lose their effectiveness and ultimately affect the credibility of the project and its activities.

Videos and Webinars. Online videos can be a great way to showcase the grant project or activities. The key is to distribute the video in a way that ultimately reaches the intended audience. According to Michael Hoffman,

"Online video is in the same stage of life as the Web was in the mid-1990s, when most organizations were beginning to recognize the role a Web presence could play but few had dedicated Web teams or budget lines. Today, even the smallest organizations invest in the Web. Similarly, many organizations have realized the importance of online video, but have yet to develop processes to maximize use of this up-and-coming tool."[19] As with many other digital tools, there are free software tools and low cost technologies to assist in the creation and distribution of web video. If appropriate, do not just tell stakeholders and others what you are doing, show them!

Other ways of presenting information regarding some aspect of the grant project is through the creation of a webinar[20] or podcast.[21] With so many emerging technologies to choose from, the grant team will need to spend some time exploring the best ways to reach its intended audience.

Building an Online Community to Support the Grant Project

Social networking sites such as Facebook,[22] Twitter,[23] and Ning[24] can be used effectively to build online communities of people that share an interest in the grant project's activities. There is no question that significant numbers of individuals are spending more of their waking time and attention on social networking and less on traditional media. If your library or grant team is trying to reach Millennials, it is doubtful that traditional media sources will get their attention.

Facebook and other social networks now have business-oriented features and options that should be evaluated as possible components of any marketing strategy. If you are new to Facebook and wondering how to use the site effectively for marketing, there is a Facebook Marketing Bible.[25] As with all social media marketing, these online communities demand an active presence, so there must be a strong commitment to keep it alive. A community web site will not manage itself. The grant team will have to devote some staff resources to supervising the community and addressing member concerns.

Overlooked Opportunities to Promote the Grant Project

Promoting the grant project is a task that never really ends. It takes imagination and perseverance to build a program or complete a project. Yet, it often seems like there is not enough time or money designated for such activities. Therefore, the grant team should view every required activity under the project, even the submission of interim reports to the funding agency, as an opportunity to promote the value of the grant project.

For example, most grant proposals include timeframes for the achievement of certain goals and activities. As such goals, objectives, or activities are met, think about whether there is some way to turn these accomplishments into promotional opportunities with just a little more effort. Not only will this enhance the visibility of the project, it will increase the morale of the grant team by allowing them to acknowledge and celebrate their accomplishments along the way. Opportunities to promote the grant might include:

- The submission of required reports. Is there some way to further publicize the report or an executive summary of the report, even if only internally?
- The hiring of grant staff or a change in key personnel. Can this be turned into a networking opportunity under the guise of introducing new grant personnel to an individual or organization?
- Attendance at conferences. Is there the opportunity for a display table or to develop a training or workshop related to the grant project?
- Stakeholder/partnership events. Is there a way to piggyback onto another organization's event? How about sponsoring a social event or offering to co-host?
- Writing an article for publication. Has there been some activity or unique experience that occurred during the grant project that would be of interest to others?

The point of this discussion is to look at every grant activity in terms of whether or not, with a little more effort, it is also an opportunity to promote the grant project.

NOTES

1. ALA JobList, http://joblist.ala.org/ (accessed September 30, 2010).
2. U.S. Equal Employment Opportunity Commission, *Age Discrimination*, http://www.eeoc.gov/laws/types/age.cfm (accessed September 30, 2010).
3. U.S. Equal Opportunity Commission, *Disability Discrimination*, http://www.eeoc.gov/laws/types/disability.cfm (accessed September 30, 2010).
4. U.S. Equal Opportunity Commission, *National Origin Discrimination*, http://www.eeoc.gov/laws/types/nationalorigin.cfm (accessed September 30, 2010).
5. U.S. Equal Opportunity Commission, *Pregnancy Discrimination*, http://www.eeoc.gov/laws/types/pregnancy.cfm (accessed September 30, 2010).
6. U.S. Equal Opportunity Commission, *Race/Color Discrimination*, http://www.eeoc.gov/laws/types/race_color.cfm (accessed September 30, 2010).
7. U.S. Equal Opportunity Commission, *Religious Discrimination*, http://www.eeoc.gov/laws/types/religion.cfm (accessed September 30, 2010).
8. U.S. Equal Opportunity Commission, *Sex-Based Discrimination*, http://www.eeoc.gov/laws/types/sex.cfm (accessed September 30, 2010).
9. U.S. Equal Opportunity Commission, *Sexual Harassment*, http://www.eeoc.gov/laws/types/sexual_harassment.cfm (accessed September 30, 2010).

10. U.S. Equal Opportunity Commission, http://www.eeoc.gov/ (accessed September 30, 2010).

11. Institute of Museum and Library Services, *Grant Recipients Grantee Communications Kit*, http://www.imls.gov/recipients/communication.shtm (accessed September 30, 2010).

12. Microsoft Publisher 2010, http://office.microsoft.com/en-us/publisher/ (accessed September 30, 2010).

13. TopTenReviews, *Desktop Publishing Software Review*, http://desktop-publishing-software-review.toptenreviews.com/ (accessed September 30, 2010).

14. SurveyMonkey, http://www.SurveyMonkey.com (accessed September 30, 2010); Zoomerang, http://www.zoomerang.com/ (accessed September 30, 2010); *Survey Software: Ask, Analyze, Improve*, http://www.surveymethods.com/ (accessed September 30, 2010); QuestionPro, http://www.questionpro.com/ (accessed September 30, 2010).

15. Dave Evans, *Social Media Marketing: An Hour a Day*, (Indianapolis, Indiana: Wiley Publishing, 2008), 37.

16. Ibid., 57.

17. Technorati, http://www.technorati.com (accessed September 30, 2010); Google Blogs, http://www.blogsearch.google.com (accessed September 30, 2010).

18. WordPress.Com, http://wordpress.com/ (accessed September 30, 2010).

19. Michael Hoffman, *Getting Your Videos Onto the Web*, February 2009, http://www.idealware.org/articles/getting-your-videos-web-0 (accessed September 30, 2010).

20. Coreography, *Creating Winning Webinar Presentations*, http://www.coreography.com/web-seminars/create-winning-webinar-presentations.php (accessed September 30, 2010); *Tips on How to Create a Webinar*, http://www.bestforwebinars.com/tips-on-how-to-create-a-webinar.htm (accessed September 30, 2010); Susan Smith Nash, *Creating Webinars Using Open Source Software*, http://elearnqueen.blogspot.com/2010/04/creating-webinars-using-open-source.html (accessed September 30, 2010).

21. Corey Deitz, *How to Create Your Own Podcast: A Step-by-Step Tutorial*, http://radio.about.com/od/createyourownpodcast/ss/How-to-Create-Your-Own-Podcast-Make-Your-Own-Talk-Show-Music-Program-or-Audio-Stream.htm (accessed September 30, 2010); Podcasting News, *Make Your First Podcast*, http://www.podcastingnews.com/articles/How-to-Podcast.html (accessed September 30, 2010); Moving at the Speed of Creativity, *Creating a Course Audio Lecturecast (podcast) with Podcast Generator*, http://www.speedofcreativity.org/2010/09/02/creating-a-course-audio-lecturecast-podcast-with-podcast-generator/ (accessed September 30, 2010).

22. Facebook, http://www.facebook.com/ (accessed September 30, 2010).

23. Twitter, http://twitter.com/ (accessed September 30, 2010).

24. Ning, http://www.ning.com/ (accessed September 30, 2010).

25. *The Facebook Marketing Bible*, http://gold.insidenetwork.com/facebook-marketing-bible/ (accessed September 30, 2010).

CHAPTER 10

Managing the Project Day-to-Day

Smooth project operations are the result of good planning and organization. When careful planning and organization are incorporated into the proposal phase, implementation becomes a procedural rather than an all-encompassing process. The parameters of every project or program are set forth in the grant proposal. Therefore, planning and organizational activities should originate from the obligations and requirements set out in that document. A thorough knowledge of all project obligations is critical to project implementation and management.

ORGANIZATIONAL STRUCTURE: THE BIG PICTURE

Every project needs an organizational structure. An organizational structure defines the lines of authority and the relationships between project components. Grant-funded projects typically include management, budget, and evaluation components. Other common components include marketing, staffing, and strategic planning. A line of authority is simply another way of saying who reports to whom.

The Principal Investigator (Project Director) may be responsible for all project components in a very small project (see Table 10.1). He or she may also be the top line of authority. However, for most projects a number of people with varied levels of authority will be involved. For example, at a college or university the departmental finance director may oversee day-to-day account entries while larger budgetary decisions are made by higher level university officials. Similarly, the departmental finance director may send monthly reports to the Principal Investigator who may then report to the

Table 10.1 Project Director Monthly Tasks

Activity	Time-frame	Notes and Comments
☐ Sign payroll forms		
☐ Monthly (full-time staff)		Submit to payroll clerk
☐ Biweekly (part-time staff)		Submit to payroll clerk
☐ Effort certifications		Submit to Budget Officer
☐ Check financials		Receive from Budget Officer
☐ Report from Budget Officer		
☐ Cost share documentation		
☐ Credit card statements (approve for staff)		
☐ Credit card statements (send to library administrator)		
☐ Prepare reports		
☐ Narrative report on project progress		
☐ Update project web site (if applicable)		
☐ Update project portfolio site (if applicable)		
☐ Review reports		
☐ Project reports		
☐ Subcontractor reports		
☐ Consultant reports		
☐ Other reports for grantor/funder		

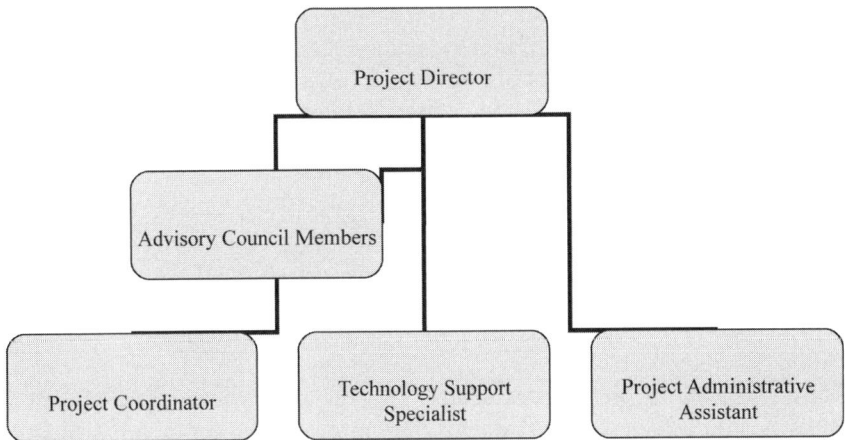

Figure 10.1   Grant Organizational Structure

grantor. The more complex the organizational structure, the more important knowing all aspects of that structure becomes. Much frustration can avoided by thoroughly understanding the project's organizational structure and how that structure fits into the larger library organizational scheme and that of the parent organization.

Organizational structures are often displayed in a graphical format. The project management field provides a number of organizational models. Many of these models are complex and more complicated than necessary for routine grant-funded projects. A simple organizational structure will generally best serve the needs of grant-funded projects. An example of a simple grant organizational structure appears in Figure 10.1. However a project's organizational structure may be complicated by the library's organizational structure. While it is imperative that the Principal Investigator understand the full organizational framework—both the project's structure and how the project and its components fit into the parent organization—creating a simple and separate organizational structure for the project itself is useful. It clarifies the lines of authority within the grant team and promotes positive team dynamics and communication.

ROLES AND RESPONSIBILITIES: THE DETAILS

Well-defined roles and responsibilities are the foundation for smooth project implementation and management. For the purposes of this text, a role is defined as one's relationship with others within the larger scheme of a project or organization; responsibility refers to the duty to complete a task; and tasks are simply the many things that must get done.

All team members should understand their roles in the grant project. To promote good communication and positive team dynamics, team members should also know the roles of fellow team members. Part of a team member's role is defined by his or her job title and description. For example, a Principal Investigator's role as final decision maker is inherent in the Principal Investigator title. For hired staff, job descriptions may be used to define the individual's role. Generally job descriptions will include information like managerial responsibility, working relationships, and job duties. Where job descriptions are inadequate, the Principal Investigator should convey expectations to the employee and team.

Likewise, for team members who are colleagues or coworkers and not hired specifically for the project, written roles and expectations should be developed prior to implementation. This is especially important where the relationship between coworkers is different for the project than during normal operations. Grantors customarily require proposals to include fully developed job descriptions for key personnel and contracted services. An example of key project staff roles appears in Table 10.2.

Defining roles and assigning responsibility begins in the proposal phase and may continue throughout the project period. For every activity, objective, and outcome included in a grant proposal, a corresponding responsibility should be assigned to a project team or staff member. Further, grant activities and obligations should be broken down to the task level with individual tasks assigned to appropriate team or staff members.

Most project activities and obligations are set out in the proposal. Tasks are derived from these activities and obligations. For example, a project objective may call for marketing materials to be created and distributed through targeted mailings, regional information sessions, and at national conferences. The obvious tasks involved in achieving this objective include creating and assembling the materials, completing the mailing, and attending information sessions and conferences. Other less obvious tasks may include selecting the most effective type of marketing material, proofreading and/or approving copy, contracting for services, creating a mailing list, coordinating with other institutional marketing efforts, reserving a conference booth, and the like. While one team member may be responsible for marketing, the many tasks involved in the process may be divided among a number of people. Keeping track of project tasks and deadlines is critical to successful project management.

In addition to the responsibilities and tasks found in the proposal, responsibilities and tasks may also be created by the policies and procedures of the library and its parent organization. All organizations have policies and procedures that must be followed in the course of everyday work. Generally, grant-funded projects and programs are required to abide by all of the parent institution's rules and procedures. For example, some organizations may require all contracts to be reviewed by a staff attorney or legal

Table 10.2   Project Staff Key Responsibilities

Project Director
- responsible for all aspects of the program;
- recruitment of mentors, students, and teachers;
- database development, web site creation;
- presentations to libraries, schools, community agencies, companies, and government agencies;
- fund raising;
- program evaluation; and
- the supervision of staff members.

Technology Specialist
- responsible for technology planning and implementation;
- oversees technology issues; and
- presents to libraries, schools, community agencies, companies, and government agencies on the uses of technology in education.

Content Specialist
- responsible for all fiscal and project management;
- building and maintaining relationships with state, regional and national groups;
- managing curricular frameworks project; and
- developing assessment tools.

Communications Specialist
- production of library publications;
- communication and strategic planning;
- internal communication and organizational climate;
- marketing;
- government relations; and
- special project planning.

---

department before being executed. Others may have strict rules regarding institutional branding and the use of the institution's trademarks. Institutional policies such as those listed above create the types of responsibilities and tasks that may be "hidden" and must not be overlooked.

Clearly defined roles and responsibilities are important because they create accountability. For every project, the Principal Investigator is ultimately accountable for all aspects of the project's implementation and management.

However, as most projects involve many people completing many tasks, it is unreasonable to expect a Principal Investigator to be directly involved in every aspect of implementation and management. Delegating responsibility and tracking the completion of tasks allows a Principal Investigator to maintain control without the burden of micromanaging. Should deadlines be missed or work not be completed to a high standard, the Principal Investigator need only reference his or her list or matrix of responsibilities to address the issue in a timely and controlled manner.

Additionally, clearly defined roles and responsibilities create a positive work environment for team members and staff to do their jobs efficiently and effectively. It is extremely important that project team members and staff know what is expected of them. If roles and responsibilities are left ambiguous, a project runs the risk of falling into lethargy and disarray. This is especially true if the team consists of colleagues and/or coworkers. All too often, preconceived work relationships may lead colleagues and coworkers to make assumptions about responsibilities and duties within a grant-funded project. In order to avoid misunderstandings and project setbacks, it is always best to clearly define and communicate roles and responsibilities at the start of the project.

Finally, a Principal Investigator should not assume that staff members will take the initiative to complete non-delegated tasks. When implementing smaller projects, the Principal Investigator may be able to identify and delegate the necessary tasks for all project activities and obligations. However, for larger and more complex projects or programs, the Principal Investigator will find it necessary to assign some of that work to other team members. Where the budget allows, the Principal Investigator may choose to hire a project coordinator or assistant to help with planning and everyday management responsibilities.

OPERATIONS

Operations are the day-to-day activities that keep grant-funded projects and programs up and running. Grant activities range from the mundane (e.g., responding to email and answering the phone) to the essential (e.g., data collection, reporting, and the creation of deliverables). Generally the collaborative work of many people is required for project operations to run smoothly. Consequently, a project's success often hinges on the people management skills of the Principal Investigator and other project leaders.

Good communication is essential when managing people. Organization and attention to detail are necessary at all levels and should be modeled by the Principal Investigator and team leaders. Established recordkeeping practices assure that data needed for evaluation and reporting purposes is accumulated, organized, and stored in a logical and easily accessible manner.

Keeping good records also aids in creating deliverables and information about the project's success and progress.

Managing People

Managing people is an important part of every grant-funded project. All of the good things that grant-funded projects and programs accomplish would not happen without the effort and talents of people. Grant-funded projects generally require the supervision of four categories of people: colleagues and coworkers, partners, hired staff, and volunteers. Supervising members of each category requires a slightly different management style. All categories benefit from good communication and strong leadership. While most of the people management duties usually fall to the Principal Investigator, other team members may find themselves responsible for managing lower level staff and/or volunteers.

Management Styles

An immense volume of literature, including books, articles, and online resources, has been written about managing people. People are a resource common to every business, organization, and profession. For many organizations, people are the most important (and most costly) asset. Getting the most out of people is the topic of much discussion and study. The importance of good people management for grant-funded projects and programs cannot be stressed enough.

Every grant-funded project and program benefits from managers with good people management skills. Inexperienced Principal Investigators and individuals new to management responsibilities should read and consult introductory texts.[1] Seasoned managers should consider updating their skills with a review of current practices and trends.[2] Managers of all experience levels will benefit from recognizing the unique needs of the different groups of people that generally work on or for grant-funded projects.

Colleagues and coworkers. Grant teams often consist of coworkers and internal and external professional colleagues. Managing coworkers and colleagues is very different from managing hired employees. A collaborative approach is usually best when dealing with members of this group. Principal Investigators and other project managers should always remember that the relationships created with colleagues and coworkers extend beyond the end of any particular grant-funded project. Managers need to remain aware that their professional reputations will be affected by the way they treat their colleagues. Best practices for managing coworkers and colleagues include the following:

- Schedule meetings well in advance. Setting a regular meeting day and time is a good way to accommodate multiple busy schedules.
- Take meeting notes and distribute them to the grant team in order to keep everyone informed of the project's progress.
- Work collaboratively with individual coworkers and library colleagues when assigning responsibility for project tasks.
- Recognize coworkers' and colleagues' efforts in departmental or professional publications or events.
- Be diplomatic when dealing with participation or work product deficiencies.
- Share the lead. Although the Principal Investigator is ultimately responsible, responsibility for individual activities may be shared with others.

Partners. Similar to managing colleagues and coworkers, managing project partners requires special care and attention. Partners playing a large role and partners from other divisions of the library should be treated like coworkers and colleagues. They should be included in all project activities and collaboration should be stressed. However, many grant-funded projects have formal and informal partnerships with organizations and individuals performing only small or time-limited functions. A clear understanding of the partnership parameters, good communication, and a definite timeline are essential when managing these types of partners.

Formal partners will have a written partnership agreement detailing their role in the project. The Principal Investigator should meet with each formal partner early in the implementation stage to ensure a mutual understanding of the partnership terms. If possible, the Principal Investigator should provide each formal partner with a definite timeline detailing their involvement at the handoff meeting. Formal partnerships are recommended for partners that will play a critical role in any project.

Informal partners should also be reminded of their pledged support early on in the implementation stage. Depending upon the nature of the partnership and the partners' established relationship with the library or the Principal Investigator, this may be done in person, as a group, or by phone or email.

Ongoing communication is essential for both formal and informal partners. All partners should be kept in the loop throughout the project period. Even if a particular partner's role in the project is months or even years away, it is important that they be kept up-to-date on the project's progress. One way to accomplish this is to send out a newsletter or project update on a regular basis. Keeping small and limited partners aware of the project's progress will keep excitement levels high and encourage further cooperation and support.

Staff. Staff members include employees hired specifically for a funded project and support staff of the parent organization with dedicated project responsibilities. Each type of staff requires a slightly different management approach. Hired staff should be treated like the project or program's staff. Usually they will report to the Principal Investigator or another authorized individual and not to a library supervisor. Because their primary responsibility is to the project, duties for hired staff should generally be limited to activities directly supporting the grant. Depending on the grantor, hiring staff may require special documentation or prior approval. Replacing hired staff that are either removed from their position or leave for some other reason may also require grantor approval and/or special documentation.

Many organizations have staff members who support grant-funded projects or programs as part of their daily duties. These individuals include budget and accounting officers, IT staff, departmental support staff, and the like. From a Principal Investigator's viewpoint, managing these individuals is different from managing staff hired with grant funds. Care should be taken to ensure that the library's boundaries are respected and that staff members have a clear understanding of their role and responsibilities in the grant-funded project or program. It is also important that the Principal Investigator works closely with the library and its departments when assigning new duties and tasks to these individuals.

Volunteers. Many projects use volunteers to squeeze the maximum impact out of limited resources. Volunteers make significant contributions to libraries and provide another way to involve interested community members in the project or program. Using volunteers for appropriate project activities often creates community goodwill.

However, using volunteers to accomplish project goals does not come without its challenges. It is important for the Principal Investigator and grant team members to remember that volunteers are not paid employees. They should not be relied upon as a primary resource for completing project activities and obligations. Occasionally, volunteers can be unreliable and some may not take project goals and objectives seriously. When using volunteers, additional time and oversight should be built into their contributions. Additionally, managing volunteers can be very time intensive. Because volunteers are not paid employees, they often require increased direction for tasks and supervision.

Although not always the case, many volunteers also expect more face time with managers and increased accolades to recognize and validate the value of their donated time and effort. In small projects where the Principal Investigator has little management support, working with volunteers may exceed the time and resources available. However, when managed and used appropriately, volunteers can contribute significantly and bring a positive aspect to projects or programs. Generally, individuals volunteer their time and talents because they have a special interest in the project or program. They also often bring with them special skills that the project or program might not otherwise have at its disposal.

Leadership and Team Building

Teams are built by leaders. Experienced grant writers and managers know that grant-funded projects and programs rely on strong leadership as an essential ingredient for success. Without a strong leader, many projects will fall into lethargy, lose sight of grant objectives, or fail to move the project forward in a positive and productive manner. Leaders depend upon their teams to support them and get the job done. Where a project lacks a strong leader, there can be disconnects among the goal, objectives, and activities that lead to varying degrees of failure.

> **Communication.** Leadership and teambuilding begin with good communication. Good communication is important to project management and begins with the first meeting of the grant team and staff. The Principal Investigator is responsible for ensuring that those involved in the project understand their roles and responsibilities. Everyone who works on the project must be included in the communication loop. Given the potential of electronic communication, the Principal Investigator can rely on email, blogs, tweets, and instant messages to keep in contact with the project team. That's all good news. However, experienced managers recognize that leading a team is easier when everyone is located together. They understand that technology cannot replace talking face to face. Nevertheless, the Principal Investigator can use straightforward strategies to manage a dispersed grant project team.[3]
> **Create the right attitude.** The Principal Investigator and team members must be diligent and sensitive to collaboration. Individuals working off-site from the main project team must be assertive about keeping in contact with their colleagues.
> **Establish good communication processes.** Principal Investigators must adopt proactive communication strategies to ensure that everyone

works well together. The team is well-served when they gather regularly for meetings so that progress can be monitored, problems and concerns identified, and adjustments made for the next tasks to be accomplished on the schedule. Technologies can be used to facilitate communication within the grant team. For example, Adobe Connect[4] enables team members to meet when they are dispersed geographically or are working with an advisory group or consultants who live away from the project site, and Skype[5] allows individuals to make telephone calls over the internet on a pay-as- you-go or subscription basis.

Provide the right technology. The Principal Investigator is responsible for ensuring that every grant team member has the hardware, software, and other equipment needed to do their assigned tasks. Every individual must have the computing, telecommunications, and other equipment needed to create an efficient, productive work environment.

Meeting the Challenge. Project managers must recognize that there is inherent risk associated with remote team members. To a certain degree, the risk increases the farther away the team members are because of time differences. However, a proactive project manager can work through the difficulties by looking holistically at the people concerns, process concerns, and technology concerns. You can set up a plan to mitigate the risk and ensure that a dispersed team works well together for the common good of the project and everyone associated with it.

DEADLINES, CALENDARS, AND TIMELINES

The Principal Investigator is responsible for ensuring that all project objectives are completed and all obligations are met. A thorough review of the proposal is the first step to achieving this goal. Because the proposals for comprehensive projects are many pages long and include numerous sections (each of which may have been written by a different person), reliance on memory for verifying deadlines, setting calendars, and establishing timelines is not recommended.

A detailed review of the proposal may reveal forgotten obligations or tasks that were not fully developed or understood during the writing process. When reviewing the proposal, the Principal Investigator should create a list or table of project tasks, calendar deadlines, and key responsibilities (see Table 10.3). If possible, the Principal Investigator should also identify the individuals who will take a leadership role to ensure the achievement of each objective on time. While time-consuming, this necessary step is well worth the effort because it provides a measure of perspective, creates a

Table 10.3 Project Activities, Calendar, and Key Responsibilities

Activity	Due Date	Person(s) Responsible
Establish external funding account with Business Office	03/09	Project Director
Convene project Advisory Committee; review of employers' IT-employee needs; IT curriculum review	03/09–06/11	Project Director, DACUM Facilitator
Submit new IT degree and/or Certificate programs to State Higher Education Coordinating Board	01/10, 01/11	College President
Develop employers' self-reporting questionnaire measuring satisfaction with IT personnel	06/30/09	Project staff
Develop IT career pathways requested by employers	09/09–08/10	Project Director, Project staff
Develop customized placement service to match pre-screened IT graduates with specific employers' needs	09/10–02/11	Project Director, Placement Office, Project staff
Design program announcements and student recruitment materials; recruitment campaign	03/09–08/09	Marketing Department
Requisition equipment, supplies; receive and install 44 PCs	04/09–08/09	Project Director, Purchasing Staff, Computer Center

Contract with Microsoft and consultants for faculty in-service programs	07/31/09	Project Director Human Resources
Identify, recruit, and enroll 80 students pursuing IT-related careers as experimental subjects in this program	09/15/09	Project Director, OIRE Office, Admissions Office
Identify, recruit, and enroll 80 students as control subjects in this program	09/15/09	Project Director, Admissions Office
Divide 80 experimental subjects into four cohort groups of 20 individuals each	09/15/09	Project Director
Divide each cohort group into study teams of four individuals each	09/15/09	Project Director
Instruct cohort teams in study skills and cooperative learning methods in lessons presented by tutors	09/15/09–05/15/11	Project Director
Develop tutorial sessions which parallel developmental and core curriculum courses	09/30/09–04/30/11	Project Director
Design structured interviews measuring students' perceptions of inclusion of Hispanic family values in the academic and social climate	09/09, 07/10	Project Director, Project Staff

(*Continued*)

Table 10.3 (Continued)

Activity	Due Date	Person(s) Responsible
Administer structured interviews for 10 percent of experimental and 10 percent of control subjects	09/09, 02/10, 10/10, 01/11, 05/11	Project Staff
Implement, update, and maintain project web site with ancillary learning materials	04/09–06/11	Computer Center Staff
Assign cohort to each tutor, establish times for daily two-hour tutorial sessions for developmental and core curriculum courses	09/15/09	Project Director
Assign counselor and social workers to help cohort members with registration, financial aid applications, problem-solving sessions, etc.	09/15/09	Project Director
Visit Mentor Library sites (to be selected)	05/09, 05/10	Project Director
Schedule 16 half-day sessions for library development to sensitize faculty to the language and culture of diverse students, introduce intrinsic learning styles, introduce cooperative learning instructional strategies	09/15/09	Project Director
Schedule library and faculty development Microsoft Certified Network Engineer sessions	09/15/09	Computer Center Staff

Develop library and faculty self-reporting questionnaire measuring incorporation of instructional methodology that supports significantly increased student-faculty interactions through the development of learning communities	09/30/09	Project Staff
Administer faculty self-reporting questionnaire incorporation of instructional methodology that supports significantly increased student-faculty interactions through the development of learning communities	09/09, 11/09, 02/10, 05/10, 07/10, 09/10, 11/10, 02/11, 05/11, 07/11	Project Staff
Record attendance at each faculty development in-service presentation to determine the number and percentage of IT faculty enrolling in and participating in in-service program	09/09, 10/09, 11/09, 12/09, 02/10, 03/10, 04/10, 05/10, 09/10, 10/10, 11/10, 12/10, 02/11, 03/11, 04/11, 05/11	Project Director
Develop faculty self-reporting questionnaire to determine the extent to which faculty integrate into classroom instruction the results of research on the learning styles of diverse students that correlates with academic achievement, retention, and completion	09/30/09	Project Director, Project Staff

(Continued)

Table 10.3 (Continued)

Activity	Due Date	Person(s) Responsible
Administer faculty pre-test to determine the extent to which faculty integrate into classroom instruction the results of research on the learning styles of diverse students that correlates with academic achievement, retention, and completion	09/09	Project Director, Project Staff
Administer faculty self-reporting questionnaire to determine the extent to which faculty integrate into classroom instruction the results of research on the learning styles of diverse students that correlates with academic achievement, retention, and completion	09/98, 11/09, 02/10, 05/10, 07/10, 09/10, 11/10, 02/11, 05/11, 07/11	Project Staff
Administer faculty post-test to determine the extent to which faculty integrate into classroom instruction the results of research on the learning styles of diverse students that correlates with academic achievement, retention, and completion	06/11	Project Director, Project Staff
Administer faculty pre-test to determine the extent to which faculty integrate into classroom instruction the results of research on the learning styles of diverse students that correlates with academic achievement, retention, and completion	09/09	Project Director, Project Staff
Develop faculty self-reporting questionnaire to determine the extent to which faculty integrate into classroom instruction		Project Staff

cooperative learning strategies that correlate with academic achievement, retention, completion, and transfer	09/98, 11/09, 02/10, 05/10, 07/10, 09/10, 11/10, 02/11, 05/11, 07/11	
Administer faculty post-test to determine the extent to which faculty integrate into classroom instruction the results of research on the learning styles of Hispanic students that correlates with academic achievement, retention, and completion	06/11	Project Director, Project Staff
Administer faculty pre-test to determine the extent of IT faculty utilizing web page development	09/09	Project Director
Determine the percentage of IT faculty utilizing web page development which will be considered covert proof of the faculty's overall utilization of technological innovations determined through actual count of web pages published	06/11	Project Director, Project Staff
Administer faculty post-test to determine the extent of IT faculty utilizing web page development	06/11	Project Director, Project Staff
Submit project quarterly narrative and financial reports	06/09–06/11	Business Office
Submit final narrative and financial report; post on project web site	07/11	Project Director
Distribute Executive Summary to community partners	08/11	Project Director

sound framework for implementation, and gives a good overview of the project or program's anticipated life.

During the initial review, the Principal Investigator should also create a timeline listing all objectives, activities, and deadlines (see Table 10.4). All grantors require project reporting and provide a schedule for narrative and financial reports. Libraries and their parent organizations may also have a review process for submitting reports to grantors as well as internal reporting requirements. Launching a project with a definite reporting schedule prevents missing deadlines and unforeseen unpleasant "surprises" throughout the funding period. A clear understanding of all reporting requirements makes everyone on the team and library administrators aware of the types of data and documents that will need to be collected, organized, and submitted throughout the project's lifespan. The reporting process and timeline should be shared with team members and other individuals or offices responsible for preparing sections of narrative and financial reports. An example of a reporting process and timeline appears in Table 10.5.

For a small project involving a limited number of people and a single report at the end of the funding period, the project team may choose to create its own timelines, budgets, calendars, and reporting schedules. This type of planning can be highly effective for a small project because it ensures that team members are intimately familiar with the project's objectives and obligations. However, for larger and more complex projects involving many individuals or multiple partners, project management software will help the Principal Investigator and team members facilitate planning and organization.

The grant team can select from a number of standalone project management software packages available in the marketplace. A majority of the programs include collaboration tools (e.g., group calendars, timelines, and email/contact integration), resource management tools (e.g., employee tracking and materials/supplies tracking), and project management tools (e.g., task statistics, charts and graphs, budget spreadsheets, and document management). Popular standalone programs include Microsoft Office Project,[6] Matchware Mindview 3 BE,[7] and Project KickStart.[8] Because there are several versions of each program, a careful review of product features is necessary when making a decision.[9] Additionally, one product may be preferred over another based on specific project needs or limitations. Some issues to consider include cost, training, support, and compatibility with existing software.

In addition to standalone programs, there are also a number of online project management solutions on the market. Online project management services provide the same types of collaboration and management tools as their standalone counterparts. The main difference is that online project management services are SaaS (software as a service) programs and are accessed online rather than installed on individual computers.[10] Growing in popularity, online project management services offer a number of advantages.

Table 10.4 Project Objectives, Activities, Outcomes, and Deadlines

Objectives and Activities	Outcomes
Objective 1. To improve student reading proficiency through participation in 90-minute afterschool programs four days a week. • **Activity 1.** Appoint seven people to an Advisory Committee for the project (August 1 of first year). • **Activity 2.** Select professional development presenters and consultants in consultation with the Advisory Committee (October 31 each year). • **Activity 3.** Secure the participation of teachers, school media personnel, and public librarians and discuss with them the project goal and objectives (October 1 of first year). • **Activity 4.** Convene at least six meetings of the Advisory Committee during each project year (Odd-numbered months each year) • **Activity 5.** Establish structured afterschool programs for elementary schools in 13 districts (October 1 each year).	**Outcome 1:** By September 30, 2011, 2,330 learners will demonstrate an overall improvement in academic achievement and State academic achievement test scores of third- and fourth-grade students will reflect a cumulative decrease of 25% in the number of "unsatisfactory" and "partially proficient" categories. **Outcome 2:** By June 30, 2011, 106 elementary teachers, 16 library media specialists, and 13 public children's librarians will have increased their awareness and understanding of the literacy needs of students and their families. **Outcome 3:** By June 30, 2011, 106 elementary teachers, 16 library media specialists, and 13 public children's librarians will have participated in 18 formal and informal professional development opportunities.
Objective 2: To strengthen familial involvement 25% in the literacy development of 2,330 emerging readers (K-5 students) through participation in three formal workshops	**Outcome 1:** By June 30, 2011, 3,495 parents, guardians, and caregivers will have increased their awareness of the importance of pre-literacy and literacy skills in

(Continued)

Table 10.4 (Continued)

Objectives and Activities	Outcomes
and 15 informal sessions for 3,495 parents, guardians, and caregivers with 16 school library media specialists and 13 public library children's librarians. • **Activity 1.** Select presenters and consultants in consultation with the Advisory Committee (September 1 each year). • **Activity 2.** Secure the participation of principals, parental involvement coordinators, teachers, school media personnel, and public librarians and discuss with them the project goal and objectives (ongoing). • **Activity 3.** Strengthen collaborative activities for parents at the school and public library through the design of family-focused literacy activities (ongoing). • **Activity 4.** Establish a mini-grant fund for school-public library teams (November 1 first year). • **Activity 5.** Develop mini-grant award guidelines (November 1 first year). • **Activity 6.** Conduct six family-focused literacy activities during the spring and summer (June 1 each year).	development of their children's reading proficiencies. **Outcome 2:** By June 30, 2011, 3,495 parents, guardians, and caregivers will have attended 18 formal and informal sessions. **Outcome 3:** By June 30, 2011, the number of families participating in the literacy development of their children will increase by 25%.
Objective 3: To enrich library media centers' and local public libraries' resources so that by June 30, 2011, and	**Outcome 1:** By June 30, 2011, 3,495 parents, guardians, and caregivers will have increased their awareness of the

| subsequent academic years, through the addition and cataloging with academic standards into the respective online catalogs of appropriate books (reading levels 1.0 through 3.9);
• **Activity 1.** Establish a materials mini-grant fund for school libraries and children's departments in the public libraries (November 1 first year).
• **Activity 2.** Develop mini-grant award guidelines in conjunction with school district coordinators and public library collection development managers (December 1 first year).
• **Activity 3.** Conduct training on cataloging with state content standards for 26 school district and public library technical services personnel (March 1 first year). | resources and programs available at school library media centers and community public libraries.
Outcome 2: By June 30, 2011, 16 library media centers and 13 public libraries will have received mini-grants to enrich their resources through the addition and integration into the online catalog of appropriate books per student (reading levels 1.0 through 3.9).
Outcome 3: By June 30, 2011, the circulation of reading materials for young emerging readers will have increased by 50%. |
| **Objective 4:** To establish school-community partnerships which enrich the learning environment and encourage continued collaboration.
• **Activity 1.** Enhance the visibility of social service agencies and community-based organizations into the local communities of learners (ongoing).
• **Activity 2.** Increase the involvement of social service agencies and community-based organizations through tutoring (ongoing). | **Outcome:** By June 30, 2011, the 13 districts' structured after-school programs will be established and funded locally. |

(Continued)

Table 10.4 (Continued)

Objectives and Activities	Outcomes
• **Activity 3.** Develop a seamless one-stop service delivery framework in each learning community that integrates all of the service providers while maximizing the benefits of each (ongoing).	
Objective 5: To manage and evaluate the project. • **Activity 1.** Hire project staff (August 1 first year). • **Activity 2.** Outline project activities for Advisory Committee (August 1 first year). • **Activity 3.** Oversee, coordinate, and evaluate all project activities (ongoing). • **Activity 4.** Gather pre-project data (September 30 each year). • **Activity 5.** Design post-project instruments (August 31 each year). • **Activity 6.** Formalize partners' consortium, file for incorporation, and apply to the Internal Revenue Service for non-profit 501(c)(3) status (December 1 first year). • **Activity 7.** Prepare and submit required reports to the U. S. Department (quarterly each year).	**Outcome:** By June 30, 2011, the project will accomplish its goal and objectives.

Table 10.5 Project Reporting Process and Timeline

Project Document	Deadline	Drafting	Reviewing
Narrative quarterly report (Quarter 1, Year 1)	October 1, 2009 (due to grantor)	Project Coordinator, Project Director	Project Director, Library Administrator (due September 15, 2009)
Financial quarterly report (Quarter 1, Year 1)		Budget Officer, Project Director	
Narrative quarterly report (Quarter 2, Year 1)	February 1, 2010 (due to grantor)	Project Coordinator, Project Director	Project Director, Library Administrator (due January 18, 2010)
Financial quarterly report (Quarter 2, Year 1)		Budget Officer, Project Director	
Semi-annual report to Project Advisory Council	February 15, 2010 meeting	Project Director	Library Administrator (due February 1, 2010)
Narrative quarterly report (Quarter 3, Year 1)	April 30, 2010 (due to grantor)	Project Coordinator, Project Director	Project Director, Library Administrator (due April 16, 2010)
Financial quarterly report (Quarter 3, Year 1)		Budget Officer, Project Director	

(*Continued*)

Table 10.5 (Continued)

Project Document	Deadline	Drafting	Reviewing
Narrative quarterly report (Quarter 4, Year 1)	July 31, 2010 (due to grantor)	Project Coordinator, Project Director	Project Director, Library Administrator (due July 16, 2010)
Financial quarterly report (Quarter 4, Year 1)		Budget Officer, Project Director	
Annual report to Project Advisory Council	August 15, 2010 meeting	Project Director	Library Administrator (due August 1, 2010)

They are easy to set up and may be used from any computer with Internet access. And unlike standalone programs, there is no drain on client system resources or upkeep costs since the licensed programs are hosted on remote servers.

For both standalone and online options, the key factors to consider are functionality, reliability, and usability. Most importantly, a program's features should match the project's needs. A careful evaluation of realistic needs will allow for the best match. Those needs may be compared with a vendor's feature list or, better yet, evaluated through a trial offer. Some issues to consider when making a final decision include the following:

- For a standalone product, what happens if you experience technical difficulties? Is there a live hotline, or do have to rely on your in-house IT department for assistance? Does tech service incur an additional fee? Will the vendor provide on-site training, or is all training done through online tutorials?
- For an SaaS product, what happens to data if the company goes out of business? Is your data secure? How long has the company been around? How do they deal with connectivity disruptions or server failure?

Finally, it is wise to consider only products that are likely to get used. Even the best or most expensive program is worthless if it is left "on the shelf." Sometimes simple and effective is better than complex if it means a product will be used consistently. When choosing project management software, do not underestimate the value of good training options and/or previous familiarity with the software's functionality.

PLANNING FOR THE UNEXPECTED

Even the best laid plans occasionally go awry. Despite careful planning and organization, grant-funded project and program managers often find themselves facing unanticipated difficulties and hurdles. While no amount of planning will remove all uncertainties, expecting and planning for the unexpected will allow a project to respond to issues quickly and effectively.

Contingency planning may be done as a group or may be a task the Principal Investigator prefers to do individually. Group planning offers the benefit of perspective; however, for certain eventualities such as problem employees or personality conflicts, the Principal Investigator may choose to do the planning independently. Contingency plans may range from written strategies to deal with certain events to simply brainstorming problems and thinking about potential solutions. Typical "problem" situations include (but are not limited to) the following:

Personality Conflicts. Personality conflicts often occur when current working relationships are changed by a grant-funded project. Personality conflicts may also arise when partners have differing views on such things as management style, meetings, recording keeping, and the like. Well-defined project roles and responsibilities may prevent some personality conflicts; however, project managers should be prepared to deal with some conflict in every project or program.

Loss of Key Personnel. Losing a key staff member can negatively affect a grant-funded project. One way to lessen the impact of losing key personnel is to write general job descriptions for key positions instead of creating positions based upon the skill sets of particular individuals. While following this approach will not lessen the impact of losing a key member of the project team, it will ensure that the project's success does not hinge on one individual's specific skills or abilities.

Loss of a Partner. Project managers should be aware that partners are sometimes unable to fulfill their pledged obligations. Because of the binding nature of most formal partnerships, Principal Investigators may reliably count on formal partners to complete their commitments. If a formal partner cannot fulfill its obligations, then the Principal Investigator or the grantor may avoid taking legal recourse by revising project objectives. Informal partners may be less reliable. It is good practice to have "back-up" informal partners should one partner not be able to fulfill its pledge.

Loss of Support and Facing Institutional Roadblocks. Receiving funding for an important project often generates considerable attention and support at most libraries and parent organizations. However, project managers should be aware that the tides of internal support can change quickly once funding is received and a project is underway. Priorities and organizational direction often change leaving existing projects in limbo. Office politics and changes in administration may also lead to priority shifts. Skilled Principal Investigators can prepare for such shifts by maintaining good networks within the library organization and communicating frequently with the institution's administration.

Poor Work Product. The poor work product of one person can put an entire project in jeopardy. Poor work product issues must be addressed as soon as they arise. For hired staff members, additional training, improved direction, or increased oversight may resolve the problem. For team members and project partners, a sit down with the Principal Investigator to pinpoint the source of problem may be necessary.

Nonresponsive or Underperforming Team Member. Most grant-funded projects and programs require the cooperative effort of many people to be successful. Nonresponsive or underperforming team and staff members can disrupt workflow, create delays, and cause stress. Dealing with nonresponsive or underperforming team members is never easy. Sometimes a frank discussion will resolve the issue. In other instances, the Principal Investigator may be forced to remove the individual from the project team or redistribute responsibility.

Unmet Expectations. Grant-funded projects and programs often provide financial support to selected individuals. For example, many grant-funded programs help students pay for educational expenses (e.g., tuition, fees, and insurances). In exchange for the financial support, a set of expectations is tied to the recipient's grant-funded assistance. The Principal Investigator should anticipate that some recipients will be unable to meet all expectations. Disciplinary or dismissal procedures should be created before they are needed, not after a situation arises.

Under/Over Budget. Grant budget items are often estimated years into the future. The challenge of estimating expenses (e.g., tuition, travel, equipment purchase) for a multi-year project can be daunting. While careful financial planning will help avoid major shortfalls, the budgeting process is often imperfect. Costs may rise or unforeseen expenditures may require amendments to the budget. Similarly, projects may under spend in areas where budget projections were too high. Principal Investigators must monitor expenses within budget categories on a monthly basis. When needed, the Principal Investigator should work with the grantor's program officer and the library's finance director to request modifications so that the grant team can meet actual conditions as the work progresses.

Changed Circumstances/Unachievable Objectives. Even the best planned project may find some objectives unachievable. Enthusiasm during the planning and drafting of the proposal may lead to some unreasonable objectives. Sometimes projects may get redirected through changes in circumstance. The granting agency should be informed as soon as it is evident an objective will not be achieved.

Change in Project Focus. It is not uncommon for projects to change their focus during the funding period. As grant team members gather data or experience, it may become evident that their initial focus was misguided or that there is a better way of achieving project goals. Any major change in a project's focus should be discussed with the grantor's program officer as soon as it becomes apparent.

Change in Space. Grant-funded projects are sometimes seen as temporary and therefore not deserving of permanent space. Project and/or office space may be taken away or changed during the course of a project. Being flexible is a key to dealing with these types of changes.

NOTES

1. Moi Ali, George P. Boulden, Terence Brake, and Robert Heller, *Successful Manager's Handbook* (New York: DK Publishing, 2002); Warren G. Bennis and Robert J. Thomas, *Geeks & Geezers: How Era, Values, and Defining Moments Shape Leaders* (Boston: Harvard Business School Press, 2002); Alice H. Eagly and Linda L. Carli, *Through the Labyrinth: The Truth about How Women Become Leaders* (Boston: Harvard Business School Press, 2007); Robert Heller and Tim Hindle, *Essential Manager's Manual* (New York: DK Publishing, 1998); Robert Kegan and Lisa Laskow Lahey, *Immunity to Change: How to Overcome it and Unlock the Potential in Yourself and Your Organization* (Boston: Harvard Business Press, 2009); Thomas W. Malone, *The Future of Work: How the New Order of Business Will Shape Your Organization, Your Management Style, and Your Life* (Boston: Harvard Business School Publishing, 2004); Joseph R. Matthews, *Strategic Planning and Management for Library Managers* (Westport, CT: Libraries Unlimited, 2005); Barbara B. Moran and Robert D. Stueart, *Library and Information Center Management*, 7th ed. (Westport, CT: Libraries Unlimited, 2007); Alan Murray, *The Wall Street Journal Essential Guide to Management: Lasting Lessons from the Best Leadership Minds of Our Time* (New York: Harper Business, 2010).
2. William Band, *The Top Eight Customer Management Trends for 2010*, http://www.customerthink.com/article/top_eight_customer_management_trends_for_2010 (accessed September 30, 2010); Klint Finley, *3 Trends in Idea Management*, http://www.readwriteweb.com/enterprise/2010/09/3-trends-in-idea-management.php (accessed September 30, 2010); Donna A. Reed, *2010 Trends in Project Management*, http://www.cmcrossroads.com/cm-journal-articles/13194-2010-trends-in-project-management (accessed September 30, 2010); Patricia Layzell Ward, "Trends in library management," *Library Review* 49, 9 (2000): 436–442.
3. Tom Mochal, *Five Tips for Managing a Dispersed Project Team*, http://blogs.techrepublic.com.com/five-tips/?p=333 (accessed October 9, 2010).
4. Adobe Connect, http://www.adobe.com/products/acrobatconnectpro/ (accessed September 30, 2010).
5. Skype, http://www.skype.com/intl/en-us/home (accessed September 30, 2010).
6. Microsoft Project Professional 2010, http://www.microsoft.com/project/en/us/default.aspx (accessed September 30, 2010).
7. Matchware, Mind Mapping Software, http://www.matchware.com/en/products/mindview/default.htm (accessed September 30, 2010).
8. Project Kickstart, http://www.projectkickstart.com/ (accessed September 30, 2010).
9. TopTenReviews, *Online Project Management Review*, http://online-project-management-review.toptenreviews.com/ (accessed September 30, 2010).
10. Software as Service, http://searchcloudcomputing.techtarget.com/sDefinition/0,,sid201_gci1170781,00.html (accessed September 30, 2010); SaaS Showplace, *Welcome to the Software-as-a-Service (SaaS) Showplace!* http://www.saas-showplace.com/ (accessed September 30, 2010).

CHAPTER 11

Project Accountability

Grant awards bring accountability for monies invested in the library and its projects. Government agencies use grants as important tools to achieve societal goals at local, state, regional, and federal levels. Prior to applying for and accepting grant awards, a library and its parent organization must put an infrastructure in place that includes checks and balances for financial and programmatic performance. The internal grant management system enables the library to provide evidence of procedures and policies required to assess grant results and use those results for continued improvements in programs and services. Throughout all grant management activities, the Principal Investigator must work with those individuals who provide and assist in monitoring institutional control over financial policies, accountability requirements, professional development, and sharing of information within the library.

Library staff members who seek and are awarded external funding must have sufficient accountability and financial support to guarantee that grant monies are invested solely in the services and activities described in the grant application and supporting documents. Grant management systems serve as the basis for ensuring to the grantor that monies will be used solely for the intended purposes and will be managed efficiently and effectively. If the library does not have sufficiently developed internal grant management systems, Principal Investigators will have a difficult task when monitoring, managing, and reporting progress toward the achievement of the project goal. Staff members will benefit from a single location to access all policies, documents, forms, and related information for the successful management of a grant award.

In order for the Principal Investigator to track all of the actions and requirements that are part of project implementation, a complete set of documents should be assembled and maintained from the time of grant award acceptance to the project closeout.[1] The Principal Investigator needs to rely on four systems for project monitoring and accountability:

- management plan of goals, objectives, and activities to be implemented;
- compliance with federal requirements for working with human subjects, animals, or handling hazardous materials;
- financial and accounting system to track an established budget and expenditures; and
- purchasing system for equipment, furniture, capital expenditures, and office disposables.

The Principal Investigator is responsible for justifying the appropriateness of direct costs budgeted and charged to the project in accordance with government regulations, sponsoring agency guidelines, conditions made as a part of an individual award, and the library's policies and guidelines. The Principal Investigator is responsible and accountable to the library administrators for the proper conduct of individuals working on the project, including (but not limited to) compliance with policies and procedures concerning the use of human subjects or animals in research activities and environmental safety; fiscal oversight and administration; and approval of monthly account reconciliations and reporting.

FISCAL MANAGEMENT

The project budget is a pivotal tool to determine the extent of time that an activity is expected to require, a baseline to monitor progress (or lack of progress), and a measure of success. Understanding the way in which costs were estimated during the budget development process enables the Principal Investigator and project team to keep the activities moving forward in a timely manner.

As the grant team develops the application and budget, careful attention needs to be paid to the potential for risks of unforeseen events. Unless the Principal Investigator is aware of these elements, an unforeseen event can occur and affect project success. A modest contingency fund should have an allowance for this type of occurrence. The stewardship of grant funds and the accountability for their expenditure causes tension when developing a budget. Although prudent risks need to be acknowledged as possibilities, estimating the potential costs is a challenge. An experienced Principal Investigator can determine the probability of delays, inexperience, changes in the library workplace, and new administrative priorities.

Every project has the potential to be affected by risks. Because employees are essential to carry out a grant-funded initiative, allowances must be made for illnesses, holidays, and vacations. Because the Principal Investigator recognizes that no one is indispensible, an experienced leader will assign a percentage of the budget to this area. An average 12-month initiative brings with it a 5 percent risk. When the project runs for a number of years or is carried out by a smaller group of people, the risk increases proportionately.

Regardless of how close the budget projections come to actual expenditures, Principal Investigators and library administrators prefer that grant expenditures are less than the estimated costs at the end of the funding period.

A capable finance director is critical to the successful implementation of a grant-funded initiative. In addition to attending the project handoff meeting, the finance director will meet with the Principal Investigator to identify the budget categories, library procedure for purchasing and paying for items, and invoicing (when necessary). Grant funds are required to be tracked in a set of separate accounts and cannot be comingled with other monies.

As the project budget is developed, the Principal Investigator will use the library's chart of accounts. This process ensures that when funds are received, they are allocated to the correct expense account. When the Principal Investigator works with the finance director and they follow this process, the project budget will align with the accounting system that the library uses. If the grant budget has anticipated expenses that do not align with the categories customarily used, the finance director will be able to provide guidance about the ways in which these costs can be allocated.

After the grant is awarded, the Principal Investigator should work with the finance director to set up a separate account. The forms require the Principal Investigator to identify the anticipated expenses and the account number, to identify every account from which funds will be expended, and to allocate dollar amounts for each object code. An account will be set up for the grant as outlined in the approved budget.

Accounting and Financial Management

The Principal Investigator needs to possess basic skills in accounting and financial management. Expecting other members of the project team or library employees to manage grant finances is clearly inappropriate. Financial management starts in the critical areas of cash flow and accurate recordkeeping, which must be handled according to financial controls to ensure integrity in the process. New principal investigators must learn how to read and analyze financial statements to understand the financial condition of the grant.[2]

A form of fund accounting, the Principal Investigator should handle the grant budget, in accordance with the requirements set forth by the grantor and the internal procedures at the library.[3] The basic task each month is to determine how closely the actual expenditures align with the budget (see Table 11.1).

Table 11.1 Budget Allocation and Expenses Report

Category	Annual Budget	Qtr. 1	Qtr. 2	Qtr. 3	Qtr. 4	Total Expenses	Difference
Personnel							
Project Director	$48,000	$12,000				$12,000	$36,000
Technology specialist	$39,000	$9,750				$9,750	$29,250
Content specialist	$36,000	$9,000				$9,000	$27,000
Evaluator	$7,500	$0				$0	$7,500
Librarians	$9,000	$2,250				$2,250	$6,750
Benefits							
Project Director	$11,664	$2,916				$2,916	$8,748
Technology specialist	$9,477	$2,369				$2,369	$7,108
Content specialist	$8,748	$2,187				$2,187	$6,561
Evaluator	$1,823	$0				$0	$1,823
Librarians	$2,187	$547				$547	$1,640

(*Continued*)

Table 11.1 (Continued)

Operating						
Supplies	$360	$30			$30	$330
Printing (workshop materials)	$1,500	$250			$250	$1,250
Refreshments (155 people @ $15)	$2,325	$300			$300	$2,025
Travel (local, 200 miles)	$110	$11			$11	$99
Travel (Grand Junction RT (488), hotel, per diem, 2 people)	$416	$416			$416	$0
Travel (Pueblo RT (230), hotel, per diem, 2 people)	$275	$0			$0	$275
Travel (Greeley RT, hotel, per diem, 2 people)	$217	$0			$0	$217
Totals	$178,602	$9,805		$0	$42,026	$136,576

A library may receive one of four types of grant funding. The four major sources of funding are as follows:

- **Federal:** sponsored agreements funded directly by the United States federal government.
- **Federal Pass-Through:** sponsored agreements where the library is not the prime contractor from the United States federal government, but is acting in the capacity of a subcontractor (federal requirements/restrictions *are* passed through the prime recipient from the federal government to the library).
- **Private:** sponsored agreements funded by a private foundation or corporation.
- **State:** sponsored agreements funded directly by the state.

The Principal Investigator must become familiar with commonly used terms in grants accounting. These terms include the following:

- **Allowable cost:** For purposes of OMB Circular A-21, an expense that can be included in the facilities and administrative cost rate proposal or included as a direct cost to federal sponsored agreements and is not specifically excluded by government regulations or by the contract/grant/cooperative agreements.
- **Budget:** Principal Investigator's financial plan that lists the categories of expenditures and dollar amounts required to carry out objectives and activities.
- **Budget period:** An interval of time by which the project period is divided for budgetary purposes.
- **Carryover (carry forward):** The remaining available budget balance of a project that may be used to increase the budget of the next budget period. Carryovers are not always automatic and are not always allowed by a funding agency.
- **Cost Accounting Standards (CAS):** Requires consistency in estimating, accumulating, and reporting costs. Federal grant recipients must comply with CAS standards (see Table 11.2).
- **Cost Reimbursable Contract:** A cost reimbursable contract provides for payment to the library based on actual cost experience in performing and completing the contract.
- **Cost Sharing:** The sharing of the costs of a grant by the library. Cost sharing can either be provided by released time, cash, indirect cost differential, or a combination of all. Cost sharing accomplished through the first two (release time and cash) must be recorded in a library cost sharing account.
- **Direct cost:** Cost that can be clearly identified and directly allocated to a specific grant.

Table 11.2 Cost Accounting Standards[1]

Educational institutions that receive federal grants and contracts must comply with certain federal rules and regulations. OMB Circular A-21, entitled *Principles for Determining Costs Applicable to Grants, Contracts and Other Agreements with Educational Institutions*, sets forth the governing rules for determining the various costs that can be charged to grants and contracts, and for establishing whether those costs may be charged directly, or charged through the application of the institution's Facilities and Administration (Indirect Cost) rate. Incorporated in the Circular specifically, and by reference as well, are four Cost Accounting Standards (CAS) with which universities are required to comply.
CAS 501—Consistency in estimating, accumulating and reporting costs. The purposes of this standard are to (1) assure consistency in estimating, accumulating, and reporting costs as well as (2) provide a basis for comparison of such costs. The same practices should be used when estimating costs for the proposed budget, accumulating costs in the accounting system, and reporting costs to the sponsor.
CAS 502—Consistency in allocating costs incurred for the same purpose. The educational institution is required to charge similar costs in the same manner, either as direct costs or indirect costs.
CAS 505—Accounting for unallowable costs. This standard does not include additional guidance on unallowable costs. Educational institutions will, therefore, continue to follow A-21 for guidance on what is unallowable.
CAS 506—Cost accounting period. An educational institution must use either its fiscal year or a fixed annual period approved by the government as its cost accounting period.

[1]Office of Management and Budget, *OMB Circular 21*, revised May 10, 2004, http://www.whitehouse.gov/sites/default/files/omb/assets/omb/circulars/a021/a21_2004.pdf (accessed September 30, 2010).

- **Disbursement:** Payment made by the library for goods and services.
- **Encumbrances/Obligations:** The dollar amount of items ordered, services rendered, contracts awarded, or similar purchases that are outstanding or unpaid.
- **Equipment:** Items, nonexpendable in nature, such as furniture, instruments, or repairable machines with a useful life of more than two years and a threshold cost of $2,000.
- **Fixed Price Contract:** A firm fixed price contract provides for a payment to the library that is not subject to any adjustment on the basis

of the cost experience in performing and completing the contract (i.e., billings are not based on actual expenditures).
- **Indirect Cost:** Costs associated with sponsored projects that cannot be clearly identified with or allocated to an individual project.

The project budget is analogous to a bank account opened in the Principal Investigator's name that can be used during the award period. It is the Principal Investigator's responsibility to ensure that project funds are spent in a timely manner and in compliance with the grantor's requirements and the library's internal accounting practices. All grant expenditures must align closely with the anticipated costs that were included in the application. If this is not the case, the Principal Investigator must request a budget modification from the grantor's program officer. Unless these steps are taken, the grant funds are not likely to pass an audit, causing the library to pay back those funds that were not spent according to the approved plan.

The documentation of expenditures is essential throughout the grant period. Unless the Principal Investigator carefully monitors all expenses, a possibility exists for the funds to be misallocated, and important activities may need to be cancelled or modified due to the lack of funds. The Principal Investigator must also be aware of under-spending in budget categories when costs are less than the anticipated amounts. In these cases, the grantor may permit funds to be moved to another category. The Principal Investigator should use the library's accounting system at least once a month to review the project's financial expenditures. The Principal Investigator must also check monthly expenditure reports from the finance director to ensure accuracy. If the Principal Investigator finds a discrepancy, he or she should check with the finance director and not automatically assume that the figures are wrong. The Principal Investigator should then recheck both data sources to identify the cause of the errors and consult with the finance director to determine the difference and correct entries (if needed). Working together, the Principal Investigator and the finance director can monitor expenses throughout the funding period and follow the grantor's requirements for financial reporting and auditing. (For a list of OMB Circulars, see Table 11.3.)

Budget Modifications

A grantee may wish to modify his or her budget for many reasons. Grantees sometimes receive overlapping funding from other sources, or are forced to change costs of certain items due to project delays or difficulties. The grantor outlines a process for requesting a change to the grant budget in the guidelines for accepting, managing, and reporting.

The process customarily includes the submission of the original budget, a modified budget, and reasons for the adjustment (see Table 11.4). Grantors approve a majority of budget alterations. The budget as submitted with the

Table 11.3 Office of Management and Budget Circulars (OMB Circulars)[1]

For Educational Institutions

OMB A-21: Cost Principles for Educational Institutions (05/10/2004)—This circular establishes principles for determining allowable costs applicable to grants, contracts and other agreements with educational institutions. All federal agencies that sponsor research and development, training, and other work at educational institutions shall apply the provisions of this circular in determining allowable costs. The principles shall also be used as a guide in the pricing of fixed price or lump sum agreements.

OMB A-110: Uniform Administrative Requirements for Grants and Other Agreements with Institutions of Higher Education, Hospitals and Other Non-Profit Organizations (11/19/1993) (further amended 09/30/1999)—This Circular establishes uniform administration requirements for federal grants and agreements awarded to institutions of higher education, hospitals, and other non-profit organizations.

OMB Circular A-122: Cost Principles for Non-Profit Organizations (05/10/2004)—This Circular establishes principles for determining costs of grants, contracts and other agreements with non-profit organizations. It does not apply to colleges and universities which are covered by Office of Management and Budget (OMB) Circular A-21, "Cost Principles for Educational Institutions"; state, local, and federally recognized Indian tribal governments which are covered by OMB Circular A-87, "Cost Principles for State, Local, and Indian Tribal Governments"; or hospitals.

OMB A-133: Audits of States, Local Governments, and Non-Profit Organizations (06/24/1997, includes revisions published in Federal Register 06/27/03)—This Circular establishes audit requirements for federally sponsored awards and defines federal responsibilities for implementing and monitoring higher education and other non-profit institutions that receive federal awards.

For State, Local, and Indian Tribal Governments

OMB Circular A-16: Coordination of Geographic Information, and Related Spatial Data Activities—This Circular provides direction for federal agencies that produce, maintain or use spatial data either directly or indirectly in the fulfillment of their mission. This Circular establishes a coordinated approach to electronically develop the National Spatial Data Infrastructure and establishes the Federal Geographic Data Committee (FGDC).

OMB Circular A-87: Cost Principles for State, Local, and Indian Tribal Governments—This Circular establishes principles and standards for

(Continued)

determining costs for federal awards carried out through grants, cost reimbursement contracts, and other agreements with state and local governments and federally recognized Indian tribal governments (governmental units).

OMB Circular A-97: Provisions of Specialized and Technical Services to State and Local Governments—This Circular promulgates the rules and regulations which the Director of the Bureau of the Budget is authorized to issue pursuant to Section 302 of the Intergovernmental Cooperation Act of 1968 (P.L. 90-577; 82 Stat. 1102). It also provides for the coordination of the action of federal departments and agencies (hereinafter referred to as "Federal agencies") in exercising the authority contained in Title III of said Act as directed by the President's Memorandum of November 8, 1968 (33 F.R. 16487).

OMB Circular A-102: Grants and Cooperative Agreements with State and Local Governments—This Circular establishes consistency and uniformity among Federal agencies in the management of grants and cooperative agreements with state, local, and federally- recognized Indian tribal governments. This revision supersedes Office of Management and Budget (OMB) Circular No. A-102, dated March 3, 1988.

OMB Circular A-133: Audits of States, Local Governments, and Non-Profit Organizations—This Circular is issued pursuant to the Single Audit Act of 1984, P.L. 98-502, and the Single Audit Act Amendments of 1996, P.L. 104-156. It sets forth standards for obtaining consistency and uniformity among Federal agencies for the audit of states, local governments, and non-profit organizations expending federal awards.

[1] Office of Management and Budget, *Circulars*, http://www.whitehouse.gov/omb/circulars_default (accessed September 30, 2010).

application narrative cannot be changed without written permission from the grantor. Budget modification should be discussed and approved by the library's finance director before submitting a written request to the grantor.

Cost Share

Contributions from the applicant of record and its community partners are frequently required by selected state and federal agencies. Without written assurances that these organizations will bring local resources to the project, funding awards may not be forthcoming. When the award is

Table 11.4   Process to Submit a Request for Budget Modifications[1]

Regular Budget Modification
- Request letter signed by Project Director and Budget Officer.
- Provide budget information in table/chart format, including proposed budget revision.
- Provide justification for revision; include information regarding effect on objective, activities, and timeline completion; and include timeline revisions (if applicable).
- Requests must be received by the grantor at least 60 days prior to the end of the current budget period.

Requirements for no-Cost Extension Requests

No-cost extensions require preapproval from the grantor. At least 75% of the total grant period must be completed prior to an extension request. Extension requests must be submitted at least 60 days in advance of the end of the grant period.

- Requests must be received by the grantor at least 60 days prior to end of the grant period.
- Request letter signed by Project Director and Budget Officer.
- Provide projection of funds anticipated to remain at end of grant period.
- Provide justification for the no-cost extension; discuss specific reasons for under-spending, incomplete objectives and activities, and provide plans for completing them during the extension period.
- Final amount applicable to the extension period will be determined after receipt of the applicable Annual Financial Report.

Requirements for Requests to Spend a Budget Surplus

Requests to spend budget surplus funds are submitted to the grantor when objectives and activities are completed and unexpended funds are identified to remain. *Expenditure of surplus funds requires pre-approval from the grantor.*

- Requests must be received by the grantor during the grant period.
- Request letter signed by Project Director and Budget Officer.
- Provide projection of funds anticipated to remain.
- Surplus revision requests must include scientific narrative describing the new work proposed, and be accompanied by new milestones and timeline for their completion. Surplus expenditure requests may be referred by the grantor to outside expert review.

> • Final amount of surplus funds will be determined after receipt and approval of the last invoice applicable to milestone completion.

[1]Requirements for re-budgeting of unexpended funds (i.e., "annual carry forward") within an annual budget to a subsequent budget period (i.e., "carry forward") *requires preapproval from the grantor*. Unexpended funds may only be re-budgeted into the subsequent budget period.

received, the grantor will include a statement about the requirement and amount of cost share. When the grant award has a required cost share component, the Principal Investigator must keep careful records of the contributions from the library and each of its partner organizations. At the end of each fiscal year, the calculations of values ascribed to the efforts and items directly contributed to the project must be documented. While the grantor may not specify the form in which these records need to be kept, official statements of the dates, individuals who participated, and value of their time (salary plus fringe benefits) can be sent to the Principal Investigator on the partner organization's letterhead. The totals from each of the partnering organizations can be calculated and kept as the permanent record of meeting cost share requirements. Meeting cost share requirements is part of the financial audit. If an auditor cannot find appropriate documentation, the entire grant may be in jeopardy, and portions of the funds may need to be repaid to the grantor.

Cost sharing is that portion of the total costs, direct and indirect, of a grant that meets the following criteria: It is not provided by the grantor, and the library has agreed to fund it; and it is included in the itemized costs for the project that has been approved. Cost sharing as defined above may be included in either of the following categories: mandatory cost share is a contribution required of the grantee by the grantor as a condition of the award (e.g., matching requirements of awards); and voluntary cost share is a contribution voluntarily offered by the applicant (i.e., the library and its parent organization) and accepted by the grantor.

Costs financed by the library or partner organizations may be claimed as a cost sharing contribution for a federal grant if they are directly identifiable with the project activities and are contributed during the funding period. The Principal Investigator must use caution when compiling a cost share statement as part of the grant application. Library expenses which duplicate the types of costs included in the indirect cost rate (IDC) cannot be used as part of cost sharing.

Typically, cost sharing is derived from library-funded salaries and wages with fringe benefits of employees in partner organizations who work on the grant project (see Table 11.5). A payroll authorization to allocate a portion of wages as cost share to the grant needs to be created to put the

Table 11.5 Calculation of Cost Share

Annual Cost Share

Individual	Affiliation	Hourly Rate	Hours / Month	Applicant Personnel	Adjunct Faculty	Community Partners
Technology Specialist	Technology	35.00	4.00	1,680.00		
Principal Investigator	Applicant	80.00	4.00	3,840.00		
Reference Librarian	Applicant	30.00	8.00	2,880.00		
Adult Services Librarian	Applicant	35.00	8.00	3,360.00		
LIS faculty member	Applicant	35.00	4.00	1,680.00		
LIS Staff Liaison	Applicant	35.00	16.00	6,720.00		
LIS adjuncts (2, yrs 1 and 3)	Various	50.00	4.00		9,600.00	

(*Continued*)

Table 11.5 (Continued)

Annual Cost Share

Individual	Affiliation	Hourly Rate	Hours / Month	Applicant Personnel	Adjunct Faculty	Community Partners
LIS adjuncts (3, yr 2)	Various	50.00	4.00		7,200.00	
Local Public Library	Various	30.00	24.00			8,640.00
Collaborating Public Librarians	Various	30.00	24.00			8,640.00
State Library Association	Various	45.00	16.00			8,640.00
Professional Development Presenters	Various	45.00	16.00			8,640.00
Public Lecture Speakers	Various	300.00	16.00			19,200.00
Totals				20,160.00	16,800.00	53,760.00

90,720.00

appropriate personnel on and off the cost share account. Once the form is fully signed, the original should be sent to the finance director. In the case of community partners, a formal letter on the organization's letterhead giving the individual's wages with fringe benefits and associated costs (e.g., travel to and from meetings) is submitted to document contributions to the project.

LEGAL OVERVIEW AND ISSUES

Grant awards are legal contracts. Yet, less experienced principal investigators often have minimal knowledge of contract law. An understanding of basic contact law and legal issues is necessary to manage a grant project successfully. Most people deal with contracts on a regular basis without even realizing or thinking about it. Individuals submit credit card applications and are subject to the terms and conditions, a couple enters into a contract to have a new home built, or a business person executes an employment agreement for a new job. In all these cases some type of contract is involved.

In its simplest terms a contract is a legal obligation to do or to not do something. *Black's Law Dictionary* defines a contract as, "an agreement between two or more parties creating obligations that are enforceable or otherwise recognizable at law."[4] An important fact to note is that a contract can be either a positive or a negative commitment. This means that a contract can require an individual to take some type of action or perform some type of service, or it can require an individual to forgo a specific action.

Three elements are necessary in order to create a valid contract: an offer, an acceptance, and consideration. An offer occurs when a party determines that he or she is ready to enter into a contract and communicates or publishes that to another party.[5] An important point to remember is that a request to enter into negotiations is not equivalent to an offer and as a result cannot constitute a binding contract.[6] An offer occurs when the other party actually receives it, whether verbally or in writing. Additionally, the party receiving the offer must reasonably believe it has been made in order for it to constitute a valid offer.[7]

Once an offer has been made, the party receiving the offer can choose to accept it, reject it, or make a counter-offer. In order for a contract to be formed, the offer must be accepted. Without such acceptance there is no contract or "meeting of the minds." If the party rejects the offer, a contract is not formed. Once rejected, the party cannot change its mind and later attempt to accept the original offer.[8] A third option is that the party may make a counter-offer, which is in essence a rejection of the original offer and the making of a new offer that can either be accepted or rejected by the original offering party.

The final element required to form a binding contract is consideration. According to *Black's Law Dictionary*, consideration is "something (such as an act, a forbearance, or a return promise) bargained for and received by a promisor from a promisee."[9] Consideration must be given by both parties to the contract, and is the component that distinguishes a contract from a gift or mere promise. Consideration is the price that is bargained for between the parties and is generally a profit or interest accruing to one party and a detriment or forbearance by the other party.[10] While consideration often takes the form of money—one party agrees to pay a sum of money (the detriment or forbearance) to the other party (the profit)—that is not always the case. Consideration can also be a tangible item (a painting or some other object) or a commitment from one party to refrain from taking an action (never traveling overseas). While the consideration can be great or small, it must be something of actual value.[11]

Another aspect of contract law is whether a contract must be in writing to be enforceable. Unless specified by statute, a contract does not have to be in writing to be legally binding. While an oral agreement may be an enforceable contract, it is a best practice to commit all contracts to writing so that they are more easily enforced. Pursuant to statute, there are a number of contracts that must always be in writing to be enforceable and these include: (i) any contract for the sale of land; (ii) any contract that cannot be performed within a one-year period; (iii) any contract for the sale of goods or securities for more than $500; and (iv) any contract where one party agrees to be responsible for the debts of another party. One final aspect of contract law that is important to remember is that parties cannot enter into a contract that requires them to engage in illegal acts. If the contract requires one of the parties to perform an illegal act (the sale of prescription drugs) or goes against public policy, the contract is not enforceable and is an invalid contract.[12] See Table 11.6 for contract formation examples.

Table 11.6 Contact Formation Examples

Example One: Sally sends John an email offering to clean his home's windows for $250. John responds to Sally's email saying he accepts her offer to clean his windows for $250 and will pay her upon completion. Sally's email to John is the offer. John's email response to Sally is the acceptance. The agreement of Sally to clean the windows and of John to pay the $250 upon completion is the consideration. A contract has been formed.
Example Two: Sally sends John an email offering to clean his home's windows for $250. John responds to Sally's email stating he already retained Brian to clean his windows. Sally's email to John is an offer. John's email to Sally is a rejection. No contract has been formed and John cannot later change his mind and accept Sally's offer because he has already rejected it.
Example Three: Sally sends John an email offering to clean his home's windows for $250. John responds to Sally's email saying he accepts her offer to clean his windows, but is only willing to pay her $200 upon completion.

Sally's email to John is an offer. John's email to Sally is a rejection and a counter-offer. No contract has been formed and can only be formed if Sally accepts John's counter-offer.

Example Four: Caryl calls her son Joseph and states that she will pay him $400 if he agrees to never chew gum for the rest of his life. Joseph accepts her offer and states that he is spitting out his last piece of gum as they speak.

Caryl's statement to Joseph is an offer and Joseph accepted the offer. Caryl's payment of money and Joseph's forbearance of chewing gum constitute the consideration. A contract has been formed.

Example Five: Chris, in a conversation with Claire, offers to sell her his family's heirloom vase for $1,500. In that same conversation, Claire says she definitely accepts Chris' offer to purchase the vase and she'll bring a check tomorrow.

Chris has made an offer and Claire has accepted his offer. Chris's parting with the vase and Claire's payment for the vase constitute the consideration. However, no contract has been formed because this is a sale of goods for more than $500, so the contract must be in writing to be enforceable. Since Chris's and Claire's discussions were oral and never formalized in writing, there is no legally binding contract.

Components of a Contract

While every contract is unique, most contracts contain similar provisions. This section briefly discusses the standard provisions that are generally contained in a contractual agreement (The provisions described below are adapted from Haggard & Kuney.)[13]

1. *Title*—Most contracts will have a title at the top of the initial page of the agreement. This title should briefly and accurately describe the type of contract. Some examples of titles include Employment Agreement, Independent Contractor or Consulting Agreement, or Grant Award Agreement.
2. *Introduction*—Every contract should contain an introductory paragraph that sets forth the legal names of the parties to the agreement, including how such parties may be referred to throughout the contract, and the date that the agreement is being entered into.
3. *Recitals*—Most contracts contain a list of recitals prior to the main body of the contract that set forth the general background for the agreement. These statements generally give insight into why the parties are entering into this particular contract.

4. *Statement of Consideration*—At the beginning of the main body of the contract, there is typically a statement of consideration. This statement indicates that the parties to the contract agree to the terms set forth in the main body in exchange for adequate consideration.
5. *Definitions*—Most contracts define specific terms so that all parties clearly understand the meaning ascribed to that word. Some contracts may contain a formal definition section, while other contracts may define terms when they are initially used in the text of the agreement.
6. *Substantive Provisions*—Every contract contains substantive provisions and it is these sections of the agreement that constitute the meat of the contract. Substantive provisions set forth the rights and obligations of the party under the contract. These are the provisions that contain the unique terms and conditions that apply to this particular agreement.
7. *Default/Remedies*—Every contract should contain a section that sets forth what constitutes a default under the terms of the agreement. In addition, this section should stipulate the remedies available to the party that has not committed a default.
8. *Term/Termination*—Most contracts, when appropriate, set forth the term of the agreement; how long it will remain in effect. In addition, every contract should contain language regarding how the agreement can be terminated, if at all.
9. *Boilerplate Provisions*—Every contract has a section towards the end of the agreement that sets forth standard or boilerplate provisions that are contained in most contracts. These provisions include such items as how the contract may be modified, how the contract can be assigned, how notices to the parties must be sent, the governing law, the severability clause, and other items.
10. *Signatures*—Every contract contains a section where the parties to the agreement must sign and agree to be bound by the terms of the contract. In some cases the signature may require a third party witness or a notary.
11. *Exhibits*—Subsequent to the main body of the contract, exhibits, addendums, attachments, or schedules are included. In some cases, these documents are relevant to the agreement made between the parties but are not part of the actual contract. In other cases, these documents may be an actual part of the contract. Examples of these types of documents may include a lease agreement, financial statements, a list of contracts, etc.

Contract Terms and Their Importance

It is crucial for any party entering into a contract to carefully read, consider, and understand the entire agreement. This includes both substantive and boilerplate provisions. It is the entire agreement's terms and conditions that govern the relationship between the parties and their performance under the contract. In addition, the language of the contract determines the resolution of issues or disputes that may arise between the parties. In order for a contract to be effective and serve its purpose, it should be clear, concise, and as specific as possible.

In conjunction with being well-drafted, a contract should reflect the actual intent and purposes of the parties to the agreement.[14] The final contract should be comprehensive and should accurately represent the understanding of the parties as discussed and negotiated prior to memorializing the terms in writing. Any person reading the contract should have a clear understanding of what the parties agreed to and intended.

While it seems like common sense to state that a contract should clearly and accurately reflect the parties' intentions, contracts often do not achieve this goal. The agreement may fail to express all the aims of the parties or a material term of the contract may be vague or uncertain as to its meaning. When these types of circumstances occur, the contract may be said to be indefinite or ambiguous. These types of contracts often result in litigation between the parties if or when an issue arises regarding the vague or ambiguous term or provision.

One of the reasons that a contract may not contain all the relevant terms is due to the parties themselves. In some cases one of the parties to the agreement may draft the contract and in other cases an attorney for one of the parties may draft the contract. No matter which situation exists, each party should have a representative, other than their lawyer, responsible for thoroughly reading the contract to ensure that it specifically meets the intentions of that party. In addition, it is crucial that a party to a contract take the time and effort to review the contract themselves and not rely on third parties, whether a lawyer or someone else, to ensure that the final contract clearly sets forth the terms that were agreed upon by the parties. A well-drafted contract plays a significant role in preventing future litigation when issues arise between the parties.

In certain situations a binding contract can be formed through oral discussions and agreement between the parties. However, it is never wise to enter into an oral agreement for a variety of reasons. When the contract has not been memorialized in writing, there is no concrete proof as to the parties' intent. As a result, it is one party's word against the other when an issue arises. In addition, it is much more difficult to enforce an oral contract for similar reasons. The court will not have a written document to look to in order to determine the parties' intent, and so must base a decision on hearsay, unverifiable information provided by each party to the agreement. It is always the best course of action to solidify every contractual relationship in a written document that is reviewed and executed by all parties involved. This is a first step in preventing future confusion as to the actual agreement and intention of the parties.

General Contract Tips

1. *Use plain language*—When drafting contract provisions, the best course of action is to avoid the unnecessary use of "legalese." Using plain language generally results in a clearer and less confusing contract. In this same regard, keep the sentences short and to the point. Long, run-on sentences create confusion and can result in misinterpretation.
2. *Define terms*—When drafting a contract, do not hesitate to define technical or unique terms so that the parties have a clear understanding of their meaning. In addition, if a term or phrase could be construed in different ways by different parties, that term should be defined. By defining potentially confusing terms, the parties can prevent ambiguity in the contract.
3. *Use punctuation carefully*—When drafting contract provisions, be aware of the use of punctuation. A misplaced comma can change the meaning of a sentence. In addition, be cognizant of the connectors, "and" and "or." Choose your connector carefully, as it can completely change the meaning of the principle set forth.
4. *Be comprehensive*—When drafting a contract, address all possible contingencies. Do not intentionally leave a relevant provision out of the agreement and allow chance to dictate the outcome. While boilerplate may seem unnecessary, it serves a purpose. Do not omit sections addressing notice requirements, governing law, and attorneys' fees.
5. *No oral modifications*—When drafting a contract, require that all changes to the contract, no matter how large or small, be in writing and executed by all the parties. By requiring changes to be in writing, the parties can clearly keep track of all provisions of the agreement, whether agreed to originally or modified subsequently by the parties.
6. *Avoid passive voice*—When possible, avoid the use of the passive voice in contracts. This type of language often creates confusion and ambiguity.
7. *Engage a lawyer*—While the party entering into the contract should understand it, it is also wise to hire an expert to review your agreement and suggest changes and clarifications.

Grants versus Contracts

In its basic form, a grant is an award of money for a specific purpose. The granting agency (or grantor) stipulates the guidelines that must be followed and adhered to by the grantee once the award has been made. Whether or not a grant rises to the level of a traditional contract varies with each individual situation. As discussed previously, a contract requires an offer, acceptance, and consideration. While a grant creates a relationship between the parties—the grantor and the grantee—it does not always create a contractual relationship in the sense of contract law and principles.

In some circumstances, the granting agency may require the grant recipient to execute an agreement titled a Grant Award Contract. When this is the case, a clear contractual relationship has been formed and the Grant Award Contract governs the terms and conditions of the grant. The Grant Award Contract generally contains provisions regarding how the funds can be utilized, the types of reporting required, and the manner in which the award can be terminated.

In other situations, the granting agency requires the grant applicant to execute a type of commitment form or pledge letter that is submitted with the grant application. This form generally states that the applicant certifies that all statements made in the grant application are complete, true, and accurate. The grant applicant also agrees to comply with all terms of the grant if they are offered and accept the grant award. Additionally, the applicant often acknowledges that any false or fraudulent statements made in the application may be subject to administrative, civil, or criminal penalties. This commitment form or letter, upon acceptance of the grant award, creates a contractual relationship between the granting agency and the recipient, and requires the recipient to comply with all terms and conditions of the grant.

Lastly, in some circumstances no true contractual relationship is formed. The grant applicant simply applies for a grant award and is awarded the funds. The grantee is not required to execute a Grant Award Contract or a commitment form or pledge letter. In this situation, the parties have entered into a relationship, but not a traditional contractual one.

Specific Types of Agreements in the Grant Context

1. *Memorandum of Understanding*—The memorandum of understanding describes and sets forth the relationship between two or more parties. In most instances, the parties are agreeing to come together and collaborate on a proposed grant or to act as partners on the grant project. This document expresses the intent of the parties as to the actions each will undertake. It indicates which party will serve as the lead or applicant for the grant and which party serves in a partnership capacity. A memorandum of understanding may be entered into either before or after the application for the proposed grant has been submitted.

   The memorandum of understanding essentially takes the place of a verbal commitment and handshake between the parties to work together on some aspect related to the proposed grant. As a result, it may or may not be viewed as an enforceable contractual obligation. The issues regarding its status as a contract pertain to whether there is an offer and acceptance and, more importantly, whether there is consideration. If the memorandum is not viewed as a contract, there is little power on either side to enforce its terms.

The memorandum of understanding should list the parties to the arrangement, including a brief background of each party. It should also describe the history of the relationship, including the reasons the parties are collaborating on this particular project. The memorandum should clearly set forth the responsibilities and roles of each of the parties including a relevant timeline. Lastly, the parties should set forth their commitment to collaborate and act as partners in regard to this proposed grant project.

2. *Letter of Support*—This letter is a statement of an outside party's support or endorsement of a proposed grant project.[15] Letters of support may be written by businesses or organizations in the community, persons or other departments within the academic institution, or any person or organization that supports the proposed project. A letter of support does not entail any type of financial or in-kind support; it simply sets forth a discussion of the worthiness of the project. This letter can play an important role in whether or not the proposed grant project is funded.

A letter of support should be succinct and to the point. The letter should: (i) identify the proposed grant project that is supported; (ii) discuss the relationship between the writer and the party applying for the grant; (iii) set forth the rationale for the support; and (iv) state the writer's endorsement of the proposed project (see sample letter in Table 11.7).

3. *Letter of Commitment*—This letter is a statement of commitment by an outside party to actively participate in the proposed grant project.[16] In essence, this letter demonstrates the outside party's belief that the project is important enough to commit resources to it. Each letter of commitment is unique to the circumstances of the particular grant and the collaboration agreed to by the parties. The outside party may commit monetary support or in-kind support, such as services, office space, equipment, or supplies.

A letter of commitment should be concise and generally only one page in length. There is no standard format for a commitment letter. However, most contain the following elements: (i) the name of the organization the letter is submitted on behalf of; (ii) the proposed grant project that the third party is committing to; (iii) the type of commitment being made and specific details regarding that monetary or in-kind commitment; and (iv) the name and signature of a party who has the authority to make the commitment. Additionally, the letter should clearly communicate the writing party's

Table 11.7 Letter of Support

September 1, 2010

Dear Project Director:

Our Local Community-Based Organization enthusiastically endorses and supports the School-to-Work application prepared by the County Library District team. Working collaboratively with implementation ideas from educators, business leaders, and community representatives, the team has created a universal School-to-Work Opportunities system that is harmonious with the State's vision and is designed to serve two customers: employers and students.

Built on the cooperative, focused initiatives for the city and county, the plan integrates school-based learning, work-based learning, and connecting activities. Easily accessible and appealing to both students and adults, the School-to-Work system is responsive to the needs of the private sector, emphasizes academic integration of the SCANS Workplace Know-How and contextual methodologies, and establishes a continuous improvement process.

The public education community is ready for full mobilization of resources toward the common goal of building a School-to-Work system. We welcome the opportunity to work with our colleagues and neighbors to bring work-based training for all students and adults. Implementation of this plan will create "wins" for all stakeholders, meeting the needs of employers and students and helping the children and adults in the city and county to move from economic dependence to independence.

We look forward to working with students, educators, community representatives, and business leaders to achieve the mutually beneficial goals of the School-to-Work application.

Sincerely,

Executive Director

enthusiasm for the proposed grant project and their participation in that project.

In some instances, the letter of commitment may be the only agreement between the parties. However, in other cases the parties may enter into a more formalized agreement, such as a consulting agreement, cost share agreement, or partnership agreement. Whether a more formalized agreement is entered into depends on the circumstances of each particular grant, as well as the requirements of the organizations involved (see sample letter of commitment in Table 11.8).

Table 11.8 Letter of Commitment

September 1, 2010

Dear Project Director:

Our Community-Based Organization enthusiastically endorses and supports the *Academics 2000: First Things First* application prepared by your library grant team. Working collaboratively with implementation ideas from educators, business leaders, and community representatives, the team has created an innovative project that is harmonious with our shared vision of exemplary early childhood and elementary education.

Built on the cooperative, focused initiatives for the Local Elementary, the project integrates local improvement planning, professional development sessions, and pre-service activities for the school and library community. The application is responsive to local needs, emphasizing the importance of ensuring proficiency in reading, language arts, mathematics, social studies, and science for all students by the end of fourth grade.

Local Elementary welcomes the opportunity to work with our colleagues to bring innovative training and capacity building to the faculty of our school and local public library. The implementation of this plan will create "wins" for all stakeholders, meeting the needs of teachers, paraprofessionals, librarians, administrators, parents, students, and the community by ensuring an academically strong, learner-centered educational environment focused on student achievement and success.

We look forward to working with students, educators, community representatives, and business leaders to achieve the mutually beneficial goals of the *Academics 2000: First Things First* in our community.

Sincerely,

Executive Director

4. *Consulting Agreement*—This agreement sets forth the relationship between the grant recipient and an outside party or entity that agrees to provide specific services or support related to the grant for a fee. The agreement may be with an individual or with some type of entity—such as another educational institution or a for-profit or non-profit corporation—and creates a contractual relationship between the parties.

   The consulting agreement should clearly set forth the services or duties that the consultant will provide to the grant recipient (see statement of work for consultant in Table 11.9). In many cases,

Table 11.9 Statement of Work for Consultant

Date	Event	Responsible Individuals
October 2008	Formal contract signed and payment I due	Library and Consultants
October 2008 through July 2009	**Planning Phase**	Consultants
	• Conduct campus conversations with teachers and focus groups with students;	
	• Interview teachers and administrators at campuses with similar information literacy initiatives;	
	• Promote collaboration among teachers and librarians at public and academic libraries to highlight available print, online, and electronic resources;	
	• Identify emerging technologies in the access, retrieval, repackaging, and delivery of information to students; and	
	• Publicize information about library resources, including (but not limited to) web sites, bookmarks, and emails to students, parents, and teachers.	
	Deliverables:	
	• Findings from local library, other campus, and community interviews;	
	• Compilation of emerging technologies; and	

(*Continued*)

Table 11.9 (Continued)

Date	Event	Responsible Individuals
	• PR materials about library resources for community.	
July 31, 2009	**Payment II due**	Library and Consultants
August 2009 through December 2009	**Implementation Phase—Part I**	Consultants
	• Provide technical assistance for teachers to transform history courses (using curriculum maps) into information literacy curriculum of interest and significance to students and faculty;	
	• Deliver information literacy sessions to students, parents, and faculty;	
	• Administer pre-test and training session to students;	
	• Work with teachers to review and enrich content of history courses to achieve information fluency;	
	• Track web site use (number of visits, types of queries, resources accessed, and the like); and	
	• Identify trends in access, retrieval, repackaging, and delivery of information.	
	Deliverables:	
	• Modified history curriculum maps;	
	• Directory of local, state, regional, and national sites for information literacy in high schools;	

Date	Event	Responsible Individuals
	• Results of pre-tests (Fall 2009) administered to students; and	
	• Use data for white boards and information literacy website.	
December 31, 2009	Payment III due	Library and Consultants
January 2010 through April 2010	**Implementation Phase—Part II**	Consultants
	• Administer post-test to students;	
	• Track web site use (number of visits, types of queries, resources accessed, and the like); and	
	• Prepare a framework for the information literacy initiative.	
	Deliverables:	
	• Results of post-tests (Spring 2010) administered to students;	
	• Use data for white boards and information literacy web site; and	
	• Framework for the information literacy initiative.	
April 30, 2010	Payment IV due	Library and Consultants
April 2010 through July 2010	**Evaluation Phase**	Consultants
	• Formative and summative evaluation components;	
	• Analysis of outcomes; and	
	• Final report.	

(*Continued*)

Table 11.9 (Continued)

Date	Event	Responsible Individuals
	Deliverables:	
	• Draft report (completed research, emerging community partnerships with public and academic libraries and analysis of options to sustain and enhance information literacy framework); and	
	• Final report (PowerPoint presentation with executive summary report).	
July 31, 2010	Payment V due	Library and Consultants

the grantee should set forth a timeline for the completion of the services, including a strict deadline. In most circumstances the consultant agrees to provide its services at an hourly rate and this rate should be stipulated in the contract. In addition, the agreement should set forth other expenses that the consultant may be reimbursed for such as travel or meals. The agreement may also contain a maximum amount that can be charged by the consultant for completion of the duties. While the agreement will contain many of the standard provisions and terms of any contract, it should also specifically state that the consultant is an independent contractor and as such is not an employee of the grant recipient and in no way can take any action or make any commitment that binds the grant recipient.

Understanding contract law is no easy feat. It takes time, practice, and patience to become proficient at reading and understanding contracts. However, it is crucial to understand every contract that is entered into and also to know whether a contract is appropriate for a given situation. Contracts ultimately protect all parties to the agreement. The contract's terms and conditions govern the relationship between the parties and provide guidance to the parties and the courts when issues or disputes arise. In order for a contract to meet its intended purposes, it should clearly set forth the intent of the parties and address the relevant concerns and issues that may arise as a result of the contractual relationship (see Table 11.10 for Cautionary Tales).

Table 11.10 Cautionary Tales

Example One: Sylvia, the grant's principal investigator, talks to Bruce, an outside expert in curriculum development, regarding his assistance in planning the curriculum for the new degree offering supported by the grant. Bruce indicates that he would act as a consultant and states that his rate is $250 per hour. Sylvia negotiates with Bruce over the phone and convinces him to lower his hourly rate to $200 per hour. Both parties hang up the phone happy and the idea of a written consulting agreement is never discussed. Over the next month, Sylvia works closely with Bruce on the curriculum development. At the end of that time, Bruce submits an invoice for payment and charges his time at $225 per hour. Upon receipt of the invoice, Sylvia contacts Bruce to discuss the discrepancy in the hourly rate. Bruce insists that $225 per hour is what they agreed to orally when first discussing his work as a consultant and Sylvia adamantly disagrees and states that they agreed to $200 per hour. Sylvia states that she will not pay the invoice until it is adjusted and Bruce states that he will not provide any further services and is going to sue for his payment.

This is the type of situation that can arise as a result of an oral contract. When there is a discrepancy between the parties, it easily turns into a "he said, she said" type situation. If this dispute winds up in court, because there is no written consulting agreement that sets forth the terms and conditions that the parties agreed to, the judge or jury will have to make a determination based on the oral evidence presented by both parties. Had this arrangement been in writing, either party could have presented that writing to verify the hourly rate and likely avoided this entire situation.

Example Two: Sylvia, who learned a lesson from her dealings with Bruce, retains another curriculum developer, Carter, to assist with the remainder of the project. Before Carter provides any services, Sylvia presents him with a written consulting agreement that sets forth the terms and conditions regarding the services to be provided, including his hourly rate of pay. The consulting agreement simply states that the consultant will provide curriculum development services. Sylvia provides Carter with a detailed description of the new degree offering and requests that he provide her with a list of potential curriculum offerings, including proposed course syllabi. After six weeks, Carter provides a list of potential course offerings and proposed syllabi, along with an invoice. Sylvia reviews the information and contacts Carter to inform him that this is not what the consulting agreement required and that she will not pay his invoice. Carter states that he complied with the terms of the consulting agreement and must be paid or he will sue.

This is the type of situation that can arise when contract terms are not specifically set forth or defined. In this case, the consulting agreement stated that Carter was to provide curriculum development services. Carter claims that he provided these services and Sylvia claims that he did not.

Because the definition of services to be provided under the agreement was vague and ambiguous, Sylvia will have a difficult time establishing that Carter did not provide what was contracted for or intended. In this case, the consulting agreement should have specifically set forth the exact services that were to be provided by Carter, including the manner for review and approval of the services ultimately rendered.

Example Three: Chris, the grant project coordinator, enters into a contract with the Printing Store for the preparation of business cards and marketing brochures to support the grant project team. Claire, a graphic designer for the Printing Store presents a contract to Chris, which he carefully reviews and Sylvia, the principal investigator, executes. Claire then counter-executes the contract and provides a fully executed copy to Chris for the grant project's files. After three weeks, Chris contacts Claire to inquire about the status of the business cards and brochure. Claire indicates that her boss does not want to do this small of a project and so Claire has done no work. Chris reminds Claire that they have an executed contract requiring the work to be performed. Claire tells Chris that he should speak with the owner of the Printing Store, George. The next day Chris contacts George to demand that the work be performed. George tells Chris he has no idea what he is talking about and is not aware of any contract for these services. Furthermore, George indicates to Chris that the only person with authority to enter into a contract on behalf of the Printing Store is George and since he did not enter into this contract he is not going to honor the promise of the business cards and brochures.

This is the type of situation that can arise when a contract is entered into, but the person who executes the contract does not have the authority to do so. As a result, it can be argued that no contract exists and the party is not obligated to perform the services required pursuant to the contract. While Chris may have an argument that the Printing Store should be required to fulfill its obligations under the contract even though Claire did not have the authority to execute the agreement, George will argue that no such contractual obligation exists. While not always evident, it is crucial for any party entering into a contract to make sure that they have the authority to execute the agreement and that the counter-executing party has the authority and power to enter into the agreement as well.

PROJECT EVALUATION

"Evaluation is the systematic assessment of the operation and/or the outcomes of a program or policy, compared to a set of explicit or implicit standards, as a means of contributing to the improvement of the program or policy."[17] Experienced grant team managers recognize the importance of evaluations and their linkages to constant review, assessment, and improvement.

An evaluation strategy is part of the grant proposal process (see Chapter 5). When evaluation is integrated into the project, a review and analysis of each activity or program can be conducted so that team members understand what worked, what failed, and the reasons for each. An astute Principal Investigator will assemble a collection of "lessons learned" so that each experience has value and strengthens the project team and its abilities to improve as the funding period progresses. This approach to evaluation differs significantly from the end-of-project review because experienced Principal Investigators understand that post-facto evaluation has limited value and applicability to the situation at hand. If final evaluation reports are the sole review of a project, the probability is that copies will sit on a bookshelf or in a file and will not be discussed, distributed, or shared with partners and stakeholders.

Conducting Evaluations

Effective evaluation enables the Principal Investigator and team members to consider evaluation as a dynamic process, one that continues throughout the life of an initiative, and "lessons learned" contribute to the body of knowledge in the discipline. An effective evaluation process requires:

- planning for evaluation from the time of drafting a grant application;
- monitoring and documenting progress, correcting the course (as needed);
- conducting a summative evaluation at the conclusion of a grant project; and
- sharing project results, both good and bad, with colleagues.

When planning the strategies to conduct project evaluations, components embedded in the grant application need to be considered. In addition to identifying them on the project calendar, the Principal Investigator and team members can benefit from strategic evaluation planning. Benefits of using carefully constructed evaluation strategies include the following:

- Determining evaluation goals helps to establish clear expectations, roles, and responsibilities within the project team.
- Understanding baseline data at the time the project implementation begins enables the project team to make a more informed assessment about the grant's impact and potential sustainability.
- Measuring the regular progress of each activity as it builds to the achievement of an objective and the project goal helps the team determine whether the initiative is progressing well or changes are merited.

- Defining evaluations for each activity enables the Principal Investigator and team members to demonstrate progress and detect concerns and potential barriers.
- Sharing intermediate results enables the Principal Investigator and team members to keep community partners, stakeholders, and the grantor engaged in the activities.
- Preparing the final report is easier when the grant team has conducted evaluation activities throughout the funding period.

Writing Project Reports

Writing project reports is an opportunity for the Principal Investigator to articulate progress, focus on continuous quality improvement, and monitor performance during a funding period. Most grantors require the Principal Investigator to prepare a grant report semi-annually and annually. When the Principal Investigator submits a well-written, comprehensive grant report, the program officer at the funding agency will be positively influenced, and the potential for future funding is increased. Information in the report can be incorporated into the library's web site and public relations materials. Results can be used as evidence of effective project management and stewardship of funds invested in the library and its programs and services. For tips on writing a grant report, see Table 11.11.

A typical report contains several key elements. Each discussion point enables the Principal Investigator to highlight activities, successes, challenges, and opportunities for the future. In addition to a financial report, key components of a well-written report include the following: project results and impact; lessons learned; and sustainability potential.

> **Results and Impact of the Project.** If the grant proposal stated quantifiable goals, the written report must address a measure of achievement. If the project team did not meet the goals, the Principal Investigator needs to explain the reasons for falling short of the targets. Because the grant report addresses the overall impact, measures are helpful so that the program officer can understand the positive impact the funding agency's investment had on the target audience, stakeholders, and community at large. When the project's impact is long-term, intermediate measures of success should be reported.
>
> **Lessons Learned.** A grant report should include a description of the major achievements, information about the activities, and unexpected challenges. An insightful description of the problems, issues, and concerns that the project team encountered, with honest explanations of the ways in which they were resolved or mitigated, will demonstrate effective grant project management and the prudent nature of the grantor's investment.

Table 11.11 Tips for Writing a Grant Report

1. Organize the report. The easier it is for a program officer to read a grant report and locate important information, the more effective it will be. To help guide readers through your grant report, use highlights for major sections with bold-text headings and organize key points into easy-to-read bulleted lists.

2. Use charts and graphs. If the grant initiative resulted in achievements that can be numerically quantified, consider expressing the information in a chart or graph. Since the grant report may contain a significant number of statistical data, displaying key successes or findings in a chart can help call attention to important points.

3. Include stories about the people impacted by the project. The project goal is to impact the lives of a target audience. The Project Director can include anecdotes from selected individuals who benefited from the grant initiative.

4. Be brief. The grantor may specify the length for a written report. The Project Director should make certain that the report contains sufficient information to meet the reporting requirements while striving for brevity. If no length is specified, five to 10 pages will suffice.

5. Meet the deadline. Just as most funders set a deadline for submitting grant proposals, they also place deadlines on when grantees should submit reports. You should make every effort to meet this deadline, but if for some reason your report will be late, be sure to contact the funder. Most funders will have an understanding attitude regarding tardy grant reports as long as you give advance notice.

6. Thank the grantor. Use common courtesy and thank the program officer for working with the project team.

Sustainability Plans. If the grant project was a success and met each of the goals and objectives, the Principal Investigator may find that the library will decide to continue or expand the initiative. In this case, the grant team may be asked to find additional external funding. Outlining an initial plan to sustain the project can help convince the program officer to renew the grant or encourage the submission of a new proposal.

In most cases, the Principal Investigator will benefit from using office productivity software to prepare the report.[18] Writing the grant report is not a chore, but rather presents an opportunity to strengthen the relationship with the grantor and set the stage for future funding.

Deliverables

Deliverable is a term used in grant project management to describe a tangible or intangible object produced as a result of the activities that are intended to be delivered to the grantor and internal or external stakeholders.[19] A deliverable could be a report, a document, a server upgrade, or any other building block of an overall project.

A deliverable may be composed of multiple smaller components. It may be either an outcome to be achieved or a program, service, or product to be created and provided. Using the goals, objectives, and activities that the grant team defined while drafting the proposal, the Principal Investigator and project team can create a list of "things" (i.e., deliverables) that they need to deliver in order to complete the project successfully. The project team members should specify when and how each item must be completed and add an estimated delivery date.

NOTES

1. Henry Flood, *Essentials for Grants Management: A Guide for the Perplexed*, http://www.tgci.com/magazine/Essentials%20of%20Grants%20Management.pdf (accessed September 30, 2010).

2. Carter McNamara, *Basic Guide to Non-Profit Financial Management*, http://managementhelp.org/finance/np_fnce/np_fnce.htm (accessed September 30, 2010).

3. *Critical Issues in Financial Accounting Regulation for Non-Profit Organizations*, http://www.muridae.com/nporegulation/accounting.html#expenses_operations (accessed September 30, 2010).

4. *Black's Law Dictionary*. 8th ed. Bryan A. Garner, ed. (St. Paul, MN: Thomson West, 2004).

5. Bryan M. Carson. *The Law of Libraries and Archives* (Lanham, MD: Scarecrow Press, 2007); Matthew J. Canavan. *American Jurisprudence 2d: A Modern Comprehensive Text Statement of American Law State and Federal*. Volume 17A: Contracts. (St. Paul, MN: Thomson West, 2004).

6. Carson, 2007.
7. Canavan, 2004.
8. Carson, 2007.
9. *Black's Law Dictionary*, 2004.
10. Canavan, 2004.
11. Carson, 2007.
12. Ibid.
13. Thomas R. Haggard and George W. Kuney. *Legal Drafting in a Nutshell*. 3rd ed. (St. Paul, MN: Thomson West, 2007).

14. Ibid.

15. RIT Researcher News (2006, March 3). "Grant Writing Tips: Writing Effective Letters of Commitment," http://www.rit.edu/research/srs/news/index.php?option=com_content&task=view&id=149&Itemid=208 (accessed January 12, 2009)

16. Ibid.

17. Carol H. Weiss. *Evaluation: Methods for Studying Programs and Policies*. 2nd ed. (Englewood Cliffs, N.J.: Prentice-Hall, 1998).

18. Brian Satterfield. "An Introduction to Grant Reports: Tips and Tools for Preparing Reports for Your Funders," http://www.techsoup.org/learningcenter/funding/page7036.cfm (accessed September 30, 2010).

19. *Deliverable*, http://en.wikipedia.org/wiki/Deliverable (accessed September 30, 2010).

CHAPTER 12

Project Closeout

For a multi-year project, the Principal Investigator (Project Director) should determine if budget modifications or programmatic changes need to be requested from the grantor about one fiscal year quarter before the funding period ends. This request is the first step in beginning to close out the grant. Several steps need to be taken to ensure that the project will be closed, audits can be conducted, and reporting is completed. Concurrent with the beginning of the project closeout, the Principal Investigator needs to verify the amount of unencumbered funds and the status of expenditures to ensure that budget categories have not been over- or under-expended. Any unused project funds should be encumbered not more than 30 days before the end of the grant period. All equipment purchased should be inventoried and a project evaluation should be completed.

The Principal Investigator should notify the project team and human resources office to ensure that forms are filed and library employment requirements for termination are prepared. When all of the project activities have been completed, the Principal Investigator must work with the library's finance director to prepare financial and programmatic reports for the grantor. Completing the financial work for the project includes paying all invoices, collecting any monies due, and closing out accounts. The project account will be closed on the last day of the funding period. The experienced Principal Investigator will share narrative and financial reports with library administrators before submitting them to the grantor.

Programmatic and financial audits may be conducted to ensure that the grant funds paid for the activities described in the grant application. The Principal Investigator may work with a library representative and the program officer to conduct the audits, or an outside auditor may come and conduct them. The experienced Principal Investigator will notify library administrators when audits of a grant-funded initiative are being conducted.

A financial audit is the most frequent kind of audit applied to externally funded projects. Actual expenditures contained in progress reports and projected expenditures detailed in the original approved proposal are compared by category. Some budget codes are selected at random for a detailed review. In addition, a random detailed review of an individual staff member's expenditures may be performed.

Another, less frequent, kind of audit is the operational audit. This audit examines the project's total range of activities in an effort to determine the overall effectiveness of the project. Before the project can be formally closed out, the Principal Investigator must conduct an internal audit to verify that all required work has been completed. The audit takes three steps:

Verify that all activities are completed. Sometimes called a functional audit, a review of all project activities against the requirements in the grant proposal will indicate that everything is complete and evaluated. Discrepancies must be identified and resolved.

Validate all support documents. Any grant documents and materials (whether they be paper or electronic copies) must be validated by comparing them to the requirements in the grant proposal. To prevent problems, the documents should be collected and stored in a secure location during the funding period.

Verify all deliverables are available. When the project requires the production of deliverables, the Principal Investigator needs to conduct an audit to verify that all are present. This is sometimes called a "physical configuration audit."

When the Principal Investigator has reached the end of the audits, submitted the final reports, packed away all of the documents, and worked with the library administrator to make sure everything has been completed, the paperwork is done, and no stones are left unturned, the project is closed. It's been quite an adventure—and time for another!

GLOSSARY OF GRANT TERMS

Abstract. Summary description of a program or project. Usually less than one page in length, it concisely states the main components of the proposal, including the needs assessment, goal, objectives, activities, and evaluation plan.

Accountability. Responsibility of the grantee to account for and report project activities and the expenditures from grant funds. An audit may be part of this process.

Action grant. A grant awarded to support action research.

Action research. Exploration of a situation or service that occurs as part of regular activity within an organization conducting research. Action research attempts to resolve a local problem or provide a service. This immediate, specific application distinguishes action research from empirical research, which is conducted to make a contribution to theory or a body of knowledge within a discipline.

Applicant. An individual, group, or agency requesting a grant award.

Application for supplement. A process of asking the funding agency for additional moneys to support a project.

Application kit. A complete package of materials issued by the funding agency that generally includes instructions and required forms.

Application notice. An announcement that a funding agency is accepting applications for a particular program. The notice may include a brief program description, anticipated funding levels, award amounts, contact information, and the deadline.

Applied research. Research primarily aimed at solving a specific human problem.

Approval/disapproval time. The period of time taken by a funding agency to review and select applications to fund.

Assurance of compliance. Documentation demonstrating that an applicant pledges to act in accordance with regulations governing such areas as affirmative action, rights of human subjects, humane treatment of animals, and appropriate certification of personnel.

Basic research. Research conducted to expand knowledge.

Behavioral objectives. Statement of anticipated, measurable outcomes designed to change target participants' actions.

Bid list. Compilation of registered, potential respondents to a Request for Proposal, contract, or grant. Those on the list may receive early notification of funding opportunities.

Biographical sketches. Background information regarding the key project personnel that is routinely required by a funding agency as part of the application. The information includes education, experience, unique skills, memberships, and publication.

Block grant. Categorical federal grants falling within broad subject areas. Control is delegated to local or regional authorities.

Boilerplate. Sections of a grant proposal that are used frequently and are standardized features so as to require minimal changes for each application.

Broad, long-term objective. The project goal proposed in a grant application.

Budget. A document detailing project expenditures for a given period of time.

Budget justification. The portion of the grant application that provides a narrative rationale for the funds itemized in the budget. Also called "budget detail" or "line-item budget."

Categorical grant. A governmental grant (usually at the federal level) issued under specific program guidelines that delineate, in detail, considerations such as eligibility requirements, program time frames, and intended beneficiaries.

CFDA number. A unique number assigned by the federal government in the *Catalog of Federal Domestic Assistance*.

Challenge grant. An award from a funding agency that requires the applicant to raise a specified amount in order to receive the award.

Channeling. The process whereby a tax-exempt, more credible, and more visible intermediary organization accepts funds from one grantor and passes them directly on to a predesignated grantee.

Client. The person or group designated as the target recipient of the programs and services described in the grant application.

Conceiver. The person credited with the concept from which a grant project can be designed.

Conceiver's disease. Term used to describe a continuous generation of ideas for grant-supported projects.

Conceptual dexterity. Skill at expressing ideas in terms to which the funding agency, program participants, and other partner organizations can relate and understand.

Consortium. Two or more entities that are allied contractually for a shared program or common mission. Funding agencies require documented assurance that consortium members will comply with all applicable laws and policies.

Contingency funding. Support offered with the proviso that the grantee comply with specified requirements.

Glossary of Grant Terms

Contract. A document that facilitates the award of funds.

Contract Opportunity Notice (CON). A public announcement indicating an organization's interest in obtaining a particular type of service. Less specific than a Request for Proposal, this document is used primarily to determine "most qualified" applicants.

Cost-benefit. Method of evaluating a product or service through a formal comparison of acquisition and maintenance against utility.

Cost sharing. The allocation of expenses among organizations that expect to benefit from a project.

Data collection procedures. Processes designed to gather data as part of project evaluation.

Data sharing. Detailed examination of data gathered in preparation for or as part of a grant-funded project.

Deadline. Date by which a grant proposal must be submitted to or received by the funding agency.

Defunding. Expression used to describe a decision by a funding agency to postpone or withhold the release of funds.

Demonstration grant. Funds awarded to support an innovative or unique project. May also be called a "pilot project."

Direct costs. Expenditures associated with the implementation, management, and evaluation of a program or project.

Discretionary funds. Monies that can be expended at the discretion of the Project Director or other appropriate official.

Discretionary grant. A grant that empowers the recipient to decide the type and level of support for a program or project.

Dissemination. The process of distributing information related to a funded program or project. May include (but is not limited to) reports, press releases, journal articles, conference presentations, Internet presence, web sites, and portfolios.

Documentation. The paper, electronic, and digitized records related to a program or project.

"Doing your homework." An expression used to describe the process of learning as much as possible about a funding agency before applying for a grant. Activities may include research, studying the publications of the funding agency (e.g., annual reports, newsletters), and networking with previous grant recipients.

Donor. An individual, organization, corporation, or other entity that contributes money, products, or services.

Donor control. The amount of influence that a donor has over the disposition of a grant award.

Effectiveness. The measurable impact or result of a project.

Efficiency. The relationship of expended effort to achieve anticipated results.

Enabling legislation. Federal or state statute to authorize a grant or funding program.

Endowment. Donated funds that are invested rather than expended by the recipient.

Evaluation. A rigorous quantitative and qualitative measurement of the degree to which the project goal and objectives are achieved.

Exemplary project. A project distinguished by the funding agency as one that sets a standard for excellence.

Expository writing. Narrative writing intended to clarify or explain the topic at hand. Employed in grant writing, applications, scholarly articles, and similar documents.

Formative/process evaluation. An analysis of the methods and techniques used to implement and manage a project or program.

Formula grant. Financial award based on predetermined set of criteria.

Foundation. An organization established for charitable purposes.

Funding agency. An entity that awards grant monies.

Funding cycle. Period of time frequently at set intervals beginning with the announcement of funding opportunities, proposal review, and grantee notification.

Funding period. The period of time during which a project is funded with grant monies.

Goal. Vision of the change that a grant will support.

Grant. An allotment of resources from a funding agency that supports the goal and objectives described in a proposal.

Grantee. Recipient of a grant award.

Grant-in-aid. Another term for "grant."

Grants officer. A funding agency employee who administers a grant program.

Grantsmanship. The process of identifying and securing grants.

Grantspeople. Individuals responsible for the grant process. Also referred to as "grant seekers" or "grant writers."

Grievance procedure. Process through which applicants of unfunded proposals can appeal the decision.

Guidelines. The funder's stated goals, priorities, eligibility criteria, and application procedures.

Hard match. Money identified from the applicant and partner organizations to support a grant-funded program or project.

Hard money. Dependable, long-term funding sources.

Human services. Programs that provide assistance to people (e.g., homeless shelters, day care) as opposed to those that support research, purchases of equipment or facilities, etc.

Indirect costs. A category in a budget that represents the calculated proportion of internal expense incurred by a grantee to accept, manage, and report on grant-funded activities.

Information overload. The inability to focus on critical information when faced with data, reports, statistics, and the like.

Glossary of Grant Terms

In-kind contribution. Noncash contribution to a project or program from the applicant and partner organizations.

Intervention. Deliberate action taken to keep a problem from becoming worse.

Joint funding. Supporting a program or project from more than one funding agency or monetary source.

Letter of commitment. A statement that accompanies a proposal and indicates the commitments to the project from partner organizations, community-based organizations, and others.

Letter of inquiry. Correspondence to a funding agency that includes a description of a proposed program or project and requests a level of interest and application documents.

Letter of intent. A statement required by a funding agency that indicates the applicant's intent to submit a proposal.

Letter of support. A statement that accompanies a proposal from persons and organizations to express endorsement of a grant award.

Leveraging. The use of one grant to obtain another. Also called "dominoing" or "pyramiding."

Mandate. A requirement imposed by a government agency.

Matching. A proportion of a request that the funding agency requires the applicant and partner organizations to contribute to a program or project.

Multipocketed budgeting. The process of securing financial support from more than one source.

Narrative. The section of the proposal that describes the proposed program or project.

Needs assessment. Compelling statements that convince the funding agency to provide financial support to a program or project.

Packaging. Communicating the essentials of a proposal to address specific priorities, objectives, and guidelines.

Payout requirement. Legal mandate directing private foundations in the United States to distribute funds according to the calculation of the larger of two amounts: the net investment return or 6 percent of the total investment corpus.

Peer review. The process of reading, evaluating, and scoring a proposal by experts in the discipline and program officers. Also called a "technical review."

Preliminary studies. A section within a proposal that describes earlier research and data that support the proposed project.

Preproposal. A concise document that outlines a proposed program or project used to select submissions of merit for further consideration. Also called a "preliminary proposal," "discussion paper," or "preapplication."

Primary reviewer's reports. Comments and evaluation by peer reviewers of the strengths and weaknesses in a proposal as measured by the funding agency's state criteria.

Principal Investigator (PI). The individual in charge of a project.

Pro bono publico. Latin phrase meaning "for the public good." This term refers to people or organizations who volunteer time and professional services to charitable causes.

Proposal. Document submitted to apply for a grant.

Public sector. The entities that are funded with tax dollars to supply designated public services. Within the grant sector, it includes federal, state, and local governments as well as community foundations and some tax-exempt organizations.

Request for Application (RFA). A formal notice from a funding agency inviting qualified applicants to submit funding requests.

Request for Proposal (RFP). A formal announcement from an entity that requests information from potential suppliers or contractors for specific services, products, or programs.

Research design. Methodology used to test a hypothesis or answer a research question.

Revenue sharing. A federal or state formula grant program that requires the distribution of tax monies to local jurisdictions on a discretionary basis within broad limits.

Reviewers' comments. Comments and evaluation by peer reviewers of the strengths and weaknesses in a proposal as measured by the funding agency's stated criteria.

Risk capital. Funds available to invest in new ventures, programs, and services.

Sacrifice trap. The tendency of a funding agency to support applicants continuously in an attempt to rationalize initial awards.

Seed grant. A small monetary allotment provided by a funding agency or organization to motivate the applicant to implement a potential program or project.

Service delivery system. An infrastructure that is employed to provide programmatic components in a proposal to the target participants.

Set-aside. Funds designated for specific groups of persons or organizations in advance of the application process.

Sign-off. Written authorization from an authorized representative on required documents, compliances, assurances, and legally binding agreements.

Site visit. A funder's first-hand look at the grantee, programs, and services.

Soft money. Grant funds or donated monies that cannot be predicted in advance; funds whose frequency of receipt cannot be predicted.

Specific aims. Brief notations of the research intent in a grant application.

Spinoff disease. Diverting time and energy from an existing program or project to develop extensions, variations, and secondary initiatives related to the basic plan.

Spinoff projects. New programs or projects developed to address previously unrecognized needs arising out of an original grant project.

Subcontract. A contract between the grantee and other individuals, groups, or organizations to provide resources and services.

Summative/product evaluation. The process of determining whether and to what extent a funded program or project occurred.

Supplemental grant. Additional monies provided to a supported program or project by the same funding agency in addition to the original award.

Support services. Nonprogrammatic activities that facilitate the accomplishment of an organization's primary functions.

Target population. Identified participants and beneficiaries of a grant-funded program or project.

Technical assistance. Information, professional development, and training support from the grantor available to applicants and grantees.

Unexpended funds. Grant monies not yet encumbered or spent during a funding period.

Unrestricted funds. Grants awarded without previously established conditions or requirements dictating expenditures.

Unsolicited applications. Grant programs not dictated by firm application deadlines.

Vanity funding. Funding that results from a grantor's desire for ego gratification as opposed to altruism or a commitment to a particular type of program or project.

BIBLIOGRAPHY

This list of resources is by no means exhaustive. Like the annotated bibliography in *Grants for School Libraries* (Libraries Unlimited, 2003) and *Grantsmanship for Small Libraries* and *School Library Media Centers* (Libraries Unlimited, 1999), this bibliography has been compiled based on the recommendations of educators and librarians working in the area of seeking and managing grants. This bibliography supplements and builds those in the earlier works. While more recently published and available resources are listed here, many of the items in the previous bibliographies are still worth consulting. Although all these resources have components related to education, not all specifically or exclusively concern libraries.

Regarding Internet sources, URLs for web sites may change, new sites are frequently developed, and established sites (for various reasons) may be modified or entirely removed. It is a useful practice to browse sites, follow links, and maintain contacts with others in the field to stay current and share "new finds."

RESOURCES FOR DISCOVERING FUNDING SOURCES

Print Resources

Annual Register of Grant Support. Indianapolis, Ind: Marquis Who's Who. Annual.
    This listing of organizations offering grant support includes education-related sources.

The Big Book of Library Grant Money. Chicago: American Library Association. Annual.

Lists over 2,500 private and corporate donors who have shown interest in or have previously provided funding for libraries.

Brewers, Ernest W., Charles M. Achilles, and Jay R. Furiman. *Finding Funding: Grantwriting from Start to Finish, Including Project Management and Internet Use.* 4th ed., Thousand Oaks, Calif.: Corwin, 2001.
Provides a comprehensive overview of the grant-seeking process, as well as specific sections on exploring grant opportunities in education and using the Internet to discover funding sources.

Brown, Larissa Golden, and John Martin Brown. *Demystifying Grant Seeking: What You Really Need to Do to Get Grants.* San Francisco: Jossey-Bass, 2001.
The authors describe the grant-seeking cycle in five parts: learn—about your organization, your community and your potential funders; match—your needs with the funder's interests and performance; invite—the funder, through the proposal, to invest in the organization and the community; follow up—on the program and the partnership; and, evaluate—the grant-seeking process to fine-tune it before renewing the cycle.

Catalog of Federal Domestic Assistance. Washington, D.C.: Superintendent of Documents, U.S. Government Printing Office, https://www.cfda.gov/.
Comprehensive listing of federal domestic programs, with index.

Federal Register. Washington, D.C.: Superintendent of Documents, U.S. Government Printing Office. Daily.
Publishes announcements of grants along with upcoming changes in related rules and regulations. Federal depository libraries receive this and other relevant documents published by U.S. government agencies, http://www.access.gpo.gov/su_docs/.

Funding Sources for K-12 Education. Westport, Conn.: Oryx Press. Annual.
Entry numbers for sources appropriate for school libraries are listed in the subject index under "Libraries, School." Entries include description, requirements, restrictions, and examples of programs previously funded.

Grants for K-12 Schools. Mollie Mudd, ed. Gaithersburg, Md.: Aspen Publishers, 2001.
Designed as a guide to the complete process of seeking a grant, including how to establish an office of grants development.

Grants for Libraries and Information Services. New York: The Foundation Center. Annual.
One of several resources related to education published by The Foundation Center, this one includes information on providers of grants to libraries.

The "How To" Grants Manual: Successful Grantseeking Techniques for Obtaining Public and Private Grants. 4th ed. Phoenix, Ariz.: American Council on Education/Oryx Press, 1995.
Covers all phases of the grant-seeking process; includes chapters on government funding and the difference between public and private funding.

Karsh, Ellen, and Arlen Sue Fox. *The Only Grant-Writing Book You'll Ever Need: Top Grant Writers and Grant Givers Share Their Secrets.* New York: Basic Books, 2009.

The authors rely on years of experience and interviews with dozens of foundations, associations, and government organizations to provide readers the best current thinking around a very tedious subject. The book includes 16 lessons, each prefaced with a truth-is-stranger anecdote and expanded via a series of questions and answers, discussion, and tested with pop quizzes from fill-in-the-blanks to independent study.

New, Cheryl Carter, and James Aaron Quick. *Grantseeker's Toolkit: A Comprehensive Guide to Finding Funding.* New York: Wiley, 1998.

Details the grant-seeking process from developing the project to be funded, through researching and finding a funder, to developing and writing the proposal. Also note other related works by these same authors described under "Resources to Support the Project" in this bibliography.

Internet/World Wide Web Sites

American Library Association. *American Association of School Librarians.* c. 2003. Available: http://www.ala.org/ala/mgrps/divs/aasl/index.cfm (Accessed September 30, 2010).

Provides information about the American Association of School Librarians (AASL) and its programs, including "Resource Guides for School Library Media Program Development," a description of funding opportunities, and a "Proposal Writing Short Course."

The Foundation Center. *The Foundation Center.* c. 1995–2010. Available: http://foundationcenter.org/. (Accessed September 30, 2010).

Includes grant seeker tools, "Online Librarian," and links to grant maker web sites.

Government Publications Office. *Federal Register.* c. April 4, 2002. Available: http://www.gpoaccess.gov/fr/. (Accessed September 30, 2010).

See annotation for *Federal Register* under "Print Resources."

Hewlett-Packard Co. *Hewlett-Packard Company.* c. 1994–2010. Available: http://www.hp.com. (Accessed September 30, 2010).

Describes corporate philanthropy for K-12 schools and their students.

Scholastic, Inc. *Scholastic, Inc.* c. 1996–2010. Available: http://www2.scholastic.com/browse/index.jsp. (Accessed September 30, 2010).

Lists awards and grants in the "About Scholastic" section.

TGCI. *The Grantsmanship Center.* Available: http://www.tgci.com. (Accessed September 30, 2010).

Features searchable proposal abstracts, links to funding sources, and access to the full text of selected articles from *The Grantsmanship Center Magazine*.

United States Department of Education. *U.S. Department of Education*. Available: http://www.ed.gov. (Accessed September 30, 2010).
Provides an array of resources covering funding, policy, a proposal guide, and relevant legislation. Check this site for research and statistics as well.

RESOURCES TO SUPPORT THE PROJECT (FROM INITIATION TO EVALUATION)

Print Resources

Abshire, Sheryl. "Grant Writing Made Easy." *School Library Journal* 48 (February 2002): 38–39.
Features tips specifically for writing technology-related grants.

Anderson, Cynthia. *Write Grants, Get Money*. Worthington, Ohio: Linworth Publishing, 2002.
Addresses the entire grants process from identifying a need through writing and editing the proposal and conducting an evaluation. A chapter is devoted to reasons that a proposal may be rejected and actions to take should rejection occur.

Bauer, David G. *The Teacher's Guide to Winning Grants*. San Francisco: Jossey-Bass, 1998.
Includes worksheets and a section on writing the needs statement as well as a section on contacting the grantor before starting to write the proposal.

Brown, Larissa Golden, and Martin John Brown. *Demystifying Grant Seeking: What You REALLY Need to Do to Get Grants*. New York: Wiley, 2001.
Describes a five-step process to use when seeking a grant, beginning with learning about the local organization, community, and funders, and concluding with evaluation of the results and procedures used.

Burke, Jim. *I'll Grant You That: A Step-by-Step Guide to Finding Funds, Designing Projects, and Writing Powerful Grant Proposals*. Portsmouth, N.H.: Heinemann, 2000.
Begins with discussion of an initial strategic assessment; continues with each step that follows, including budget development; and concludes by considering design of evaluation and assessment methods.

Carlson, Mim. *Winning Grants: Step by Step*. New York: Wiley, 2002.
Covers the grant process using a workbook format and includes in the "Special Resources Section" a portion titled "How to Evaluate a Proposal Through a Funder's Eyes." The accompanying CD offers samples of winning proposals as well as a template for local use.

Clarke, Cheryl A. *Storytelling for Grantseekers: The Guide to Creative Nonprofit Fundraising*. San Francisco: Jossey-Bass, 2001.

Uses the analogy of storytelling and such elements as characters, problem/tension, and resolution, and even preparing for a sequel, to guide readers through the grant-seeking process.

Farmer, Lesley S. "Encumbering Grants: Managing the Money." *Book Report* 21 (May/June 2002); 12–14.

Ferguson, Jacqueline. *The Grantseeker's Answerbook: Fundraising Experts Respond to the Most Commonly Asked Questions.* 2nd ed. Gaithersburg, Md.: Aspen Publishers, 1999.
Questions cover such issues as where to start when new to grant writing and linking strategic planning to grant development.

Hofmann, Mary R. "Think Money in the Bank for Your School," *Book Report* 17 (May/June 1998): 22–23.
Suggests guidelines to follow for each of the eight typical parts of a grant proposal; author has written as well as read and scored grant proposals.

New, Cheryl Carter, and James Aaron Quick. *How to Write a Grant Proposal.* New York: Wiley, 2003.
Offers detailed treatment of every section of a grant proposal, alternative names that sections may be called, and what should be included. Each chapter contains a checklist; and a CD with guidesheets and templates accompanies the book. A related work by these authors appears in the "Resources for Discovering Funding Sources" section of this bibliography.

Quick, James Aaron, and Cheryl New Carter. *Grant Seeker's Budget Toolkit.* New York: Wiley, 2001.
Offers detailed treatment of budget and project development and planning with careful attention to definitions, types of costs, and preparation for the budget narrative.

Internet/World Wide Web Sites

These are in addition to those listed in the "Resources for Discovering Funding Sources" section of this bibliography. A number of those sites also offer resources related to grant application and administration.

American Association of School Administrators. No date. Available: http://www.aasa.org/. (Accessed September 30, 2010).
The "Resources" category includes a "Grants and Funding" section.

Beginning Grant Writing: An Educator's Guide. No date. Available: http://www.uml.edu/College/Education/Faculty/lebaron/GRANTBEGIN/. (Accessed September 30, 2010).
Designed to help the first-time grant writer.

The Foundation Center. *Online Training Courses.* c. 2010. Available: http://foundationcenter.org/getstarted/training/online/. (Accessed September 30, 2010).

The course (free) treats each part of the proposal and also surveys the research process that precedes the writing.

Grant Station. c. 1999–2010. Available: http://www.grantstation.com/index.asp. (Accessed September 30, 2010).
GrantStation is an online funding resource for organizations seeking grants throughout the world. Providing access to a comprehensive online database of grant makers, as well as other valuable tools, *GrantStation* can help your organization make smarter, better-informed fundraising decisions.

SchoolGrants. c.1999–2010. Available: http://www.schoolgrants.org. (Accessed September 30, 2010).
Site includes sections on grant opportunities, writing the grant proposal, and samples of proposals. *SchoolGrants* also provides links to grant management, grant writing, and state agency sites. *Note:* Regional, state, and local education and library agencies and associations are another valuable resource for grant seekers.

INDEX

Abstract, 70
Academic achievement, 173
Academic library: administrative team in, 12; budget preparation worksheet for, 152–56; demographic data submitted by, 170; formative evaluation by, 103; librarians in, 97; mission statement of, 86; Office of Management and Budget principles used by, 141; organizational structure of, 12; policy development surveys, 105–6; proposals written by, 46; staffing in, 92; summative evaluations by, 105; teaching in, 96
Acceptance: of award, 199–201; of contract, 267–68
Accountability: fiscal management. *See* Fiscal management; overview of, 253–54; Principal Investigator's role, 229; roles and responsibilities, 229; systems for, 254
Accounting: Principal Investigator's understanding of, 255; software used in, 147; terminology used in, 258–60
Action verbs, 45–46, 48
Activities: deadline setting for, 236–42; goals and objectives aligned with, 112–26, 142–43; listing of, 243–46; proposal description of, 228; responsible parties for, 236–42; tasks derived from, 228; types of, 230
Advertising of job position, 211, 213
Advisory Group: establishing of, 59–60; members of, 58–60; orientation for, 60
Affirmative action, 206
Age Discrimination in Employment Act, 215
Agreements: consulting, 276–80; oral, 268, 271; partnership, 197. *See also* Contract
Allowable cost, 258
Americans with Disabilities Act, 215
Announcements, 16, 18
Appendices: academic achievement, 173–79; benchmarks, 173–79; bibliography of resources, 180; curriculum standards, 173–79; demographic data, 170–72; description of, 80, 167; literature review, 173–79; material included in, 168; reasons for, 167; roles of, 167–68
Aptitude tests, 108
Articulation liaison, 93
Assurances, 168–69, 192

Audits, 289–90
Award: acceptance of, 199–201; accountability issues, 253; announcing of, 219–23; hiring considerations, 207–8; internal promotion of, 219; media coverage of, 197; reviewing information about, 200
Award notification: celebration after, 195–96; partner organizations, 197–99; procedure for, 186; timeline for, 185; waiting period for, 185

Benchmarks, 173
"Best practices" site visits, 56
Bibliography of resources, 180
Bid decision form, 13
Blogs, 221
Boilerplate provisions, 270–71
Brochures, 220
Budget: adjustments and amendments to, 164; cost principles that affect development of, 141; definition of, 143, 258; description of, 78–79; drafting of, 147–62; expenditures aligned with, 256–57; expenses, 145–47; funding agencies' influence on, 163; incorrect calculations in, 192; justification narrative with, 162–63; line-item format, 163; modifications to, 260, 262–64; overestimating in, 142; padding of, 191; personnel, 151, 156–57, 207; Principal Investigator's handling of, 255; problems with, 191–92, 251; reviewing of, 163; role of, 142–43; underestimating in, 142, 251; unforeseen event risks, 254
Budget narrative, 162
Budget period, 258
Budget preparation: academic library, 152–56; accounting software used in, 147; communications costs, 161; consultant costs, 159; description of, 143–44; drafting process, 147–62; equipment costs, 158–59; forms used in, 143–44; fringe benefits, 157–58; grantor's guidelines reviewed before, 144; miscellaneous expenses, 162; public library, 148–51; recommendations for, 144–45; supplies and materials costs, 161–62; travel costs, 160–61; worksheets used in, 148–62
Budget summary, 79
Budget surplus, 263

Calendar, proposal development, 28–33
Carryover, 258
Case studies, 52–53, 134
Cash matches, 146
Causality, 135
Chart of accounts, 255
Charter school, 4, 11
Civil Rights Act, 215
Collaboration: grant writing, 197; with institutional representatives, 50–58; in project design, 50–58
Colleagues: discussions with, 54, 56; management of, 231–32; notification of award, 197
Communication: description of, 32; leadership through, 234; management uses of, 230, 232; with partners, 232; teambuilding through, 234; technologies for facilitating, 235
Communications, 161
Communications specialist, 229
Community-based organizations, 25
Community representatives, 23–24
Comparison group design, 134
Comprehensive proposal, 66
Conceptual design meetings, 35
Conferences, 223
Conflict, 38
Consideration, 267–68, 270
Consultants, 159, 207–9
Consulting agreement, 276–80
Content specialist, 229
Context of problem, 43
Contingency planning, 249
Continuing education, 58
Continuous planning, 10

Contract: acceptance of, 267–68; boilerplate provisions, 270–71; components of, 269–70; comprehensiveness of, 272; consideration, 267–68, 270; cost reimbursable, 258; definition of, 267; elements necessary for, 267; examples of, 268–69; fixed price, 259–60; Grant Award Contract, 273; grant versus, 272–73; illegal acts and, 268; intent of parties expressed in, 271; language used in, 272; law regarding, 267–68; modifications to, 272; offer, 267; oral, 268, 271; signatures, 270; terms of, 270–72; tips for, 272; in writing, 268
Cooperative programming, 25
Cost(s): allowable, 258; description of, 79; direct, 145, 254, 258, 264; indirect, 145, 260, 264; unforeseen, 251
Cost Accounting Standards, 141, 258–59
Cost Accounting Standards Board, 141
Cost estimates, 144
Cost reimbursable contract, 258
Cost reimbursement, 164–65
Cost sharing, 145–46, 258, 262, 264–67
Cover letter, 80, 211
Cover sheet, 70
Coworkers, 231–32
Critical incident reports, 109
Curriculum-related projects, 52
Curriculum standards, 173
Curriculum vitae, 170–71, 173

Data analysis: project evaluation report, description of, 138–39; statistical software for, 135; techniques for, 135; web site resources for, 136–37
Data collection instruments, 135; description of, 106–7; document reviews, 111; interviews, 110; observations, 109–10; pencil-and-paper ability tests, 106, 108; pencil-and-paper self-reporting tests, 106, 108–9; performance tests, 110; project evaluation plan incorporation of, 134; project evaluation report description of, 138; web site resources for, 134–35
Data presentation, 135–36
Day-to-day operations. *See* Operations
Deadlines: listing of, 235–42; setting of, 32–33; for submission, 192–93
Declarative sentence, 45
Delegation, 32
Deliverables, 286
Demographic data, 170–72
Diaries, 109
Direct costs, 145, 254, 258, 264
Disbursement, 259
Discrimination, 214–16
Dissemination of findings, results, and products, 77–78
Document reviews, 111
Donations, 146

Editing, 37–39
Educational technology sessions, 58
Education Department General Administrative Regulations, 168
Employees: hiring of, 207; management of, 233; motivating of, 10–11; personality conflicts, 250; position descriptions for, 209–13, 228; rewarding of, 10–11. *See also* Project personnel; Staff
Encumbrances, 259
Equal Employment Opportunity Commission, 217
Equipment, 158–59, 218, 259
Evaluation. *See* Project evaluation
Evaluation teams: external, 132; internal, 127, 132
Evaluators, 127, 132
Executive summary, 137
Exhibits, 270
Expenditures, 142, 260
Expenses, 145–47, 256–57
Experimental designs, 51, 53
External evaluation teams, 132

Index

Face-to-face interviews, 110
Family involvement, 61–62
Federal demographic data, 170
Federal equal employment statutes, 215–16
Financial audit, 290
Financial management, 255
Financial resources, 14
Financial statements, 169
Findings section, of project evaluation report, 139
Fiscal management: accounting, 255; financial management, 255; overview of, 254–55
Fiscal paperwork, 201
Fixed price contract, 259–60
Fixed price subcontract, 165
Flyers, 220
Formal partners, 197, 199, 232, 250
Formative evaluation, 102–3, 132, 137–38
Friends of the Library organization, 169
Fringe benefits, 157–58
Full-time equivalents, 156
Funding: eligibility for, 169; non-traditional sources of, 193; sources of, 258; strategies after denial of, 189–90
Funding agencies: budget formatting affected by, 163; contacting of, 186; evaluator requirements, 127; indirect costs allowed by, 145; parental involvement, 100; project personnel requirements, 87, 90
Funding opportunities: appropriateness determination of, 19; information resources about, 16; potential of, 18–19; review of, 16, 34; types of, 3–4

General Services Administration, 160
Goal(s): activities and, 112–26, 143; adequate presentation of, 44; definition of, 72; development of, 45–48; examples of, 47; objectives and, 47–50, 112–26, 143; problems with, 49–50; proposal description of, 72
Goal statement, 45–48
Graduate student, 93
Grant(s): applications for, 6, 163; contract versus, 272–73; definition of, 272; development of, 7, 14; funding opportunities for, 3–4; management systems, 253; preparation of, 4; recipients, 187–89; team involved in. *See* Grant development team; terms associated with, 291–97
Grant assurances, 168–69, 192
Grant award. *See* Award
Grant Award Contract, 273
Grant compliances, 168–69, 192
Grant development team: charter school, 4; collaboration among, 3, 9; college campus, 4; description of, 42; established, 9; information access and availability, 15–16; members of, 4; nonresponsiveness in, 251; public library system, 4; school campus, 4; underperformance by, 251
Grantor: budget preparation after review of guidelines of, 144; definition of, 42; restatement of guidelines of, 44. *See also* Funding agencies
Grant project. *See* specific project entries
Grant seeking: collaborative nature of, 9; continuous nature of, 6; steps involved in, 42; strategies for, 8
Grant writer, 9
Grant writing: collaborative approach to, 197; reference handbooks and tools, 14–15; tips for, 285
Group planning, 249

"Hidden agendas," 41
Hiring: of consultants, 207–9; decisions regarding, 217–18; of employees, 207; interviews for. *See* Job interview; of project personnel, 201,

204–7; of volunteers, 209. *See also* Job position
Human resources department, 210

Independent contractor, 159
Indirect cost rate, 264
Indirect costs, 145, 260, 264
Informal partners, 199, 232
Information age, 214
In-kind contributions, 146–47
Institute of Museums and Library Services, 169
Institutional Review Board, 5
Instructional personnel, 95, 98–99
Internal evaluation teams, 127, 132
Internet, 16
Interviews: data collection through, 110; job-related. *See* Job interview
Introduction, 71

Job descriptions, 91, 170, 172–73, 209–11, 228
Job interview: anti-discrimination protections, 214–16; process of, 213–14; questions for, 214, 217; tips for, 216
Job position: advertising of, 211, 213; description for, 209–13; posting of, 211, 213. *See also* Hiring
Joint editing, 38–39
Joint writing, 38
Journals, 109

Leadership, 234–35
Legal issues: contract. *See* Contract; overview of, 267–68
Letter of commitment, 179–80, 274–75
Letter of determination, 169
Letter of intent, 65–66
Letter of support, 179–80, 274–76
Letter of transmittal, 80
Letter proposal, 66
Librarians: academic library, 97; job responsibilities of, 6; professional, 97; public library, 97; responsibilities of, 97; risk taking by, 16; school, 98

Libraries: academic. *See* Academic library; as communities of practice, 11; financial resources, 14; growth rate of, 12; policies and procedures of, 228; public. *See* Public library; report submission policies of, 242; school. *See* School library; self-assessments, 17–18
Library administrators: description of, 94–97; meetings with, 163; participation by, 163
Library grants officer, 187
Library technology director, 60
Limited partners, 233
Listening, 38
Literature review, 173–79
Long-term goals, 8

Management styles, 231–34
Matching funds, 146
Meetings: planning. *See* Planning meetings; project handoff, 202–3, 255; scheduling of, 232
Memorandum of understanding, 273–74
Methodologies: case studies, 52–53; curriculum-related projects, 52; experimental designs, 53; professional development projects, 52; surveys, 51–52; types of, 50–51
Mission statement: description of, 11; lucidity of, 44; project goal articulation of, 45; public library, 86
Motivation, 10–11

Narrative. *See* Project narrative
Needs statement: aspect of problem to be addressed, 44; context of problem, 43; definition of, 43; description of, 42–43; justification for project, 44; problems with, 190; purpose of, 71–72
No-cost extensions, 263

Objectives: action verbs used in, 48; activities aligned with, 112–26; budget expenses aligned with, 144;

310 Index

curriculum-related projects, 52; definition of, 72; goals aligned with, 112–26, 143; guidelines for writing, 73; listing of, 243–46; preparation of, 48–49; problems with, 49–50; project goal and, 47–50; proposal description of, 72; reviewing of, 106; types of, 107; unachievable, 251; underdeveloped, 107; well-developed, 107
Obligations, 195, 197, 199, 225, 228, 242, 259
Observations, 109–10
Offer, 267
Office of Federal Procurement Policy, 141
Office of Management and Budget, 141, 261–62
Office of Research and Sponsored Programs, 5
Online preparation, 39
Online project management services, 242, 249
Online surveys, 220–21
Operational audit, 290
Operations: communication's role in, 230; definition of, 230; leadership, 234–35; managing people, 231–34; team building, 234–35
Oral agreement, 268, 271
Organizational structure, 225–27
Organizations: complexity of, 11–12; culture of, 11–12; mission statement of, 11; partner. See Partner organizations; project award effects on, 197; rewarding of employees for contributions, 10–11
Overbudget, 251
Overestimating, 142

Parents: involvement by, 99–100; proposal development team, 23
Participating institutions, 170
Partner organizations: communication with, 232; formal, 197, 199, 232, 250; loss of, 250; management of, 232–33; notification of award, 197–99; partnership agreement with, 198–99; project governance participation by, 58; proposal development, 19, 23–24; relationships with, 197
Partnership agreement, 197
Peer networking, 132
Pencil-and-paper ability tests, 106, 108
Pencil-and-paper self-reporting tests, 106, 108–9
Performance tests, 110
Personality conflicts, 250
Personnel. *See* Employees; Project personnel; Staff
Physical configuration audit, 290
Pilot testing, 136
Plan for continued support section of proposal, 78
Planning: components of, 5–6; definition of, 5; flowchart of, 7; historical commitment to, 10; importance of, 3; inadequate, 6; information necessary for, 15–16; job description creation during, 209; ongoing nature of, 5; rationale for, 6; readiness for, 7–16
Planning meetings: conceptual design meetings, 35; description of, 33–34; initial, 34; working meetings, 35
Podcast, 222
Policy development surveys, 104–5
Poor work product, 250
Pregnancy Discrimination Act, 215
Pre-proposal checklist, 19–23
Principal, 11
Principal Investigator: accountability of, 229; approval seeking from administrative team, 12; award acceptance, 199–201; budget handling by, 255; cost determinations by, 14; decision-maker role of, 228; funding agency requirements, 87; planning meetings, 33; pre-proposal checklist, 19–23; project implementation and, 187–88; responsibilities of, 93–94, 195, 210, 225, 234; rewarding of project team by, 196–97

Printing checklist, 82–83
Problem: context of, 43; identifying of, 42–43; scope of, 44; statement of. *See* Needs statement
Professional development: opportunities for, 57; participation in, 56–57; projects, 52
Program coordinator, 92
Progress monitoring, 101, 127
Project: closeout of, 289–90; costs of, 79; design of. *See* Project design; evaluation of. *See* Project evaluation; fiscal paperwork for, 201; focus of, 45, 251; implementation of. *See* Project implementation; internal accounts for, 201; justification for, 44; management of. *See* Project management; organizational structure for, 225–27; parental involvement with, 60–62; problem situations, 249–52; promotion of. *See* Project promotion; support for, 57–58; timeline for, 128–31
Project coordinator, 92, 210–11
Project design: "best practices"sites, 56; collaborative approach, 50–58; colleague discussions, 54, 56; definition of, 50; description of, 41; dynamic process underlying, 50–58; educational technology sessions, 58; institutional representatives' participation in, 50–58; methodologies. *See* Methodologies; preliminary checklists, 50; professional development, 56–57; project support, 57–58
Project director, 226, 229, 289
Project evaluation: activities, 101–2; basics of, 106–32; checklist for, 76, 133; conducting of, 283–84; definition of, 75, 282–83; design of, 75–77, 134, 138; evaluator for, 127; expert for, 111; formative, 102–3, 132, 137; internal evaluation teams, 127, 132; methods of, 102–6; overview of, 102; planning of, 132–36; public library, 103–4; report of, 137–39; steps involved in, 136; summative, 102, 104–6, 132, 138–39; when to begin, 126–27
Project evaluation plan: components of, 132–33; data collection instruments incorporated into, 134; description of, 102; goals, objectives, and activities aligned with, 112–26, 133; importance of, 103, 106; recommendations for, 106–32; simplicity of, 126; writing of, 112
Project goal: adequate presentation of, 44; development of, 45–48; examples of, 47; objectives and, 47–50
Project governance, 58–59
Project handoff, 200–203, 255
Project idea development, 55
Project implementation: checklist for, 187; getting started, 195–200; Principal Investigator's responsibilities, 188, 230; proposal description of, 44; staffing, 201–18
Project leader, 95
Project limitations, 50
Project management: description of, 58–59; elements of, 195; individuals involved in, 225; online services for, 242, 249; operations. *See* Operations; roles and responsibilities, 227–30; software for, 242, 249
Project narrative: clarity of purpose listed in, 191; components of. *See* Proposal components; definition of, 65; fonts used in, 191; jargon used in, 190; problems with, 190–91; proofreading of, 190; staff descriptions in, 91
Project office, 218, 252
Project personnel: budgetary considerations for, 151, 156–57; capabilities statements, 90–94; cost calculations for, 157–58; curriculum vitae of, 170–71, 173; full-time equivalents for, 156–57; hiring of, 201, 204–7; instructional, 95, 98–99; librarians. *See* Librarians; loss of, 250; managing of, 231–34; mission statement and, 86; personality

conflicts, 250; Principal Investigator. *See* Principal Investigator; professional development for, 203; program coordinator, 92; project coordinator, 92; support staff, 94; training of, 203

Project promotion: brochures for, 220; electronic publications used for, 220; flyers for, 220; online surveys for, 220–21; opportunities for, 222–23; promotional ideas used for, 220; social media for, 221–22; social networking sites for, 222; traditional methods of, 219–20; web sites used for, 220

Project reports, 136, 284–86

Promotion of project. *See* Project promotion

Proposal: activities and obligations detailed in, 228; child-related provisions, 100; components of. *See* Proposal components; comprehensive, 66; definition of, 42; development of. *See* Proposal development; focus of, 43; functions of, 66–67; goal of, 48–50; identifying weaknesses in, 189–90; length of, 192; letter, 66; non-funded, 189–90; preparation of. *See* Proposal preparation; printing checklist for, 82–83; by public library system, 45; resubmitting of, 193; by school library, 46; submission of. *See* Proposal submission; timeframes included in, 222–23; writing of. *See* Proposal writing

Proposal components: abstract, 70; appendices, 80; budget, 78–79; cover sheet, 70; dissemination of findings, results, and products, 77–78; evaluation design, 75–77; goals, objectives, and activities, 72–74, 112–26; introduction, 71; needs assessment. *See* Needs statement; overview of, 67–69; plan for continued support, 78; service programs, 74–75; table of contents, 71

Proposal design, 81–82

Proposal development: checklist for, 36–37; conflict during, 38; "hidden agendas" that affect, 41; management of, 19; partner organizations, 19, 23–24; steps involved in, 24–27

Proposal development calendar, 28–33

Proposal development team: communication in, 32; members of, 23–24; rewarding of, 196

Proposal document formatting, 39–40

Proposal idea, 73

Proposal preparation: costs associated with, 14; decisions relating to, 35, 37–40; online, 39

Proposal submission: activities after, 186; checklist for, 83; deadline for, 192–93; delays after, 185, 207; electronic, 192; failure to follow guidelines for, 190

Proposal writing: elements of, 19; guidelines for, 81–82; individuals involved in, 38; issues regarding, 37–39; joint approach to, 38; steps of, 42

Public library: budget preparation worksheet for, 148–51; formative evaluations by, 103; grant development team, 4; hierarchical structure of, 11; librarians in, 97; mission statement in, 86; Office of Management and Budget principles used by, 141; proposals developed by, 45; staffing of, 91; summative evaluations by, 104; teaching in, 96

Q-sorts, 109
Qualitative methods, 50, 75
Quantitative methods, 50–51, 75
Questionnaires, 108

Ranking scales, 108–9
Rating scales, 108
Recitals, 269
Recommendations, 136, 139
Recordkeeping, 230
Reference handbooks and tools, 14–15

Reference librarians, 16
Reporting process, 242, 247–48
Request for Application, 45
Request for Proposal, 45, 208
Research findings, 15
Resubmitting of proposal, 193
Risk, 254–55
Risk taking, 16
Roles and responsibilities: delegation of, 230; listing of, 235–42; Principal Investigator, 93–94, 195, 210, 225, 234; project management, 227–30

Sampling, 138
School district, 4, 11–12
School faculty, 99
School librarians, 98
School library: formative evaluation by, 103; mission statement of, 86; proposal focus by, 46; staffing of, 91; summative evaluations by, 105; teaching in, 96
Semantic differentials, 109
Service programs, 74–75
Single subject design, 53
Social media, 221–22
Social networking sites, 222
Software: accounting, 147; project management, 242, 249; project office use of, 218; statistical, 135
Staff: funding agency requirements, 87–90; guidelines for, 88–89; hiring of, 201, 204–7; instructional, 95, 98–99; loss of, 250; management of, 233; members of, 210; office equipment for, 218; personality conflicts, 250; position descriptions for, 209–13, 228; requirements, 85–90; responsibilities of, 85; rewards for contributions by, 10–11; size of, 86; support, 94; training for, 203. *See also* Employees; Project personnel
Standards, 173
Statement of consideration, 270
Statistical software, 135
Strategic planning, 8–9
Subcontracting, 164–65, 207–9

Submission: grant applications, 6; proposal. *See* Proposal submission
Summative evaluation, 102, 104–6, 132, 138–39
Supplies and materials, 161–62
Support staff, 94
Surveys: description of, 51–52; online, 220–21; policy development, 104–5
Sustainability, 78, 285

Table of contents, 71
Teachers: participation incentives for, 99; responsibilities of, 96; school librarians and, 98
Team building, 234–35. *See also* Grant development team; Proposal development team
Technology: educational, 58; importance of, 235; staff training in, 203
Technology support specialist, 212–13, 229
Telephone interviews, 110
Timeline, 128–31, 242, 247–48
Time management, 28
Time-sampling observations, 109–10
Time-series design, 134
Travel, 160–61

Underbudget, 251
Underdeveloped objectives, 107
Underestimating, 142
Unforeseen events, 250–52, 254

Videos, 221–22
Virtual site visits, 56
Volunteers, 209, 233–34

Web 2.0, 69
Webinars, 221–22
Web sites: data analysis, 136–37; data collection instruments, 134–35; project promotion using, 220
Well-developed objectives, 107
Working meetings, 35
Writing of proposal. *See* Proposal writing

About the Authors

SYLVIA D. HALL-ELLIS is an associate professor of library and information science in the Morgridge College of Education at the University of Denver. Dr. Hall-Ellis has written *From Research to Practice: The Scholarship of Teaching and Learning in LIS Education and Grants for School Libraries*. She holds a PhD in library and information science from the University of Pittsburgh and an MLS from the University of North Texas.

STACEY L. BOWERS is the Outreach and Instructional Services Coordinator for the Westminster Law Library in the Sturm College of Law at the University of Denver. She is the principal investigator of a 2009 Wolters Kluwer Law & Business Grant from the American Association of Law Libraries. Ms. Bowers holds a JD and an MLIS from the University of Denver.

CHRISTOPHER HUDSON is the Project Coordinator for the Law Librarian Fellowship program at the University of Denver, an Institute of Museum and Library Services grant funded project. Mr. Hudson holds a JD from the University of Colorado School of Law and an MLIS from the University of Denver.

CLAIRE WILLIAMSON is the Outreach Center Coordinator for the Law Librarian Fellowship program at the University of Denver. Ms. Williamson holds a JD and an MLIS from the University of Denver.

JOANNE PATRICK is an administrator for the Sturm College of Law at the University of Denver. She holds an MA in communications from the University of Denver.

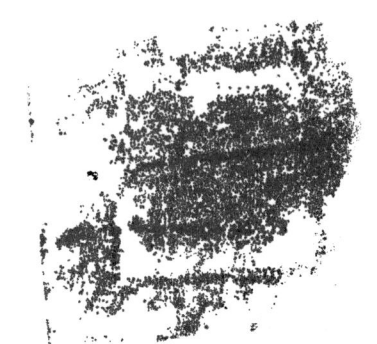